C000136391

Supermax
Controlling risk through confinement

Sharon Shalev

WILLAN
PUBLISHING

Published by

Willan Publishing
Culmcott House
Mill Street, Uffculme
Cullompton, Devon
EX15 3AT, UK
Tel: +44(0)1884 840337
Fax: +44(0)1884 840251
e-mail: info@willanpublishing.co.uk
Website: www.willanpublishing.co.uk

Published simultaneously in the USA and Canada by

Willan Publishing
c/o ISBS, 920 NE 58th Ave, Suite 300
Portland, Oregon 97213-3786, USA
Tel: +001(0)503 287 3093
Fax: +001(0)503 280 8832
e-mail: info@isbs.com
Website: www.isbs.com

First published 2009

ISBN   978-1-84392-408-1 paperback
       978-1-84392-409-8 hardback

British Library Cataloguing-in-Publication Data

A catalogue record for this book is available from the British Library.

FSC
Mixed Sources
Product group from well-managed
forests and other controlled sources

Cert no. SGS-COC-2482
www.fsc.org
© 1996 Forest Stewardship Council

Project managed by Deer Park Productions, Tavistock, Devon
Typeset by GCS, Leighton Buzzard, Bedfordshire
Printed and bound by T.J. International Ltd, Padstow, Cornwall

For Patrick

Contents

List of tables and figures

Tables

Figures

Abbreviations

ADX	Administrative Maximum Security Facility
AIMS	Adult Internal Management System
ASU	Administrative Segregation Unit
CARE	Control and Rehabilitation Effort
CCPOA	California Correctional Peace Officers' Association
CDC	California Department of Corrections
CDCR	California Department of Corrections and Rehabilitation
CO	Correctional Officer
DOC	Department of Corrections
DRB	Departmental Review Board
ICI	Institutional Classification Committee
ISP	Intensive Supervision Program
LAO	Legislative Analyst's Office [California]
MTA	Medical Technical Assistant
NIC	National Institute of Corrections
PHU	Protective Housing Unit
PSU	Psychiatric Services Unit
SAMs	Special Administrative Measures
SHU	Security Housing Unit
SMU	Special Management Unit
START	Special Treatment and Rehabilitation Treatment
THU	Transitional Housing Unit
UCC	Unit Classification Committee

Acknowledgements

This book has been a long time in the making, and many people have generously offered their time and help throughout the years. Acknowledging them all by name is an impossible task, but many friends, colleagues and family members have provided encouragement and ongoing support, listened to me patiently as I have banged on about supermax prisons over the years, and made insightful comments that have set me off in new and fruitful directions. My thanks and appreciation to them all.

I am deeply indebted to all the interviewees who are cited anonymously in this book for sharing their experiences and expertise and, in the case of former prisoners, for agreeing to talk about very painful personal experiences. Their testimonies have given this book richness and depth, and have helped me to better understand some of the pains of isolated confinement as well as the difficulties inherent in the prison as a social institution for all those involved.

This book grew out of my PhD dissertation at the London School of Economics and Political Science. The British Council generously supported the first year of my research, and awards from the Harry Frank Guggenheim Foundation and the Harold Hyam Wingate Foundation greatly assisted me during its final year. I was also supported by an award by the Department of Sociology at the LSE, and a Percy Cohen scholarship. I am indebted to each of these bodies for their generous support.

My supervisor, Stan Cohen, offered his ongoing support and unfailing friendship throughout the years. He has been a constant source of intellectual challenge to me, and saw the wider picture emerging from it all long before I did – a true mensch. As is David

Downes, who stepped in to assist supervision of my dissertation at its later stages and offered his time, support and enthusiasm, and gentle – but consistent – encouragement to write this book. My heartfelt thanks and gratitude to both of them.

Nicholas Claxton, Christie Donner, Stuart Grassian, Mary Ellen Johnson, Bonnie Kerness, Terry Kupers, Joanne Mariner, Jerome Miller, Chase Riveland, Corey Weinstein and many other US-based individuals and grass-roots organisations provided invaluable help during the early stages of research, both in giving me a sense of the depth and breadth of the supermax phenomenon and in establishing contacts with former prisoners and prison activists. My thanks and appreciation also to Craig Haney, Elaine Genders, Harvey Molotch, Caleb Mows, Tim Newburn, Andrew Rutherford, Leslie Sklair, Hans Toch, Michael Welch, Paul Williams, and my peers at the Crime, Deviance and Control seminars for their insightful comments and suggestions. Special thanks to Jes Benstock, Rachel Condry, Megan Comfort, Steve Dowding, Amanda Goodall, Stephanie Hayman, Patrick Owen, Barbara Mason, Marybeth Morsink, Nogah Ofer, Gabriella Polletta, Martha Radice and Paddy Rawlinson who supported me in different ways and at different stages of my work. Paul Rock supported and encouraged me during the process of writing this book, and has offered his friendship and experience throughout. My warm thanks to him.

Jason Oddy generously allowed me to use his photographs in this book and I would warmly recommend them to readers in their larger-scale, colour format. Thanks also to the public information office of the California Department of Corrections and Rehabilitation for providing me with images of the Security Housing Unit at Pelican Bay State Prison.

An abridged version of chapter 5 was published as Shalev, S. (2007) 'The power to classify: avenues into a supermax prison', in Downes, D., Rock, P., Chinkin, C. and Gearty, C. (eds) *Crime, Social Control and Human Rights: From moral panics to states of denial*, Devon: Willan Publishing. Parts of the section 'Degraded and alone: views from the cells' in chapter 8 were published as chapter 2 in Shalev, S. (2008) *A Sourcebook on Solitary Confinement*, Mannheim Centre for Criminology, LSE, which was written with the assistance of Monica Lloyd and Jonathan Beynon. My thanks to them both, and to the Nuffield Foundation for funding work on the Sourcebook. Finally, thanks to everyone at Willan Publishing and the production team at Deer Park Productions, for making the process of publishing this book a smooth and pleasant experience.

Chapter I

Introduction: the supermax phenomenon

> I solemnly declare, that with no rewards nor honours could I walk a happy man beneath the open sky by day, or lie me down upon my bed at night, with the consciousness that one human creature, for any length of time, no matter what, lay suffering this unknown punishment in his silent cell, and I the cause, or I consenting to it in the least degree. (Dickens 1842: 147)

This book concerns itself with the direct descendants of the 'silent cells' referred to by Charles Dickens in his excoriating essay on what was then regarded as the model prison, Philadelphia's much praised Eastern State Penitentiary. It examines the deep and far end of the American criminal justice system as it operated at the turn of the twenty-first century, and the resurrection of solitary confinement, one of the oldest forms of incarceration, in its newest incarnation in the prison setting – supermax prisons. It asks why, almost two centuries after Dickens' unequivocal condemnation of the practice of isolation, tens of thousands of prisoners across the USA are yet again subjected to the immense suffering caused by prolonged solitary confinement, and questions its use as a legitimate prison practice.

Solitary confinement

In contemporary Western penal systems, most prisoners will spend their sentence in 'congregated' or 'general population' prisons. That is, they will share a cell with one or two (and sometimes more) other prisoners, be allowed to associate with others in designated areas and at designated times, and be offered some limited form of vocational, educational and therapeutic programmes. A certain percentage of prisoners, however, will be held alone in single cells where they eat, sleep, and spend most of their days. Standard typologies distinguish between three main forms of segregation: punitive, protective, and administrative. *Punitive segregation* is used as a type of punishment for prisoners' misconduct while in custody, and is typically imposed for a set, limited period of time following some form of a disciplinary hearing. *Protective segregation* is used for holding vulnerable prisoners separately from the general prison population for their own protection. These may include, for example, sex offenders, police informants, former police or prison officers, and prisoners who might harm themselves or be harmed by others. *Administrative segregation* is used to segregate prisoners belonging to certain groups or categories such as 'escape risks', 'gang members', 'predators', 'high risk' and, more recently, 'terrorists', as an internal prison management tool. Administrative segregation is imposed on prisoners by prison personnel through administrative procedures and for managerial reasons, and is typically imposed for prolonged periods of time.

Throughout the 1990s, the overall use of segregation, in all its forms (i.e. punitive, protective and administrative), increased dramatically across the USA, at a rate which far exceeded the overall increase in prison populations: between 1995 and 2000 alone, the numbers of prisoners isolated across the USA rose by 40 per cent.[1]

Whether punitive, protective or administrative, the conditions of confinement are essentially the same, namely, prisoners are confined alone in their cells for most or all of the day. Furthermore, apart from rare cases of high-profile prisoners sentenced to solitary confinement by the court, the decision to place a prisoner in solitary confinement is always made by prison administrators. The similarities in the practice make a typology dependent on the grounds or reasons for segregating a prisoner somewhat misleading. This book nonetheless follows it in focusing on administrative segregation, which in a sense is the most extreme form of solitary confinement: it is imposed on prisoners for prolonged periods of time, for reasons that often involve risk prediction and prison management rather than actual misconduct, and through administrative procedures often lacking in due process. Furthermore, in a trend that has been labelled 'Marionization',[2] in the late 1980s the extensive use of administrative segregation started gaining popularity in the USA, where many states constructed large new prisons or units within existing prisons, designed to accommodate a regime of strict and prolonged solitary confinement, enhanced by high-tech control measures. These new isolation prisons, generically known as 'supermaxes', are the main focus of this book.

Supermax prisons in the USA

There is no one definition of these prisons. Their name, too, varies from one jurisdiction in the USA to another[3]: 'special control unit', 'intensive management unit', 'special management unit' and 'security housing unit' are some of the names used by different states to describe very similar prisons. The generic name most commonly used is 'supermax', short for super-maximum security. Acknowledging the lack of a common name for supermax prisons, a study commissioned by the US Department of Justice's National Institute of Corrections (NIC) defined supermax as:

> A highly restrictive, high-custody housing unit within a secure facility or an entire secure facility, that isolates inmates from the general prison population and from each other due to grievous crimes, repetitive assaultive or violent institutional behaviour, the threat of escape or actual escape from high-custody facility(s) or inciting or threatening to incite disturbances in a correctional institution. (Riveland 1999: 6)

A survey carried out in 2004 found that more than 95 per cent of US prison wardens surveyed agreed with this definition (Mears 2005).

Supermax prisons vary from each other, but in most one would find the following[4]:

- Cells measure 70 to 80 sq. feet.
- Prisoners are kept alone in their cells for 22½-24 hours a day.
- Prisoners exercise alone in a cage or concrete exercise yard with no recreational equipment for one hour a day.
- No congregating areas, and no group activities.
- No work opportunities and few, if any, in-cell educational programmes.
- Family visits are limited, and held through a thick glass barrier; no physical contact is allowed with visitors at any time.
- High-tech measures of control, surveillance and inspection.

In addition to their particular design features, which allow strict separation between the prisoner and others at all times, supermax prisons can be distinguished from standard punitive segregation units in two very important aspects: their overall size, and the duration of confinement in them. In terms of size, most supermax prisons are designed to hold several hundred prisoners (anywhere between 200 and 1,100) in the conditions listed above, compared to a few dozen in other segregation units. In terms of duration, prisoners can be held in supermax prisons for decades, compared to weeks or a few months in other segregation units.

At a time when prison systems across the USA are severely overcrowded and financially strained, supermax prisons with their single cells and high technology seem extravagant. Although expensive to construct and run, most states in the USA now operate at least one supermax prison. A US nationwide survey in 1997 revealed that the federal government and 34 states operate some form of a super-maximum-security prison or control units within prisons.[5] By 2004, the number had risen to 44 states (Mears 2005). These prisons are built as an addition to, not replacement of, existing segregation units in general population prisons, thus dramatically increasing the number of isolation cells throughout the USA.[6]

Supermax prisons are officially targeted at those who are deemed to be chronic troublemakers, dangerous or disruptive prisoners who cannot be controlled in general population settings, the 'worst of the worst' in the prison system. They are an extreme form of exclusion: exclusion from the prison society of those excluded from wider society. The promise of austere conditions and tight measures of control over allegedly dangerous prisoners is politically contagious, and politicians and prison administrators across the USA and elsewhere are competing to build the most secure, high-tech, fortified isolation prison. Economically depressed communities eager to get a share of the business generated by prisons place bids to have supermax prisons built in their region. As an incentive, some counties even donate the land for the prison site to the relevant department of corrections. Private companies, too, stand to profit through constructing, equipping and maintaining these prisons. Supermax prisons seem to have been the flavour of the last decade of the twentieth century, and there are few signs to indicate a reversal of this enthusiasm in the twenty-first century.

Not only are there few signs that supermax prisons are losing their attractiveness to prison administrators, politicians, rural communities, private companies or the public, but also their design and operation have been exported to other countries (including Australia, Brazil, Peru and South Africa), and to other contexts, particularly in relation to the 'war on terror'. Indeed, the design and regime in two of the permanent structures (Camp 5 and Camp 6) at the US naval base at Guantánamo Bay, Cuba, where, since early 2002, the US government has been holding 'enemy combatants' captured by its armed forces, are directly modelled on maximum security prisons in the USA.

For the most part supermax prisons remain, unlike Guantánamo Bay, in the shadows. More light needs to be the shed on the phenomenon of supermaxes and their consequences for those held inside them and the wider society. I hope that this book contributes to that task.

Explaining the supermax phenomenon

Prisoners, journalists, and other observers have described supermax prisons as 'factories of exclusion' (Bauman 2000), 'steel embodiments of the dynamics of power' (Berkman 1995), 'stark and grim modern dungeons' (Burton-Rose *et al.* 1998: 187), 'a form of psychological warfare' (Bustamente 1995), 'expensive and soul-destroying' (Commission on Safety and Abuse 2006: 59), 'a proto-techno-fascist's architectural wet dream' (Levasseur 1995), 'like being entombed in steel and concrete' (Lutalo 1995), 'temples of sadomasochism' (Miller 2000) 'quiet tombs of the human spirit' (Neumann 1998), 'high tech hell' (Parenti 1999a: 209) and 'custodial overkill' (Toch 2001). Supporters of solitary confinement, past and present, on the other hand, dismiss its critics as sentimental, bleeding-heart liberals who make exaggerated and unsubstantiated allegations.[7] Substantiating or rejecting any claims regarding supermax confinement, however, is no easy task, as few 'outsiders' have access to them. Indeed, if prisons are generally hidden from view, supermax prisons are hardly ever seen from the inside by any outsiders, including prisoners' family members, the media, academics, attorneys, prison reform groups, and so on. Any contact that these outsiders have with supermax prisons is limited to short visits or interviews with prisoners conducted in specially designed areas and through a glass partition.

In 2001, Kurki and Morris (2001: 386) commented, 'It is surprising and disturbing how little reliable information about supermax prisons is available, considering their proliferation and the moral and policy issues they raise.' Although the supermax phenomenon has been receiving growing attention in recent years, there are still

5

few comprehensive studies of these prisons.[8] Commentators seeking to explain the rise of supermax prisons tend to focus on one aspect of the phenomenon. Some view current practices as a reflection of the very nature of late modernity: exclusionary, segregative and demobilising. Bauman (2000), for example, asserts that contemporary penal policies tend to maintain order by 'resorting to a paradigm of exclusion'. In his view, supermax prisons such as the Pelican Bay Security Housing Unit (SHU) in California (discussed in detail this book), operate as a

> factory of exclusion for people habituated to their status as 'the excluded'. It is a technique of immobilisation, one of several measures of 'space-confinement' that have arisen in response to the post-modern social field, and the wasteful, rejecting logic of globalisation. (Bauman 2000: 205)

The concept of 'waste management' and immobilisation techniques is also prominent in Feeley and Simon's (1992) 'new penology' thesis. Other commentators focus on changing social sensibilities, 'moral panics, cyclical patterns of moral intolerance and anxieties associated with fundamental social changes [that] increase inclinations for adoption of harsh, inhuman and ill-considered crime policies' (Tonry 2001: 179; see also Austin and Irwin 2000). Garland (2001) views supermax prisons as one of the new strategies of 'punitive segregation' which emerged as a response to the growing insecurities which characterise modern society. For Rutherford (1996: 10–12), supermax prisons are a 'contemporary embodiment of the eliminative ideal ... [that] sits all too comfortably with ... pressures for social exclusion, with notions of a culture of contentment and of a functional underclass'.

Yet others focus on wider shifts in the US criminal justice system since the early 1980s, particularly the massive growth in prison populations, the abandonment of rehabilitative efforts, and the adoption of increasingly punitive ideologies and strategies, or the 'penal harm movement'.[9] Together, these factors resulted in overcrowded prisons where prisoners had little access to programmes:

> Supermax prisons emerged in this context – seized on as a technologically enhanced tightening screw on the pressure cooker-like atmosphere that had been created inside many prison systems in the United States. As the pressure from overcrowding and idleness increased, the screw was turned even tighter. (Haney 2003: 128)

Others focus on managerial strategies for maintaining internal order in prison systems and on the return to the managerial strategy of the concentration of troublemakers in single institutions rather than their dispersal in segregation units of various high-security prisons (Riveland 1999; Ward 1999; Ward and Werlich 2003). Yet others view these high-tech prisons as part of the 'prison industrial complex' and focus on the economic benefits of supermax prisons to rural communities and private businesses (Burton-Rose *et al.* 1998; Currie 1998; Parenti 1999b), as an expression of the racism inherent in the US penal system (Miller 1996), or, finally, as a tool for repressing political opposition and penalising the poor (Monitoring Project 1997; Reiman 1996).

Each of these factors, to a greater or lesser extent, accounts for the growing use of solitary confinement as the chosen tool of first resort for predefined groups of prisoners. But none of them is sufficient in itself, and this book, by looking across a number of academic disciplines and historic periods, seeks to offer a holistic view rather than seeking one main explanation of a complex phenomenon. While I will address macro-level issues directly relevant to the emergence and proliferation of supermax prisons, my particular interest is in the (comparatively neglected) micro-level issues. What is the reality of supermax confinement, and how does it measure up to the theory of its operation? By capturing the 'nuances and complexities' (Garland 1990: 290) of supermax prisons and reconstructing a dual narrative of justification and implementation, rhetoric and practice, I seek to provide a view of a connected whole, as well as an integrated explanation of social processes and practices which shape the penal system, and are shaped by it.

The research

My particular interest in micro-level issues reflects the access and insights gained during research conducted over the course of more than a decade. That research included extensive and lengthy (some lasting several hours) semi-structured interviews with six former prisoners who were held in solitary confinement in different countries and for varying periods, and 22 semi-structured and video-recorded interviews of varying lengths and depth with current and former supermax prisoners, health professionals, a prison architect, supermax administrators, prison officers and support staff, and conversations with human rights and legal experts. My research also draws on content analysis of administrative and legal instruments, secondary analysis of statistical data sets, and archival sources.

In 2000, I had the opportunity to visit two supermax prisons in the USA as part of a film crew making an hour-long documentary on life inside supermax prisons, for a reputable, middle-of-the-road US TV network. Although it was clear to me that conducting research in this context would have certain limitations, the opportunity to spend some time inside the most hidden parts of institutions that are closed not only to the outside world, but also to the prison society, was too important to be missed. So, obviously, I took it. In all, I spent an intensive week in each of the prisons, visiting housing units, control rooms and support facilities, and chatting to prison staff. I found great value in the 'snapshots' obtained that gave me a 'feel' for the place. I also found, contrary to my initial expectation, that prison staff were surprisingly willing to speak openly in front of a camera. Many of the comments cited throughout this book are testament to that.

The structure of the book

This book is arranged as follows: in the following chapter I review the history of the use of solitary confinement as a penal strategy since the early nineteenth century. Chapter 3 briefly examines some of the macro-level factors and actors which played a role in the creation of supermax prisons in the late 1980s and throughout the 1990s. Chapter 4 examines how supermax prisons are officially justified and what their goals are, and looks at claims regarding their alleged system-wide benefits. Chapter 5 examines how official discourses and justifications are translated into administrative categories, how prisoners are selected for allocation to supermax prisons, and how and when they can leave them. In Chapter 6, I examine the architectural design of a typical supermax unit. Following this examination of what I term the 'hardware of control', in Chapter 7 I return to the tradition of prison sociologies and go deeper into the world of supermaxes to examine daily routines and interactions in them, and some of the procedures and regulations governing their operation. Chapter 8 examines how environmental and situational factors inherent in supermax prisons affect prison officers' perception of the prisoners under their charge, and how prisoners experience, and are affected by, their time in isolation, including after their release. In the concluding chapter, I evaluate the costs and benefits of supermax prisons and consider what the future may hold.

Note on definitions and scope

Some definitional issues need to be addressed before proceeding. Prison staff and prison officials do not like the term 'supermax', but prefer to use the names 'special management unit' (Arizona, Pennsylvania), 'special control facility' (New Mexico)', 'security housing unit' (California, New York), 'long-term segregation unit' (Pennsylvania), 'communications management unit' (Indiana), 'correctional adjustment center' (Maryland), 'intensive management unit' (Washington), 'secure program facility' (Wisconsin), and so on. Prison officials also do not like the terms 'solitary confinement' and 'isolation', which they associate with historic practices that, in their view, bear no resemblance to their current counterparts. The spokesperson for one prison which operates a regime of 23 hours a day solitary confinement, for example, insisted that 'we do not put inmates in "isolation". We operate a highly interactive and programmatic approach to managing the disruptive and dangerous inmates in our population.'

Putting aside such semantics and sensitivities, I adopt the terms 'solitary confinement' and 'isolation' to describe a form of confinement where prisoners are held alone in their cells for 22½–24 hours a day and conduct daily activities in complete separation from others, and the term 'supermax' as an operational definition of prison facilities specially designed to enable the holding of prisoners in prolonged solitary confinement.

Although supermax prisons – by whatever name they are called – are justified in the bold language of control, when it comes to the administration of prisons, the language of rehabilitation still lingers. To date, with the exception of the Federal Bureau of Prisons, the departments in charge of prisons across the USA are called Departments of Corrections. Prison guards are 'correctional officers' or 'peace officers' and prisoners are 'inmates' – terms which custodial staff prefer. These sensitivities, too, will be put aside in this book, as I feel that such terms mask reality. When referring to custodial staff I will use the terms 'guards' and 'prison officers' interchangeably, and those in their custody will be called 'prisoners' or, when referring to those held in custody before trial, 'detainees'. These terms reflect more accurately the roles played by prison staff, and the reality of life for those held in their custody.

The trend of supermax confinement is not unique to the USA, but its scale is, so far, a uniquely American phenomenon. I will therefore focus in this book mainly on the USA and on male, adult, maximum-security prisoners. I do not address issues of gender (of either prison staff or prisoners) and special considerations relating to the isolation of female prisoners, juveniles[10] and mentally ill prisoners,[11] nor do I consider lower-security prisons, jails, detention centres, or other forms of confinement.

Notes

1 The increase in prison populations during the same period stood at 28 per cent. A conservative estimate of total numbers in segregation stood at 80,870 prisoners in 2000 (Commission on Safety and Abuse in America's Prisons 2006: 56).
2 After the US federal prison at Marion, Illinois, which started operating in March 1983 a complete 'lockdown' whereby prisoners were locked in their cells for 24 hours a day.
3 The USA has no central prison system and prison practices differ between states, although there are shared social, cultural, political and economic values among them. Furthermore, all states are bound by the US constitution and its interpretation by the courts, and must follow federal policies and guidelines (for example, on sentencing) in order to gain federal funding for their criminal justice systems.
4 See Human Rights Watch (1997), Amnesty International (1998), Riveland (1999). These conditions typically adhere to legal standards setting out the minimum required cell size, time for physical exercise, family visits and so on. Supermax prisons usually provide prisoners with the minimum requirements and little more.
5 National Institute of Corrections (1997). A study carried out in the same year by the Monitoring Project of the National Campaign to Stop Control Units (1997) found that 42 states and the Federal Bureau of Prisons operated 'at least one control unit/supermax prison within its prison system', whereas a study carried by Human Rights Watch (1997) listed 36 states. King (1999) found that 34 states and the Federal Bureau of Prisons operated at least one supermax unit.
6 There are discrepancies in the estimates of the number of prisoners held in supermax in the USA, not least because of the different names and definitions used for these prisons. In 2000, Human Rights Watch estimated that some 20,000 prisoners were held in supermax facilities (see also Riveland, 1999), while other estimates were substantially higher (see Monitoring Project 1997). By 2004, an estimated 25,000 prisoners were held in supermaxes across the USA (Mears 2005). The total number of prisoners isolated across the USA at any given time, including death-row prisoners who are usually isolated awaiting their execution, prisoners isolated in punitive and protective custody, and pretrial detainees who are isolated, particularly those charged with offences against the state

and in connection with the 'war on terror', is, of course, far higher. California, for example, has almost 12,000 prison beds for holding sentenced prisoners in administrative segregation, including just under 3,000 supermax (or 'SHU') beds, and 8,878 Administrative Segregation Unit (or 'ASU') beds (Office of the Inspector General, 2009).

7　See, for example, Gendreau and Bonta's heated response to critics of solitary confinement, accusing them of being 'hopelessly muddled in rhetoric, ideology, sentimentality, and the avoidance of any inductive reasoning' (1984: 468). See also Ward and Werlich (2003).

8　With the exception of Rhodes' (2004b) insightful account of practices, relationships and conflicts in Washington state's control units, supermax prisons have mostly been addressed in more general terms (see, for example, Irwin and Austin (2000); King (1999, 2007), Morris (2000), Simon (2000), Ward and Werlich (2003)), or in studies of a particular aspect of these prisons (for example, their health effects or legal issues arising from their operation).

9　Haney 2008: 950–1. See also Pratt *et al.* (2005) on supermaxes as a manifestation of the 'new punitiveness'.

10　Although there are now supermax units for women and some jurisdictions also hold juveniles in supermax prisons, raising important issues which deserve separate attention, I chose to focus here on adult, male prisoners because they make up the vast majority of those confined in supermax prisons in the USA.

11　More precisely, I will not deal with prisoners who are diagnosed as mentally ill, an issue which has been attracting growing concern in recent years and is addressed in Chapter 8.

Chapter 2

Solitary confinement as a penal strategy: a brief history

> In its intentions, I am well convinced that it is kind, humane, and meant for reformation; but I am persuaded that those who devised this system of Prison Discipline, and those benevolent gentleman who carry out its execution, do not know what it is that they are doing. I believe that very few men are capable of estimating the immense amount of torture and agony which this dreadful punishment, prolonged for years, inflicts upon the sufferers; and in guessing at it myself, and in reasoning from what I have seen written upon their faces, and what to my certain knowledge they feel within, I am only more convinced that there is a depth of terrible endurance in it which none but the sufferers themselves can fathom, and which no man has the right to inflict upon his fellow creatures. (Dickens 1842: 146–147)

The use of solitary confinement predates the birth of the modern prison in the early nineteenth century, and has been a constant and universal feature of the prison, on both sides of the Atlantic, with periodic 'waves' of accelerated use ever since. While the use of solitary confinement has been constant, however, the roles it was expected to play, and the discourses on these roles, changed substantially throughout the history of its use. In the early to mid-nineteenth century, solitary confinement was the main form of imprisonment for entire prison populations, aimed at reforming convicts into law abiding citizens. By the late nineteenth century this aim was deserted, as was the practice of keeping entire prison populations in solitary confinement.

Although the systematic use of prolonged solitary confinement was deserted, however, most prison systems continued to use solitary confinement routinely, as short-term, but severe, punishment for prisoners who broke prison rules, for preventing escapes, for protective custody of vulnerable prisoners, and for holding prisoners convicted of crimes against the state. To date, most prisons around the world, new and old, regardless of their security level, retain a number of cells or a special section of the prison dedicated to holding prisoners in solitary confinement.

In the early 1970s there was renewed interest in the USA in a more systematic use of solitary confinement, alongside its more 'routine' uses, this time as part of behaviour modification programmes. By the mid-1970s this strategy, too, was officially deserted. Towards the end of the twentieth century, prolonged solitary confinement of large segments of the prison population once again returned to the fore, this time as a tool of controlling prisoners defined as 'high risk', in special units and supermax prisons.

Solitary confinement has thus had many roles in the prison world: reformation, behaviour modification, punishment, protection, prisoner management and control. These very different, at times even contradictory, proposed roles of solitary confinement are rooted in various 'theories' about human nature, crime, punishment and society. In what follows, I examine the different roles of solitary confinement in their historic context.

Solitary confinement as a tool of moral reform

> The object of this measure [separate confinement] is twofold – to prevent the prisoner from holding intercourse with his fellow-prisoners, and to compel him to hold communion with himself. We exclude him from the society of other inmates of the prison, because experience had shown that such society is injurious; and we force him to make his conduct the subject of his own reflections, because it is almost universally found that such self-communion is the precursor of moral amendment. (Adshead 1845: x)

The systematic use of solitary confinement as a penal strategy stretches back to the new penitentiaries that emerged on both sides of the Atlantic in the early- to mid-nineteenth century.[1] These penitentiaries were the outcome of a movement to transform the crowded, filthy and undisciplined gaols of the previous centuries and introduce a new concept, namely that criminals could be reformed in prison. Viewing crime as an infectious, but curable, disease, prison reformers were concerned that 'the prison, instead of school of discipline and reform, may become the lazar-house of a moral pestilence, in which those who are dying of the plague and those who are only suspected of infection are crowded together in one promiscuous mass of disease and death' (Kingsmill 1854: 109). Separation was the proposed cure: separation of those already 'infected', from the bad influences of their sick environment outside the prison and from each other within prison. But the value of solitude 'was not just precautionary ... as isolation increased, so did its power to penetrate the heart and mind. Seclusion was simultaneously a preventive and a cure' (Evans 1982: 340). In contrast to the previous forms of public and physical punishments, the new penitentiaries were centred on offenders' minds and sought to reform them by placing them temporarily in an institution that would act as a microcosm of an orderly, disciplined, morally healthy and clean society; 'just as the criminal's environment had led him into crime, the institutional environment would lead him out of it' (Rothman 1971: 83).

The new penitentiaries and the principles of reform through solitary confinement and strict, but fair, discipline, had many different appeals. They presented a vision of order in a rapidly changing society. They appealed to contemporary cultural and societal sensitivities, in that they represented a move from body to soul in punishment, a mark of an enlightened society, where punishment was to be humane and carried out in private, away from forms of public punishments. Solitary confinement, then, was viewed as 'a pre-eminently civilized punishment. It left the body untouched and, even better, was rigorously hidden behind thick walls from almost everyone's eye' (Franke 1995: 70). The idea of reformation through separation also fitted well with Christian (particularly Quaker) theology and the belief that people are inherently good and therefore capable and worthy of redemption. When prisoners were left alone with their conscience, guided by the prison chaplain and the good words of the Bible, they would engage in inner reflection and 'contemplate their sinful past and their more law abiding future' (Sharpe 1990: 69). There were also more immediate considerations which appealed to prison administrators and wardens, in that solitary confinement was a convenient measure which enabled the management of a large number of prisoners in a secure, efficient, and orderly manner. It was thought that the orderly routines would promote discipline and obedience in the convicts, who were viewed as people with weak self-control. Further, although solitary confinement was seen as a humane treatment, its harsh nature was recognised and expected to act as a deterrent to future crime. Solitary confinement was also expected to promote public security and reduce crime through the prevention of communications relating to escape plans or future crimes between prisoners. The thick and high walls of the new penitentiaries would further both these aims of security and deterrence. They were directed also at sending a message to those outside the prison.

Architects, medical professionals, prison reformers, religious and military figures, prison financiers, administrators and staff all joined forces to create these new prisons where reform would be manufactured. But while the *principles* of the new penitentiaries were received with broad consensus, the finer points of their exact application were fiercely debated. For example, should prisoners' separation from each other be absolute, or should they be allowed to mix together, but maintain complete silence? Should prisoners be allowed to work, and, if so, should they be engaged in productive work or be given intentionally monotonous tasks? Should they work with others or alone in their solitary cells? Eventually, two different versions of these prisons were devised. The 'silent system', first implemented in Auburn Prison, New York, where prisoners slept in solitary cells but participated in congregated work and outdoor recreation while maintaining strict silence at all times, and the 'separate system', developed in Philadelphia's Eastern State Penitentiary and later in Pentonville Prison in England, where prisoners were held in strict solitary confinement at all times and were required to work in their solitary cells. Despite the similarity of both models, their respective advantages and failings continued to attract heated debate on both sides of the Atlantic.[2]

The writings of the chaplain of Pentonville Prison, built in 1842, in praise of the 'separate system', give a flavour of the debate and the emphasis on the complete isolation of prisoners: 'The silent congregated system ... is a great step towards real improvement ... [but it fails] in reformation of morals as well as correction of the offender' since, although the prisoner is prohibited from communicating with others, he is still surrounded by them, and 'the winking of the eye, the movement of the finger, a sneeze or a cough, is enough to communicate what is desired' (Kingsmill 1854: 109).[3] The separate or cellular system, it was claimed, was free from these evils, as prisoners never saw each other. It was also 'sufficiently severe as a legal punishment in itself. There is no need of harshness of manner nor loudness of voice to enforce order, nor occasion for those feelings in officers, which so often find vent in irritating language towards congregated criminals' (Kingsmill 1854: 113). Yet, even in this enlightened system, 18 months in solitary confinement proved to be too long for prisoners to endure, and the period of relentless isolation was reduced first to 12 months and then to 8 months (Ignatieff 1978).

During the last quarter of the nineteenth century, it became clear that the new penitentiaries did not reform criminals and were extremely expensive to run, and there was little proof that they were any more effective than other forms of confinement. As evidence of the devastating health effects of solitary confinement surfaced, there was also a growing moral and ethical debate about whether or not it was right to keep prisoners in strict solitary confinement for such long periods of time.[4] Additionally, a growing need for prison beds and no funds to construct new prisons created internal pressures that made it difficult to maintain prisons based on single-cell occupancy. Although prisoners in those days did not have legal rights as such, the courts were also required to rule in cases involving the use of solitary confinement. In 1890, the US Supreme Court referred back to earlier debates on solitary confinement, and noted that 'it is within the memory of many persons interested in prison discipline that some 30–40 years ago the whole subject attracted the general public attention, and its main feature of solitary confinement was found to be too severe' (Re Medley 1890: 162). The court was asked to determine whether holding a death-row prisoner in solitary confinement prior to his execution constituted an additional punishment to the one already imposed on him. Rejecting prison officials' claims that prisoners were subjected to 'close confinement' but not 'solitary confinement', the court stated, 'The matter of solitary confinement is not … a mere unimportant regulation as to the safe keeping of the prisoner, and is not relieved of its objectionable features by the qualifying language'.[5] The court then went on to review the history of the use of solitary confinement, and noted that although specific arrangements varied between different prisons, solitary confinement at best failed to reform prisoners, and at worst caused serious mental problems:

experience demonstrated that there were serious objections to it. A considerable number of the prisoners fell, after even a short confinement, into a semi-fatuous condition, from which it was next to impossible to arouse them, and others became violently insane; others still, committed suicide; while those who stood the ordeal better were not generally reformed and in most cases did not recover sufficient mental activity to be of any subsequent service to the community. (*Re Medley* 1890: 164)

In light of the severity of solitary confinement, the court accepted Medley's argument that solitary confinement in itself constituted punishment, and ordered his release: 'The solitary confinement to which the prisoner was subjected ... was an additional punishment of the most important and painful character, and is therefore forbidden by ... the constitution of the United States' (*ibid.*).

By the late nineteenth century, the isolation system was mostly dismantled on both sides of the Atlantic.[6] Many of the prisons which were constructed during that period, however, remained in operation, albeit in a modified form. Indeed, some of these prisons, including Pentonville in London and Vestre in Copenhagen, still operate today. Most crucially, solitary confinement became an integral part of prison systems.

Solitary confinement as a tool of behaviour modification

In the years following World War II, two parallel developments led to renewed interest in solitary confinement: first, the revelations of the Nazi concentration camps and, later, the testimonies of survivors, and the return of American prisoners of war from Korea exhibiting signs of brainwashing; secondly, technological advances that 'have allowed men to enter into isolation situations previously unattainable – in outer space, under the sea, on the face of the moon, in remote places on the earth's surface'.[7] These developments led researchers to experiment with techniques of isolation in the context of human behaviour in extreme social and environmental situations.[8]

The potential benefits of solitary confinement were revisited with some zeal, engaging researchers and the increasingly powerful 'psy disciplines' in new discussions on the roles it could play. The growth in prisoner numbers and the wave of prison riots that broke out in the USA in the 1960s made such research potentially valuable to prison administrations, and the prison a natural site for further studies and experimentation with forms of sensory deprivation and social isolation as tools for 'changing attitudes' or resocialisation of prisoners. It was not until the early 1970s, however, that the 'control of violence replaced more time-consuming attempts to understand its sources' (Committee on the Judiciary 1974: 2), and government funding was made available for behaviour modification programmes directed at 'immediate and efficient means to control violence and other forms of anti-social behavior' (*ibid.*).

Solitary confinement was to be the first (and essential) stage in therapeutic programmes of behaviour modification of prisoners. The logic was that an environment of unrelenting isolation would make prisoners more susceptible to the next stage of the programme: 'remoulding' through therapy and medication. These programmes were based on the principle of operant conditioning (Skinner 1953) which maintained that behaviour can be learnt by stimulating certain types of behaviours and suppressing others through the use of positive reinforcements (rewarding 'correct' behaviour) and negative reinforcements (punishing 'incorrect' behaviour or attitude). Positive reinforcement used incentives provided through token economies and similar programmes. Negative reinforcement, 'in its milder forms ... deprives an individual of privileges ... in its more coercive forms ... through what is referred to as 'aversion therapy' ... [it] used drugs, beatings and electric shocks as painful punishment for violation of rules' (Committee on the Judiciary 1974: 14).

One supporter of the use of such techniques in prisons was Massachusetts Institute of Technology psychologist Edgar Schein, who studied the cases of American POWs returning from Korea and was eager to apply some of his findings in the prison setting. In 1962, he urged the participants at a conference of US prison wardens to 'think of brainwashing, not in terms of politics, ethics or morals, but in terms of the deliberate changing of human behaviour and attitudes by a group of men who have relatively complete control over the environment in which the captive populace lives' (in Mitford 1974).

Schein's call did not fall on deaf ears. One of those who attended his 1962 talk was Dr Martin Groder, a psychiatrist employed by the Federal Bureau of Prisons. In 1973, Groder had the chance to test some of these techniques by helping to devise the control unit, 'H-unit', at the US federal penitentiary at Marion.[9] The unit had a capacity of 72 single cells, and its mission statement introduced a programme of behaviour modification, 'designed to assist the individual in changing his attitude and behaviour so he may be returned to a regular institution programme'.[10] At the unit, isolation was coupled with mandatory therapeutic programmes, called, in the spirit of the times, 'CARE' (Control and Rehabilitation Effort). Around the same time, the Federal Bureau of Prisons initiated another behaviour-modification programme, START (Special Treatment and Rehabilitative Training), at the Federal Medical Center for Prisoners at Springfield, Missouri.

The programme was aimed at troublemakers who until that time had been dispersed in various segregation units across the USA, and whose behaviour was 'out of control ... even while in the institution's segregation unit. They utilize their aggressive acting-out tendencies to manipulate situations to gain their own ends. Frequently this results in verbal attacks and physical assaults on both staff and other offenders'.[11] The programme's primary goal combined treatment and managerial objectives. It was:

> the care, control, and correction of the long term, disruptive offender ... [to] help these individuals to gain better control over their behavior so that they can be returned to regular institutions where they can then participate in programs designed to help them make a successful community adjustment. START, then, can be viewed as a type of 'pre-rehabilitation'. (Committee on the Judiciary, 1974: 264)

Rather than rehabilitating prisoners, then, programmes like START and CARE aimed to make prisoners more docile and more susceptible to rehabilitation programmes through solitary confinement. Put differently, these programmes aimed to turn the prisoner into a 'tabula rasa', a blank slate, on which useful traits and acceptable behaviours could later be engraved.[12] Participation in the START programme was not voluntary. Those who were selected to take part in it were held in solitary confinement, provided only with the bare necessities, and initially allowed out of their cells only twice a week for showers and once a week for exercise. A prisoner who behaved in a way which prison officers, who were charged with a dual role of control and treatment, determined to be 'good behaviour' for 20 days (based on a detailed list of expectations) would 'graduate' to the next stage of the programme and be allowed out of his cell for an hour and a half a day, and so on, gradually increasing the level of prisoners' privileges. 'Bad' behaviour would result in the prisoner being demoted back to the initial level of privileges.

Similar experiments with behaviour-modification programmes, some of which included the administration of mind-altering drugs, took place across the USA – for example, in California's 'adjustment centers' – segregation units where the 'worst of the worst' prisoners were held – and at California's newly built Maximum Psychiatric Diagnostic Unit, which was designed to 'provide [a] highly specialised service for adjustment center inmates who are violently acting-out and management problem cases within the California prison system'

(Mitford 1974). This increasing use of isolation units was justified by prison administrators as a non-punitive therapeutic measure: 'They usually presented the new policies as non-punitive, and [said that they] planned new segregation units so they would not be as cruel as solitary confinement. In California, where segregation has been used more than in any other state, initial expansion of segregation units was justified with a therapeutic rationale' (Austin and Irwin [2000] 1994: 112).

Behaviour-modification programmes attracted a great deal of controversy from the very beginning because of their coercive nature and the 'power [it] gives one man to impose his views and values on another', as well as inequalities in application and the use of basic privileges as incentives (Committee on the Judiciary 1974: iii). Allegations of guard abuse in isolation units also prompted a number of prisoner lawsuits and the appointment of a special committee of inquiry. Following adverse court rulings, the START programme was scrapped in February 1974, less than two years after it was first implemented. State departments of corrections soon followed suit and scrapped altogether or changed the mission statement of their behaviour-modification programmes.

Solitary confinement as a risk-management tool and the birth of the supermax doctrine

In 1978, the Marion prison was reclassified as the Federal Bureau of Prisons' highest security prison. Its newly stated purpose was to 'provide long-term segregation within a highly controlled setting for prisoners who threatened or injured other prisoners or staff, possessed deadly weapons or drugs, disrupted the orderly operation of a prison, escaped or attempted to escape' (cited in Ward 1987: 80–81). Across the USA, protest against prison conditions was mounting, and prison unrest growing. At the Marion prison alone, between February 1980 and June 1983, there were 14 attempted escapes, 10 group disturbances, 54 serious assaults by inmates on other inmates, 8 deaths, and 28 serious assaults on staff (Ward 1987).

On 22 October 1983, prisoners at Marion's control unit stabbed two guards to death and injured four others, and a regime of 24-hour 'lockdown' (which meant that prisoners were locked in their single cells for 24 hours a day) was instated throughout the prison. A week later, this regime was formalised alongside the official removal of any rehabilitative rhetoric. Although rehabilitation was no longer the official goal of the unit, however, some principles of behaviour modification remained in place. Initially, prisoners would remain in solitary confinement with only basic provisions. After 24 months without any misconduct, prisoners could 'earn' transfer to the 'transitional unit' where they would be allowed to engage in work and recreation with others, as well as communal dining. After a further 12 months without any disciplinary offences, prisoners could 'earn' a transfer to the 'pre-release unit', from where they could eventually be transferred to 'general population' prisons (Ward and Werlich 2003: 59). The general time frame of what was supposedly a 'progressive programme', then, was substantially longer than before, with a starting point of two years in strict solitary confinement with only very basic provisions. In addition to the lockdown regime, new procedures designed to maximise control of prisoners were introduced, including the removal of exercise equipment, full body searches, cell-front medical consultations, and other security procedures that later became standard practice in supermax prisons.[13] Prison officials from other states were keen to observe the regime and procedures at Marion:

> As word spread among corrections officials in troubled state prisons across the country that the Federal Bureau of Prisons had found a management strategy by which control could be established over a prison system's most disruptive inmates, a strategy that has been satisfactorily tested in the federal courts, state commissioners and wardens began to visit USP Marion to learn more about what has come to be known as the 'Marion Model'. (Ward 1999: 258)

Following such visits, several state wardens were reported to have commented that they 'had died and gone to heaven' (Ward and Werlich 2003: 59). Soon, many states which were facing prison unrest at the time followed the Federal Bureau of Prisons and 'locked-down' entire prisons for months at a time (Ward 1987: 86).

The lockdown of the Marion prison is widely seen as marking the birth of the supermax doctrine.[14]

From the mid- to late 1980s, the managerial discourse and its emphasis on prison security played a growing role in the administration of prisons and prisoners, and declared rehabilitative efforts were all but abandoned. The focus was no longer on changing the individual prisoner but on managing ever increasing prison populations in an orderly and secure manner. To do so, chronically disruptive prisoners – it was claimed – had to be isolated and tightly controlled for long periods of time, as short-term solitary confinement had failed to control them in the past.

> Ordinary techniques for segregation or transfer have provided a means for separating some disruptive inmates … however they have proven ineffective with others. Established segregation programs for short periods of restriction are not satisfactory for inmates who need a longer period of control and supervisory care. Their inability to be safely placed into the population of other institutions precludes regular transfer. (Federal Bureau of Prisons 1995: 1)

Supermax prisons, a new generation of the concentration model, designed especially for long-term isolation, were the proposed solution.[15] In contrast to the past, the perceived need for designated high-security, 'concentration' prisons was no longer within the exclusive domain of the Federal Bureau of Prisons. Starting with Special Management Unit I in Florence, Arizona, built in 1987, and followed by, among others, the Security Housing Unit (SHU) at the Pelican Bay prison, California, built in 1989, supermax prisons began mushrooming across the USA. In 1994, the Federal Bureau of Prisons opened the Administrative Maximum Security Facility (ADX) in Florence, Colorado, a 'new-generation' supermax prison, replacing Marion as the Bureau's highest security prison. By 2004, an estimated 44 states operated one or more supermax prisons (Mears 2005).

Continuities and discontinuities in the use of solitary confinement

If one traces continuities and discontinuities in the use of solitary confinement since the days of the separate penitentiaries of the early nineteenth century to its use in supermax prisons, the continuities in the practice are by far the more striking. As Table 2.1 illustrates, the one area where there has been substantial change is in the discourses on the *aims* of solitary confinement. The language of control is now articulated in bold, unapologetic terms. As I will demonstrate throughout the following chapters, supermax prisons are intentionally designed to create stark, severe and highly controlled environments, justified as absolutely necessary for managing dangerous and high-risk prisoners and to ensure prison security. Whether the 'true intentions' of those who devised the separate penitentiaries were benevolent or not, is a question which others have dealt with and is of less interest to our discussion. The intentions of those who devised supermax prisons are indisputable: the control of prisoners' body, mind, and spirit.

In addition to the different rhetoric currently used, there are, of course, other differences between present-day supermax prisons and their previous incarnations. Technological advances have made possible new degrees of physical separation, surveillance and inspection. They have also made possible the construction of increasingly larger isolation prisons. The principle of work, which was prominent in the separate penitentiaries, does not feature at all in supermax prisons.[16] Standardisation, regulation and external interventions have ensured that, for the most part and in Western democracies, at least, prisoners are provided with adequate food, shelter, and basic medical care. At its core, nonetheless, as a tactic, the practice of solitary confinement has remained exceptionally similar throughout the centuries. Rather than being a new breed of prisons, supermaxes are a contemporary version of ideas and practices conceived of in the late eighteenth century, and developed and modified throughout the nineteenth and twentieth centuries. It is not a 'new penology' (Feeley and Simon 1992) as such, but rather one that is new in scale and depth, and adjusted to trends and practices of contemporary society.

The first two 'waves' of solitary confinement described in this chapter started off, at least on the declaratory level, as attempts to affect prisoners' minds and effect an internal change in them. The first wave was initially led by morally motivated prison reformers, and then was taken over by prison administrators, in a process which Rothman (1971) describes as the dialectic of 'conscience' and 'convenience'. The second wave was led by psychologists motivated by newly developed behavioural sciences, and it was again taken over by prison administrators. The third wave of solitary confinement, as embodied in supermax prisons, has been initiated and led by prison administrators and has been accompanied by very little debate outside the prison system. But what were the conditions which allowed the managerial discourse and its proposed solutions to become dominant? In the following chapter, I examine some of the factors and actors that played a role in the creation and proliferation of supermaxes in the USA in the last two decades, and argue that, together, these factors created a very powerful confluence of interests that drove

23

Table 2.1 Continuities and discontinuities in the use of solitary confinement

	1850s	1970s	1990s
Name	Separate or Silent system	Adjustment Centers; Decompression Units	Security Housing Units; Special Management Units; Control Units; Supermax
Regime	Confinement to a single cell for most of the day; complete separation from all others; work inside cells or with others in complete silence	Confinement to a single cell for most of the day; some therapeutic programmes (initially)	Confinement to a single cell for 22.5–24 hours a day; complete separation from others; no work, therapy or educational programmes
Architecture	Single cells, solitary activities	Same	Same
Surveillance	High	High	Constant
Initiator	Penal reformers; architects; religious groups	Penal professionals; researchers; psychologists	Prison administrators; politicians
'Clients'	All convicts (uniform treatment)	Troublemakers (more political/ politically motivated prisoners?)	High-risk/violent prisoners/ gang members (more economic/drug-related crimes?)
Aim	Reform (moralise)	Modify behaviour/rehabilitate (socialise)	Control (institutionalise/ immobilise)

Role of isolation	Physically isolate; separate prisoners from all previous influences to create an 'empty vessel'	Physically isolate; strip prisoners of all previous conditioning	Physically isolate; control/incapacitate prisoners; break-down communications
Replace with…	Rules of morality and self-discipline	Rules of acceptable societal behaviour	Rules of acceptable institutional conduct
Equips prisoner with tools to…	Live as a law-abiding citizen in free society/prepare to be part of the working force	Modify his behaviour	Live as per the rules of the prison; unsuitable for free society: 'they strip you of everything but replace it with nothing' [former prisoner]
Governing penological discourse	Reformation	Rehabilitation/treatment	Control
Jargon: Prison staff Prisoners	Guards/warden Convicts	Guards/warden Inmates/clients	Correctional officers/warden Inmates
The gap	Intentions/consequences?	Rhetoric/practice?	Excessiveness? Presentation of risk/reality of clientele?

the creation of harsher, high-tech and high-security isolation prisons.

Notes

1 Prison wardens of the late eighteenth century occasionally used solitary confinement coupled with a restricted diet to deal with the 'refractory prisoner ... this punishment was to strike terror in the hearts of inmates, compel them to abide by the rules of the penitentiary life. ... The confinement of the prisoner to a cell was convenient. Wardens did not intend for it to reform or elevate the criminal, or to have general applicability among all convicts' (Rothman 1971: 92). It was not until the early nineteenth century that the concept of solitary confinement as a penal strategy, and as an architectural design, was widely applied on both sides of the Atlantic.

2 Most European states adopted the 'separate system', while America largely adopted the 'silent congregated model', but, as Rothman (1971: 81) noted, 'the debate raged with an incredible intensity ... and the fact that most prisons in the United States were modelled after the Auburn system did not diminish it. Even more startling, neither did the basic similarity of the two programmes'.

3 By 1850, 10 new prisons modelled after Pentonville had been constructed in England, and 10 others converted to the separate system. Denmark, Sweden, the Netherlands, Germany and France, among other countries, similarly constructed prisons designed to accommodate strict solitary confinement during that period.

4 In 1850, for example, 32 prisoners per 1,000 had to be removed from Pentonville Prison on grounds of insanity. In prisons not applying the separate system, the proportion was 5.8 prisoners per 1,000 (McConville 1981: 208–9).

5 In subsequent cases, the court held that 'solitary confinement' and 'close confinement' do not 'import the same kind of punishment. Solitary confinement may involve close confinement, but a criminal could be held in close confinement without being subjected to solitary confinement' (*Rooney*, (1905); see also *Rogers* (1905)).

6 In some countries, most notably in Scandinavia, the 'separate system' remained in operation well into the twentieth century: until 1946 in Sweden, the early 1930s in Denmark, and 1925 in Norway (Scharff-Smith 2004).

7 Rasmussen (1973). This body of research included field studies and controlled laboratory experiments (see Vernon (1963) for a review).

8 The period also saw a shift in the psychological discourse, away from the psychodynamic approach, associated with Freud, which places the determinates of human behaviour within the individual, and towards

the behaviourist approach, associated with Skinner, which emphasises the role of environmental factors in influencing behaviour. The pharmaceutical industry also came into age during this period, offering new means for controlling populations.

9 The Marion prison replaced Alcatraz (the 'Rock') as the Federal Bureau of Prisons' highest security prison. Marion was opened in June 1963, at the height of the 'treatment era'. It had 435 single cells, and its prisoners were offered a range of counselling, educational and vocational programmes by staff, which included social workers, psychologists, teachers, and other 'new professionals'.

10 Federal Bureau of Prisons Control Unit Policy Statement, 7 June 1973 (in King 1999: 167).

11 START Revised Program Description, November 1973. In Committee on the Judiciary (1974), Appendix item II, B (d), pp. 262–72.

12 The idea that a person's mind at birth is a *tabula rasa*, 'blank slate', upon which experience then makes its imprints, has its roots in seventeenth-century thought (Locke (1710).

13 While crude principles of behaviourism remain part of official discourses to date, isolation units dedicated to behaviour modification only operated as intended for a very brief period before becoming 'regular' lockdown units, where prisoners were held in strict solitary confinement with little or no access to programmes.

14 See, for example, Haney and Lynch (1997), Human Rights Watch (1997, 1999, 2000), King (1999) and Riveland (1999).

15 Traditionally, there have been two main models for managing prisoners who pose a problem for prison authorities. The 'concentration' model, of which Alcatraz ('the Rock') was an example, wherein prisoners who require particularly secure custody are concentrated in single, specially designed prisons, and the 'dispersal' model, wherein such prisoners are dispersed in segregation units across the prison estate. In both the USA and the UK, prison administrators alternated between these two models in managing their 'trouble' prisoners. For a discussion of the 'concentration' and 'dispersal' models see Bottoms and Light (1987), Ward (1987), Buchanan *et al.* (1988). I discuss the design features of 'new-generation' prisons and demonstrate how the concept was turned on its head in the construction of supermax facilities in Chapter 6.

16 Indeed, some argue that the absence of work discipline in supermaxes entirely distinguishes them from their earlier counterparts in general and Bentham's Panopticon in particular (see Bauman 2000).

Chapter 3

Factors and actors in the rise of supermax prisons

Prisons and jails are an 'early warning system' of sorts for a society. They constitute the canary in the coal mine, providing an omen of mortal danger that often lies beyond our capacity to perceive. (Miller 2000)

Prisons do not function in a vacuum, but are part of larger criminal justice systems, which operate within wider social, cultural, political and economic systems. Shifts in these systems are affected by, and reflected in, penal ideologies and practices. This chapter examines some of the factors and actors that played a role in the creation and proliferation of supermaxes in the USA since the late 1980s, and enabled the managerial discourse of controlling risk to become predominant. First, I examine some key themes and trends which affected the US criminal justice system in its entirety. The sections which follow move from the general to the specific and use California as a primary example to illustrate and flesh out the issues discussed. My examination of these macro-level issues is selective and brief, aimed at providing contextual background in understanding why supermax prisons emerged when they did.

The American criminal justice system – general trends

The thinking behind the prison boom has its own inexorable logic.... If crime is going up, then we need to build more prisons; and if the crime is going down, it's because we built more prisons – and building even more prisons will therefore drive crime down even lower. (Schlosser 1998: 4)

The most striking feature and one of the most widely discussed issues among legislatures, prison practitioners, prison reformers – and the subject of a large, and growing, body of academic research – is the vast expansion of prison populations in the USA, particularly since the 1980s.[1] Throughout the first half of the twentieth century, incarceration rates in the USA remained more or less stable, with small cyclical changes, peaking in 1940. In the early 1970s, incarceration rates began to climb, rising sharply in the 1980s, reaching a rate of 181 prisoners per 100,000 residents nationwide in 1985, rising to 311 in 1990, 475 in 1997, and up to 751 prisoners per 100,000 US residents in 2007. Absolute numbers are striking. At the end of 2007, more than 7.3 million people in the USA were under some form of correctional supervision including those on probation (4,293,163), parolees (824,365), jail detainees (780,581) and prisoners (1,598,316) in federal and state prisons.[2] In 2008, an estimated 5.3 million US citizens were denied the right to vote as a result of being in prison, on probation or on parole, and in some states also as a result of being former felons.[3]

Recent statistics show a minor decline in the growth rate of prison populations in some states, but absolute numbers continue to increase, and prison systems across the USA are struggling to accommodate them. This is a losing battle, as even in jurisdictions which embarked on massive projects of prison construction, many prisons operate beyond their design capacity and are severely overcrowded.

The main cause of this mass expansion of the US criminal justice system, rather than growing crime rates, was changes in penal laws and policies. Since the 1990s, when incarceration rates reached unprecedented highs and the length of prison sentences increased substantially, crime rates have mostly declined.[4] Indeed, as Zimring (2001: 165) notes, harsher policies often emerge in times of declining crime rates. Some of the contributing factors to rising incarceration rates include the 'war on drugs' of the early 1980s,[5] and the adoption of mandatory and determinate sentencing guidelines and laws with catchy names such as 'three strikes and you're out', 'truth in sentencing'[6] and 'mandatory minimum sentences'[7] by the federal government and many states across the USA throughout the 1990s,[8] alongside changes in policies regarding parole. Intended to reduce disparity in sentencing and the use of judicial discretion, these sentencing laws replaced indeterminate sentencing, which was widely used in the USA for most of the twentieth century.[9] In theory, these sentencing laws and policies aim to incapacitate habitual and dangerous offenders, but in practice they result in petty and drug offenders being incarcerated for long stretches of time in high-security prisons.[10]

Washington was the first state to adopt 'three strike laws' in 1993. On 7 March 1994, California's governor signed into law the state's own (and much harsher) version of the law, described as 'the most significant change to the state criminal justice system in more than a generation' (California LAO 1999).[11] The wide public support for the measure, which was approved by California's voters by a margin of 72 per cent, is indicative of the public and political climate of the time, and a popular demand for harsher penal policies.[12] A proposition to revise the law significantly in 2004 was rejected by California voters, though the level of support for the measure (47 per cent) suggests some shift in public sentiments (California LAO 2005). California's 'three strikes' law mandates that a person who has committed one prior violent or serious offence and who commits any new felony may receive twice the normal sentence for the new felony ('second striker'). A person who has committed two prior violent or serious offences and who commits any new felony ('third striker') will automatically be sentenced to 25 years to life in prison. The law requires consecutive, rather than concurrent, sentencing for multiple offences committed by 'strikers', and restricts the ability of repeat offenders to earn good time credits, meaning that they will have to serve the entire length of their sentence. It thus removes discretionary powers not only from the judicial system but also from prison administrations. At the end of 2008, 41,089 prisoners, almost a quarter of California's prison population, were second (20 per cent) and third (4.8 per cent) strikers (California Department of Corrections and Rehabilitation (CDCR) 2009).

Another consequence of punitive sentencing laws and penal policies is the ever increasing number of prisoners from racial minorities, giving weight to assertions about the inherent racism of the US criminal justice system and its management of the unwanted poor (Miller 1996, 2000; Reiman 1996). Commentators note that the 'war on drugs', which was a major contributor to the increase in prisoner numbers, also singled out racial minorities and that although drug consumption is roughly equal among African-American and white populations, African-Americans are imprisoned for drug offences at 14 times the rate of whites.[13] In 1990, a US nationwide study found that on an average day, one in every four African-American men aged

20–29 was either in prison or jail, or on probation/parole. By 2000, the rate had risen to one in three. Indeed, while prison populations in the USA have risen for both white and non-white male prisoners, the rate of African-Americans and Hispanics in prisons is much higher than their proportional representation in the population.[14] Tonry (2001: 525) rightly notes that while it is impossible to determine whether laws and policies such as the war on drugs were intended to target racial minorities or whether they were adopted in good faith and turned out to disadvantage racial minorities, it is undisputed that in practice these laws and policies have had disproportional effects on them.

Sentencing laws which result in more people being sent to prison for longer prison terms are only one side of the equation. Another development with direct impact on prisoners' experience of the penal system was the official abandonment of rehabilitative ideals and rhetoric (Allen 1981), and a consequent trend towards harsher prison conditions or 'increasing the severity of punishment', as part of the 'get-tough' movement. Throughout the 1990s, punishment was once again taking on a more expressive form, reflected in the re-emergence of practices such as prison chain gangs and public shaming. As Garland put it, for most of the twentieth century, the 'openly avowed expression of vengeful sentiment was virtually taboo ... in recent years explicit attempts to express public anger and resentment have become a recurring theme of the rhetoric that accompanies penal legislation and decision making' (2001: 9). This trend, articulated in the No Frills Prison Act passed by the US Congress in 1996 and adopted in various forms by many states since, reduces prisoners' access to amenities such as recreational equipment, televisions, computers and crafts. The claim behind such legislation is that the deterrent effects of prisons are adversely affected as prisons come to resemble country clubs (or hotels, or summer camps) where prisoners enjoy too many luxuries, paid for by taxpayers.[15] Such policies bring to mind the nineteenth-century, utilitarian 'less eligibility' principle, which held that prisoners are less morally deserving than free people and should therefore be kept in prison in conditions which are inferior to those enjoyed by the least well-off people in the community. High-security and supermax prisoners, of course, are often the first to be at the receiving end of pressures to reduce prisoner privileges and provisions.

Views differ on the question of whether the trends of longer and harsher prison sentences and fewer prison amenities stemmed from a public demand to which politicians reacted or vice versa, and what was the media's role in this.[16] What is undisputed among commentators is that since the 1980s crime and punishment have become part and parcel of the political discourse and that the move towards more punishment is no longer exclusively within the domain of Republican (and, in the UK, Conservative) administrations, but is promoted by both ends of the political spectrum. The 'populist punitivism' (Bottoms 1995) and hardening of attitudes to crime and punishment are attributed by some commentators to the heightened fear of crime and the uncertainty which characterises late modernity (Garland 2001), and by others to public ignorance regarding the working and financing of the penal system (Lenz 2002). These attitudes are represented in, and shaped by, media reports on crime and a growing focus on the (more photogenic) victims of crime (Simon 2000). Victim groups are increasingly involved in the criminal justice system, and sentencing laws and policies are named after victims and announced in political settings. This involvement typically manifests itself in harsher policies and a hardening of attitudes to criminals. As Zimring (2001: 164) put it,

> The rhetoric in support of new punishment proposals in current politics often seems to assume that criminals and crime victims are engaged in a zero sum contest … anything that hurts offenders by definition helps victims … of course … there is no real zero sum relationship. But assuming such a relationship generates a justification for endless cycles of increased infliction of suffering on counterfeit utilitarian grounds.

Against this background, supermax prisons with their austere conditions and near-absolute control of prisoners are presented as one of the remedies by politicians wanting to appear to be doing something about crime. Supermax prisons have become

> political symbols of how 'tough' a jurisdiction has become. In some cases the motivation to build a supermax has come not from correctional officials, but from the legislature and – in at least one instance – the governor (Riveland 1999: 5).

Suggesting that politicians react to (rather than shape) public opinion, the then assistant director of the Federal Bureau of Prisons wrote, in a prison officers magazine, that,

Criminal justice is rapidly stepping out of the shadows and becoming an area in which every citizen has an opinion. This is not new. What is new and remarkable is how much weight public opinion has gained within this new freewheeling style, decisively influencing the political machinery of government. ... All of us are deeply concerned about crime, and the number one subject in every poll in the land is public safety. Our legislative bodies are reacting to public opinion – voices are really being heard, and elected representatives are creating our future in the prison business. (Carlson 1996: 5)

I doubt that Mr Carlson's use of the words 'prison business' was intended literally, but the growth of the 'business of prison' in the last three decades alongside the expansion of prison systems is another key development in the rise of supermax prisons.

Economic interests and the 'prison industrial complex'

Societies of the Western type face two major problems: Wealth is everywhere unequally distributed. So is access to paid work. Both problems contain a potential for unrest. The crime control industry is suited for coping with both. This industry provides profit and work while at the same time producing control of those who otherwise might have disturbed the social process. Compared with other industries, the crime control industry is in a most privileged position. There is no lack of raw material, crime seems to be in endless supply. Endless also are the demands for the service, as well as the willingness to pay for what is seen as security. (Christie 1993: 11)

Financial considerations and interests are another important aspect of contemporary criminal justice systems. Prison construction and management have direct and indirect economic implications. This has been termed the 'prison industrial complex': 'a set of bureaucratic, political and economic interests that encourage increased spending on imprisonment, regardless of the actual need. [It] is not a conspiracy ... it is a confluence of special interests that has given prison construction in the US a seemingly unstoppable momentum' (Schlosser 1998: 4). Viewed this way, who were some of those standing to gain from the construction of prisons in general and supermax prisons in particular, in the 1990s?

Rural communities

Many of the new maximum-security prisons were built in rural communities, whose traditional economies – farming, mining, logging and manufacturing – have been declining for decades. In stark contrast to past public campaigns carrying the message of 'not in my backyard', many communities have lobbied to have prisons built on their land. The economic impact of prisons is huge. In addition to construction and operating expenses, prisons purchase local goods and services, and prison employees purchase local properties and spend their annual wages locally. Prisons are also recession-proof, often expanding in times of national economic downturns, and are a relatively non-polluting enterprise, a feature which enhances their attractiveness to small communities. New prisons are marketed to local communities on these premises. A publicity entry posted on the California Department of Corrections (CDC) website several years ago, for example, stated that

> Prisons make good neighbors. They provide a strong economic base, create hundreds of jobs, and supply and supervise inmate workers for vital community service projects. Corrections staff enrich community life; many actively participate in local organizations and issues.

These general advantages were then further elaborated, and a price tag placed on each promised benefit to the community:

> A prison is a clean, stable, recession-proof industry. It provides permanent employment to 600 to 1,600 people. This translates to an annual payroll of $20 million to $52 million – money that helps fuel the local economy. Every year, a prison also buys between $1 million and $4 million in goods and services from the surrounding area. As local businesses prosper, more job opportunities develop. In fact, it's estimated that one new job in the community is created for every two prison jobs. (CDC website, posted 28 December 2003)

Another aspect of high-security prisons which is marketed to the public is their tight security arrangements which make prisoner escape, riot, or any other form of violence which may affect the local community highly improbable. Hidden away on large sites outside residential areas and away from view, these big prisons generate money and jobs without imposing an uneasy or threatening presence on the local community. California's Pelican Bay, located in Crescent City (Del Norte County, a rural area in northern California, close to the border with Oregon), is a good example. Crescent City is a former logging town which was hit hard by economic downturns and suffered high unemployment rates and a declining population when the CDC announced that it was looking for a site for building its new high-security prison. Early in 1984, representatives from Del Norte County contacted the CDC with a view to having the new prison located in the county. For two years, the CDC paid visits to the area, and commissioned feasibility studies addressing issues of hydrology, archaeology, geology, seismology, traffic analysis and engineering.[17] Eventually, eight possible sites were chosen and proposed at a public meeting attended by 350 members of the community. A ballot was taken, and 86.5 per cent of the 328 votes were in favour of constructing a prison in the county. Following additional public meetings and visits to the area, a former, unused logging site located 7.4 miles from Crescent City was selected and approved in 1986. The new prison regenerated the local economy through the creation of new jobs and the purchase of local goods and services. The new prison also brought an estimated 6,000 new residents to the county (in addition to the 4,000 prisoners housed at Pelican Bay), resulting in house prices more than doubling in value after its construction (Parenti 1997).

Crescent City is far from unique. Many of the larger high-security prisons constructed across the USA in the last two decades are located in rural areas and have regenerated their economies. Indeed, these prisons are so attractive to small communities that in some cases the community donated land to the relevant departments of corrections as an incentive for building prisons in the county. This was the case, for example, when citizens of Florence, Colorado, purchased land at a cost of $128,000 and donated it to the Federal Bureau of Prisons as an incentive to build its new prison complex, including a 554-cell supermax (ADX), in the county at a cost of $222 million.

Private companies

Prison means money. Big money. Big in building, big in providing equipment, and big in running. This is so, regardless of private or public ownership. In all Western systems, private firms are involved in some way or another. (Christie 1993: 98)

The issue of privatisation or the involvement of the private sector in providing goods and services that might otherwise be provided by governments has been attracting much attention from both supporters and opponents in the last two decades. Private businesses now deal, to a greater or lesser degree, with all aspects of prison construction, maintenance, provisioning, services and management. As prison systems are expanding, so are related industries providing goods and services to them, and 'what was once a niche business for a handful of companies has become a multibillion-dollar industry with its own trade shows and conventions, web-sites, mail-catalogue orders and direct marketing campaigns' (Schlosser 1998: 14).

Examining the marketing of penal commodities and the use of security as the selling point in the US corrections market through an analysis of advertisements appearing in the trade magazine *Corrections Today* between 1949 and 1999, Lynch (2002) found that, as rehabilitation and reintegration concerns began to wane from the late 1960s and throughout the 1970s, institutional security concerns became more explicit and security became the most prominent feature in ads. Tracing back the use of the term 'supermax', Lynch found that it was first used in 1984 to advertise a lighting system: 'Tougher than any hardened criminal, supermax [lighting system] was built for abuse. The Guards like supermax. The cons leave it alone' (Lynch 2002: 313). The first marketing of actual supermax prisons appeared in 1988, advertised by an architectural firm from Arizona as 'living examples of how tomorrow's maximum-security prisons will be designed' (*ibid.*). The private manufacturers of the perforated-metal cell doors and feeding slots used in supermax prisons also advertised their products in the same issue. By the late 1980s, security was used to sell products from cell furnishings to plumbing systems, and from food services to phone and medical services.

Security, of course, is the main selling point of supermax prisons, and when it comes to security and security products, these high-tech prisons provide a particularly thriving market for prison construction companies and private-sector manufacturers of various devices from mechanical and electronic restraints to gates, locks, lighting fixtures and other products designed especially for maximum-security prisons, such as indestructible food trays and cutlery. Supermax prisons may not be the laboratory that Bentham envisaged the Panopticon to be, but they do provide fertile ground for experimentation with various weapons, and keeping in business companies that previously supplied weaponry to the army.

The type of weapons used constantly evolves with technological innovations, and includes various lethal, non-lethal and chemical weapons and products, ranging from pepper spray launchers to sponge grenades. In addition to manufacturers of these weapons, the list of other private companies which are involved in the prison business is long: architectural and construction companies, plumbers, glaziers, providers of food services and health care, prisoner transportation companies, and so on. All these businesses have been queuing to get a share of this growing industry, where the amounts of money involved are substantial.

The involvement of private companies is not limited to the provision of goods and services. Since the 1980s, private companies have also been increasingly involved in running prisons.[18] In 2008, around 7.9 per cent of prisoners (state and federal) were held in private facilities. Typically, private companies are able to build prisons more quickly at a lower cost, and run them more cheaply, as they use mainly non-unionised, poorly trained guards, a factor which earned them, at least in California, strong opposition by the powerful prison guards' union, the California Correctional Peace Officers Association (CCPOA).[19] Although California does contract with private companies to manage some of its prisons, there is currently no discussion of handing over high-security prisons to the private sector, as the state elects to retain the power over those labelled as the 'worst of the worst'.

Professional interests: the case of the California Correctional Peace Officers Association (CCPOA)

> Every day they 'walk the line' among some of the toughest, most violent inmates in the world…. These are the men and women of the California Correctional Peace Officers Association – dedicated, proud, courageous law enforcement professionals who walk the toughest beat in the state. (CCPOA magazine, *In Harm's Way*, 'Life inside the toughest beat in California', 1996)

> 'The Toughest Beat'
> The correctional officers represented by CCPOA work in a volatile world of warring gangs, drugs and violence, where they face the state's most serious and violent criminals every minute of every day. The stress can be suffocating, the danger unrelenting…. Staff shortages and severe overcrowding add to the danger, forcing officers to work long hours of mandatory

overtime, which hurts family life and jeopardizes prison safety. (CCPOA website, February 2009)

Prison employees and their representative bodies are important stakeholders in the criminal justice system and have vested interest in who is sent to prison and how prisons are managed. In California, the trade union representing prison guards and related professionals is the powerful CCPOA. The opening quotations reflect well the CCPOA's ethos, and hint at how officers view themselves and how they view those incarcerated in California's prisons.[20] The CCPOA was established in 1958 by a handful of guards, and now also organises parole officers, psychiatric and medical technicians, and correctional counsellors, with a total membership of some 31,000 correctional workers who contribute 1.3 per cent of their salary in dues. Correctional Officers (COs) in California enjoy an excellent pension plan, full medical and dental health cover, a monthly budget for staying fit, vacation leave, sick leave, and an average salary cited as being substantially higher than the national average. In 2008, a California CO with seven years' experience earned $73,728 (CDCR 2009). As the prison estate continues to grow, prison staff also have a high degree of job security. There is constant demand for more staff, even in times of economic downturn and high unemployment.

Supermax prisons are relatively safe working places, as the contact that prison staff have with prisoners is reduced to a minimum, and the CCPOA supported their creation alongside the mass prison construction wave in California in the late 1980s. The CCPOA was very well placed to promote its interests at all levels of government. Under the leadership of Don Novey, its president between 1980 and 2002 and a legendary figure, 'almost as famous for his personality as for his political achievements' (Centre on Juvenile and Criminal Justice 2002), the CCPOA focused its efforts on much wider issues than improving salaries and working conditions for its members. Novey's motto was, 'If you have an open door with an administration, you can do creative things. A lot of the money that was spent by our group was to get that door open' (ibid.). Around 35 per cent of CCPOA's budget goes to funding political activities through its Bargaining Unit 6, and it has been a major contributor to political candidates in California, both Democrats and Republicans, as well as the judiciary, from local district attorneys to State Supreme Court candidates.

Throughout the years, the CCPOA has also spent vast amounts on lobbying fees and in campaign contributions to communicate its legislative agenda. It was one of the main forces behind the adoption of 'three strikes' laws in California in 1994 and a major contributor to the campaign and, more recently, donated $1.8 million to efforts to defeat Proposition 5, or the Non-violent Offender Rehabilitation Act, an initiative to reduce punishment for drug and non-violent offenders. Proposition 5 was rejected by voters in the November 2008 elections. As a union of state employees, the CCPOA is accountable only to its members and the Internal Revenue Service. Beyond its financial contributions and persistent lobbying activities, the sheer number of prison staff, particularly in smaller communities, makes them (and their family members) a substantial body of voters.[21]

The CCPOA works in partnership with crime victims groups, including the Crime Victims Units of California, which received 95 per cent of its initial funding from the CCPOA; the Doris Tate Crime Victims Bureau, which received 78 per cent of its funding from the CCPOA; and the Polly Klass Foundation. The CCPOA sponsors an annual march of victims' families to California's government buildings in Sacramento. In the words of CCPOA's magazine editorial, the event, which 'in the past has been marked by 700 mock-coffins symbolizing the victims of those on California's Death Row' being laid on the lawns surrounding the building, received in 2000,

> a new compelling impact that swept through the crowd ... when poster-sized photographs of the victims were placed by the coffins... but through shattered lives and lost dreams, hope can emerge.... They hope for changes in the way California deals with its offenders – and with its victims – and they hope for an easier time for the victims who will surely follow. (*PeaceKeeper* editorial, summer 2000)

The alliance between prison staff and victims of crime is intended to send a strong message to both politicians and the public about 'good' versus 'evil', victims versus perpetrators, 'security' versus violent crime. The 'hope for the future', it is implied, will be realised through more and tougher prisons, run by CCPOA members.

In short, the CCPOA is a wealthy and very powerful union and a strong interest group, which promotes and extends its power base and its 'kingdom' – the prison estate. Its power was particularly felt throughout the 1990s, when California's prison system expanded at an unprecedented rate. CCPOA's alliances and financial contributions placed Bargaining Unit 6 in an excellent position when negotiating the creation of more workplaces for its members, better pay, better working conditions and better status. As one commentator put it,

39

> Along with money and organisation the CCPOA has commanded the ideological high ground of the 1990s: crime. Being tough on crime has become a right-wing litmus test. The issue of crime … has a visceral power rivalled only by the once mighty anti-Communist hysteria. The CCOPA has assiduously courted this public fear and pandered to desires for strong and simple solutions. (Parenti 1999a: 227)

Most importantly, the CCPOA's powerful position has given it unprecedented clout when demanding additional security arrangements and fixtures inside prisons, enhancing the personal security of officers at the cost of reducing prisoner activities and amenities and arguably at the cost of prisoners' mental well-being. CCPOA's power may now be waning a little. California's governor, Arnold Schwarzenegger, refused to receive CCPOA contributions in the 2003 elections, citing the CCPOA code of silence and failed negotiations over pay for its members. The CCPOA, for its part, has joined forces with victims groups to oppose prison reform proposals made by the governor. Negotiations on pay contracts between the state and the CCPOA began in July 2006 and, more than two and a half years later, had still failed to reach agreement. Yet, the sheer size of its membership and the dues they pay will undoubtedly mean that the CCPOA continues to play an important role in crime and justice politics and policies in California, not least those relating to the treatment of prisoners labelled as 'the worst of the worst'.

To sum up, the increasing use of supermax confinement in the USA must be viewed against a background of macro-level issues, including the economic crisis that affected many rural communities throughout the USA from the late 1980s; prison privatisation and the proliferation of companies providing goods and services to prisons; increasingly punitive attitudes, public feelings of insecurity and fear of crime, and the political exploitation of such sentiments; and sentencing laws ensuring longer and tougher prison sentences, resulting in an enormous growth in prison populations. These factors, combined with the huge political influence of prison guard unions promoting safer working environments for their members, facilitated the creation, and proliferation, of supermax prisons throughout the 1990s.

In the following chapters, I move from external factors affecting trends and shifts in crime and punishment, and focus on the deep end of the penal system, supermax prisons. I start by examining, in the following chapter, how official narratives justify the need for solitary confinement and supermax prisons, and how the purported goals of these prisons are set out.

Notes

1 For example, see the special issue, 'Mass Imprisonment in the USA', of the journal *Punishment and Society* (January 2001, 3(1)). See also Zimring and Hawkins 1991; Christie 1993; Miller 1996; Currie 1998; Simon 2000 and Tonry 2001.

2 US Bureau of Justice Statistics, *Prisoners in 2007* (December 2008).

3 More than 2 million of these are African-Americans (The Sentencing Project, January 2009). The disproportionate representation of African-Americans and Hispanics in the criminal justice system means that they are disenfranchised at higher rates than whites. In California, African-Americans were disenfranchised at almost 10 times the rate of whites. Hispanics, who make up 19 per cent of California's citizens of voting age, made up 36.5 per cent of those disenfranchised (California Legislative Analyst's Office (LAO) 2005: 105).

4 The relationship between crime rates and incarceration rates has always been tenuous. From 1962 to 1980, crime rates (both violent and property crimes) mostly rose, declining slightly between 1980 and 1984 and then rising again until 1991 (reaching a peak of 758.1 violent crimes and 5,139.7 property crimes per 100,000 US population), and then mostly declined through to 2007, when the rate of violent crimes stood at 466.9 per 100,000 US population (Bureau of Justice Statistics 2009). Incarceration rates during the same period, as previously discussed, mostly rose.

5 See Blumstein and Beck 1999; Caplow and Simon 1999 and Mauer 2001. California is singled out as having the most expansive version of 'three strikes' laws, with consequently 'the most draconian effects on the Criminal Justice System' (Austin 1996: 157).

6 See Austin 1996: 155–77. 'Truth in sentencing', a federal initiative enacted in 1994, requires that offenders sentenced for violent crime serve at least 85 per cent of their sentence.

7 These laws, adopted by most states across the USA, mainly target the crimes of weapon possession, driving under the influence of alcohol, and possessing and distributing drugs.

8 Since the early 1990s, most states and the federal government have also adopted some form of intermediate sanctions including intensive supervision programs (ISPs), home confinement, community services, prison boot camps and day fines, which allow a 'longer menu of sentencing choices [which] could lead to better matching of the severity of punishment to the seriousness of crimes' (National Institute of Justice 1997). These initiatives, however, often result in increased 'confinement populations' through technical violations of conditions attached to the

non-custodial sentence, and, rather than reducing the numbers of people subjected to supervision, thus serve to widen the net and increase their number.

9 Mauer 2001: 9. Indeterminate sentencing was rejected by an unusual coalition of liberals, conservatives and prisoners. Liberals thought that the system discriminated against minorities, prisoners thought it was unfair, and conservatives thought it was too 'soft'. In California, indeterminate sentencing was abolished in 1976, and punishment replaced rehabilitation as the main goal of imprisonment in California's prisons (Schlosser 1998: 29).

10 Critics point out that these laws also mean that offenders will be incarcerated well beyond the 'peak' age of criminality, cited as the early 20s. See Austin 1996; California LAO 1995, 1999.

11 Following Washington and California, at least 23 states and the federal government adopted some form of 'three strikes' laws in the 1990s (Mauer 1998; Tonry 2001).

12 Applying Durkheim's thesis on the expressive functions of punishment, one study of public support in California for these measures suggested that support stemmed not so much from judgements about the future dangerousness of offenders, as from judgements about social conditions, including the decline of the family as a social institution, lack of social consensus, mistrust in the abilities of social institutions to rehabilitate offenders, and so on (Taylor and Boeckmann, 1997).

13 Miller 2000; Perkinson 1996. Commentators single out laws relating to crack cocaine, used primarily by African-Americans, which impose greater penalties than for powder cocaine, used mainly by whites.

14 African-Americans make up around 13 per cent of the US population nationwide, but are incarcerated (in state and federal prisons) at a rate of 3,138 per 100,000 residents. Incarceration rates for Hispanics and Latinos are similarly high at 1,259 per 100,000 US residents, while the rate for whites is 481 per 100,000 residents. Put differently, out of every 100,000 US residents, 4,397 people from racial minorities were incarcerated, compared with 481 whites (Bureau of Justice Statistics 2008).

15 Lenz (2002) examined whether public support for prison amenities related to perceptions about their source of funding. The findings suggested that in general people were supportive of some prison amenities, unless they were paid for by taxpayers.

16 See Miller 1996; Garland 2000; Mauer 2001; Lenz 2002.

17 Pelican Bay State Prison Public Information Office, 1989–1999; *ibid.*, Institutional Profile, 1993.

18 More specifically, the turning point is cited as 1984 when the then US president, Ronald Reagan, approved private holding cells for immigration detainees in Texas.

19 Throughout the 1990s, conditions in many of the new private prisons, including guard conduct, resulted in a number of riots and violent incidents as well as several prisoner lawsuits.

20 The emphasis on prison officers' long working hours and working conditions in the second, and more recent, quotation, also hints at a possible decrease in the CCPOA's immense power, which has characterised its position in Californian politics since the mid-1980s.

21 I might also add that, at least in Crescent City, home to the Pelican Bay prison, prison employees are certainly a much felt presence everywhere in the city.

Chapter 4

Ideologies of control: discourses on the goals and roles of supermax prisons

It is widely appreciated that total institutions typically fall considerably short of their official aims. It is less widely appreciated that each of these official goals or characters seems admirably suited to provide a key to meaning – a language of explanation that the staff, and sometimes the inmates, can bring to every crevice of action in the institution.... Each institutional goal lets loose a doctrine, with its own inquisitors and martyrs.... (Goffman 1961: 83–4)

Propaganda that promotes control units as effective against crime – in and out of prison – perpetrates a cruel hoax on an unsuspecting and too often gullible public.[1]

As discussed in the previous chapter, a confluence of social, economic, political and professional interests pushed for the creation of supermax prisons across the USA since the late 1980s. In order to gain funding, legitimacy and support, nonetheless, the necessity and alleged benefits of these prisons had to be justified to both internal and external audiences. This chapter focuses on official narratives on the need for, and goals of, supermax prisons. It examines the dominant themes in these narratives, and aims to ascertain who are the supposed inquisitors and martyrs of the supermax doctrine.

The roles of supermax prisons

> Our number one focus is always security – safety of the public, safety of staff, safety of the inmates. [prison officer]

Implicitly, supermax prisons serve to express sentiments of punishment and retribution, and many supermaxes hold prisoners who were charged with committing a serious offence in prison, and punished by a lengthy period of up to five years in solitary confinement. The main stated role of supermax prisons, however, is the management of high-risk prisoners to ensure public safety and prison security.

Protecting the public

Isolating prisoners who are deemed to be dangerous, influential (outside or inside the prison), escape risks or otherwise a potential danger to security will, it is claimed, prevent them from carrying out any act which may endanger national, public or institutional security. National security justifications are, and have historically been, used to place politically motivated prisoners in solitary confinement.[2] The stated purpose of this is to prevent the prisoner from contact with 'terrorist' or 'subversive' groups outside the prison or, in the case of people charged with espionage, to prevent the dissemination of state secrets. Less overtly, isolating those suspected or convicted of politically motivated crimes is a means of repressing political dissent. In the USA, offences against national security are within the jurisdiction of the federal government, and those isolated on 'national security' grounds are held in federal prisons, particularly the ADX at Florence, Colorado. Detainees suspected of crimes against the state, especially in the context of the 'war on terror' will also usually be held in isolation from others, in supermax or similar units. They may also be subjected to 'Special Administrative Measures' (SAMs) if there is a 'substantial risk that a prisoner's communications or contact with persons could result in death or serious bodily injury to persons' (Code of Federal Regulations, 28 C.F.R. 501.3). These measure may include housing in administrative segregation, and limits on correspondence, telephone use and visits.

Public security justifications are also used to segregate criminal prisoners who are considered to be particularly influential 'on the outside', escape artists, and prisoners incarcerated for high-notoriety crimes, such as mass murderers and serial killers. These prisoners have not necessarily committed any offences in prison, but are considered to be too dangerous or influential to allow any risk of their escape, or unmonitored communications between them and the outside world.

Prison security

It is claimed that the only way to achieve prison security and good order is by isolating

> inmates who are difficult management cases, prison gang members, and violent maximum custody inmates ... who require [the] most restrictive and secure containment because they have proven to be the most violent, predatory and disruptive inmates in the prison system. (Cambra 1997)

The introduction of the idea of 'predators' serves a dual purpose: it reaffirms the dangerousness of prisoners destined for supermax confinement, and it also proposes the protection of those who are 'preyed upon' by them, their potential victims. It is claimed that by separating predatory and disruptive prisoners from others, not only will these prisoners be incapacitated and prevented – physically – from following their natural inclination to act violently, but also the prison system as a whole will be better managed. '[The unit] has worked as designed, in that the rest of the system is operating rather quietly. It's a management tool for us.'[3]

> In an effort to maintain a safe and orderly environment within its institutions, the Bureau of Prisons operates control unit programs intended to place into a separate unit those inmates who are unable to function in a less restrictive environment without being a threat to others or to the orderly operation of the institution. (Federal Bureau of Prisons, Control Unit Programs 2001: 1)

Isolating danger will supposedly achieve a wide range of benefits. First, the most dangerous prisoners will be incapacitated and other prisoners, prison staff and the public will be better protected. Second, security arrangements in 'general population' prisons can be relaxed. Third, programme delivery in general population prisons can be improved. Fourth, prison gang communications and activities will be disrupted. Fifth, the very existence of supermax prisons will act as a deterrent.

In what follows, I look at these proposed benefits of supermax prisons and examine how they are presented in official guidelines and by prison administrators. The success of supermax prisons in achieving their official goals is evaluated in the final chapter of this book.

The goals of supermax prisons

A state of the art design ... [for] inmates presenting serious management concerns.[4]

The prevalence of the managerial discourse is evident in official narratives on the goals of supermax confinement, which are articulated in terms of their usefulness as tools for managing prison estates.

Controlling risk/incapacitating danger

Prison officials claim that some prisoners are so dangerous that the only way to prevent them from harming others is to hold them in isolation from others and under strict controls. This reasoning stems from the incapacitation/selective incapacitation model and the proposition that, by identifying high-risk prisoners and maintaining tight control over them, the occurrence of violence can be minimised. Those isolated are prevented, physically, from engaging in violence.

There are those people in prison who would prey on people because of their violence, and you have to have some place where you can put them that at least offers a modicum of safety to the other guys that you leave out there, and largely that is going to be a [supermax] environment. [administrator]

Also present in this line of reasoning are situational crime-prevention principles: preventing the occurrence of violence through the manipulation of environmental factors so as to reduce the opportunity for, and possibility of, prisoner violence.

Your main concern is control. You want to make sure that the inmates don't have the opportunity to attack each other, you limit their opportunities to assault staff and because it is a [supermax] unit, you're not concerned with providing programming. [prison officer]

> It's not a perfect system, but definitely isolating the violence off the main General Population yards is a tool we need to have. [unit manager]

It is claimed that by isolating and tightly controlling 'disruptive' prisoners and reducing the opportunities they have to act violently, the entire prison system can be better managed, and the following additional 'operational' objectives achieved: a reduction of security arrangements in general population prisons; an increase of programme provisions in general population prisons; deterrence to prisoners in general population prisons from breaking prison rules, and; breaking down prison gangs.

Reducing security arrangements in general population prisons

The claim is that concentrating 'disruptive' or 'dangerous' prisoners in separate, specially designed facilities allows a relaxation of security arrangements in other prisons. If the most disruptive prisoners are held in separate facilities, prisoners in the general population can be held in conditions more appropriate to their security level than conditions geared to 'worst case scenario' arrangements previously necessitated by the presence of dangerous prisoners.

Increasing programme effectiveness in 'general population' prisons

The rationale is that by removing the violent and disruptive few from general population prisons, the compliant majority will be able to participate in prison programmes and thus increase their chances of successful reintegration into society upon their release. According to the Federal Bureau of Prisons guidelines on control units,

> Programs that serve the vast majority, such as industries, education and vocational training are made less effective by violence, threats of violence, and major breaches of security To protect the majority of inmates and still fulfil the Bureau's obligation to provide safekeeping, care, and subsistence to those who are violent and disruptive, special programs are needed. (Control Unit Programs 2001 at section 541.406)

> In any prison system you're going to have a need to house that percentage of inmates that either can't or refuse to get along with the other inmates. It may not seem clear from the outside, but the vast majority of inmates they don't want to be in prison

but since they're there they want to be able to get a job, do something with their days. A substantial number would like to better themselves in some way, but it is difficult when you have inmates that want to tell you how to run your life and it's our job to try to find those inmates and remove them so that the remaining inmates can get along as well as they can. That's going to mean you're going to have maximum security prisons, even within maximum security prisons. [administrator]

In other words, most prisoners simply want to 'do their time', but the dangerous few prevent the docile majority from peaceful coexistence in prisons. Through the removal of 'disruptive elements', the prison system in its entirety operates better, allowing prisoners to make more of their time in prison. This claim completely ignores issues of programme provision (or the lack thereof) in prisons, as I discuss later.

Deterrence

Prisoners, it is claimed, are rational actors who wish to maximise gain and minimise pain, and therefore will seek to stay out of the highly restrictive supermax environments. The threat of being sent to a maximum-security prison thus acts as a deterrent, and contributes to the reduction of violence in general population prisons.[5]

It's a great deterrent. We have, you know, I have interviewed inmates in other units and here. They all know about the unit. Once an inmate leaves here, they discuss the security enhancements that are provided in this unit, they tell other inmates it's not the place you want to be. Some don't believe it. Some end up here, but they become believers very fast. So it is a great deterrent within this agency to have a facility like this. [administrator]

It is also claimed that the hardship of supermax confinement will deter those who are already confined in a supermax from future misconduct.

Breaking down gang communications

This operational goal targets prison gang members. Although prison gangs are largely distinct from street gangs and their influence outside prison is limited, they wield considerable power in prison and organise much of the internal prison economy and its related violence. While most state prisons have some gang presence, their size and influence vary. I deal with the process of classification and 'validation' of gang membership in the following chapter, but here we should note that the 'war on gangs' is one of the main justifications for supermax confinement in many jurisdictions and gang members – both confirmed and alleged – form a large group among those labelled as 'disruptive', regardless of their actual behaviour in prison. Isolating gang leaders and breaking down their communication with gang members is meant to result in reduced gang activity and act as a deterrent to joining prison gangs:

> Removal of prominent gang leaders from the general population is a strategy often used to weaken the gang structure and allow marginal members to rethink their leadership with the gang and its activities. It also sends a message that proliferation of gangs will not be permitted.[6]

Different combinations of the objectives discussed above are cited by most departments of corrections (DOCs) when explaining their need for supermax prisons. A US nationwide survey of supermax confinement found that

> The need to better manage violent and seriously disruptive offenders was cited as a major factor in the development of supermax housing by 36 of 37 responding DOCs. The need to better manage gang activities was ranked as a major factor by 17 DOCs. Also of some importance were projected increases in commitments of violent adult offenders. (National Institute of Corrections 1997: 5)

These and the additional objectives listed above centre on issues of control and internal management of prisons, and earlier discourses of reformation or rehabilitation through solitary confinement are not present in the official language of control. When looking beyond official statements, nonetheless, one can trace some of the earlier discourses on the expected outcomes of solitary confinement. These 'deeper themes' are examined in the following section.

Underlying ideologies, claims, and theories about human nature

> The translation of inmate behavior into moralistic terms suited to the institution's avowed perspective will necessarily contain some broad presuppositions as to the character of human beings. Given the inmates of whom they have charge, and the processing that must be done to them, the staff tend to evolve what may be thought of as a theory of human nature. As an implicit part of institutional perspective, this theory rationalizes activity, provides a subtle means of maintaining social distance from inmates and a stereotyped view of them, and justifies the treatment accorded to them. (Goffman 1961: 87)

Supermax prisons are largely justified as an administrative prison management tool that is neither punitive nor reformative in nature, but a last-resort solution for managing prisoners labelled as disruptive or difficult to control. The growing emphasis on managerial goals in official discourses is consistent with the 'new penology', and the move 'away from an aspiration to affect individual lives through rehabilitative or transformative efforts and toward the more 'realistic' task of monitoring and managing intractable groups' (Feeley and Simon 1992: 474). I would, nonetheless, argue that while the predominance of managerial discourses in the supermax doctrine may be 'new', some of the ideologies and 'theories about human nature' (Goffman 1961: 87) that guided prison policies in the past still shape current strategies, and while the explicit discourses of moral reform and behaviour modification are absent, implicit in supermax confinement is the notion that previous destructive patterns of thought and behaviour can be broken down.

The dangerous individual

A recurring theme in official justifications for highly controlled confinement is a focus on the dangerous nature or disposition of labelled prisoners. A study of the changing shape of penality as reflected in advertisements appearing in the trade magazine *Corrections Today*, demonstrated how, as security became the main selling point of 'correctional goods' in the 1980s, where the prisoner featured,

> [H]e is now made to be an irredeemably dangerous threat to safety, security and efficiency. He is no longer the 'clever patient'

> but had become the 'bad guy' who must be contained behind bars and within sophisticated perimeter systems, and who can turn everything from toothbrushes and tobacco to sprinklers and screws into security risks. (Lynch 2002: 316)

Such 'irredeemably dangerous' prisoners must be contained in a new type of high-tech confinement, suitable for their unprecedented and industrious danger. They are, it is claimed, the worst of the worst:

> That's what this facility is for. It's for violent, aggressive, very hard to manage inmates, and we have those inmates here. We have some of the worst of the worst is what this facility holds. [prison officer]

> The baddest of the bad – the most violent, the murderers, rapists, terrorists, bombers – those who cannot be managed anywhere else … the meanest, nastiest, most intransigent criminals in the country, the ones upon whom everyone else has given up. (Molden 1997, on Administrative Maximum Security Facility prisoners)

The main culprits responsible for the need for, and introduction of, supermax prisons, then, are a 'new' type of incorrigible offenders – uncontrollable, unpredictable, highly dangerous and, crucially, beyond redemption. The claim that highly controlled confinement is absolutely necessary to deal with a 'new breed' of highly dangerous criminals, however, is not new and was also used, for example, to justify the introduction of the 'special units' in British prisons in the 1960s. 'Indeed, just the past 30 years have seen the emergence of several allegedly new criminal types, each one more fearsome than its predecessor and requiring a new level of prison security'.[7]

The huge growth in the number of prisoners categorised as 'dangerous' or 'disruptive' and allocated to supermax prisons is partially explained by the growth of gang culture and street violence. With more than a hint of nostalgia, prison officials claim that in contrast to inmates in the 'old days', who respected unspoken rules and agreements between them and prison staff, prisoners today are younger and more dangerous, and lack respect for authority. They 'don't care about anything and anyone', and 'codes of honour' mean little to them; 'A lot of the older inmates out there who once wielded influence on a Yard, are throwing up their hands saying, "You know, we can't control these youngsters"' [prison officer]. In an article on the future of prisons the former director of the Federal Bureau of Prisons made a similar statement:

> Whereas the old, traditional prison gangs attempted to get along with prison staff and presented an outward co-operative attitude, today's diverse neighbourhood based groups have demonstrated no inclination to co-operate with correctional staff.... In order to cope with this new, more violent, gang affiliated offender, many states are designing, constructing and operating administrative maximum prison facilities.... Most practitioners in the prison business today will agree that our clientele is indeed tougher and more dangerous than ever before.... I attribute it simply to the fact that our streets are more violent and the same offenders are sent to our institutions. The 'drive-by shooting' mentality has moved from the inner city right into our cellblocks. (Carlson 1996: 5)

The dangerous individual, then, brings with him, or 'imports' (Irwin and Cressey 1962) to prison the violent subcultures of the increasingly dangerous streets of inner cities. This notion of 'dangerous streets' certainly has resonance with wider audiences and a growing fear of crime. Also attributing the growing dangerousness of prisoners to wider societal shifts, one prison administrator made a similar observation and referred to some of the latest stories of random violence which shocked the nation:

> We have to recognise that our society has changed ... the inmates are not the same now as they were thirty years ago.... We see in our society, we see the news every day, where we have six year old kids picking up guns, going into school and killing other children.... We're seeing kids... teenagers getting guns, getting bombs, going into high schools and killing multiple people, blowing people away.... Those are the people that we're getting into our prison system.... Those kinds of folks weren't out there thirty years ago.... These kids going into high school and using them as war zones and battlegrounds weren't always there.

The emphasis on a 'new' type of dangerous offender, then, also acts as its own justification for any new, tougher measures that need to follow. Statements linking the dangerousness of prisoners with violent crimes outside the prison not only reassert the threat that supermax prisoners pose in a way that resonates with the public, but they also place social and moral barriers between the new generic type of the 'dangerous offender' and the rest of society. Such barriers make it easier to justify, both internally and externally, any treatment meted out to supermax prisoners.

In practice, as the following chapters demonstrate, despite the official recourse to explanations of prisoners' transgressions against society as the factor which leads to their placement in supermax prisons, these prisons mostly hold prisoners who violated prison rules rather than those who committed the worst crimes outside the prison. This creates a blurring between the notions of the 'disruptive prisoner' and the 'dangerous individual' and the prison itself emerges as a separate entity which requires protection.

Behaviour modification/changing attitudes

Ideas of behaviour modification follow conveniently once images of the dangerous, uncontrollable individual are established. Unlike their earlier incarnations, supermax prisons do not officially endeavour to reform, rehabilitate, change or 'correct' prisoners, and their design is not meant to shape prisoners' morality, but to control them and their environment to the greatest degree possible. It may, however, be claimed that supermax units, prisons within prisons, do aim to change those confined within: to turn them into better, more obedient prisoners. In the 'separate' penitentiaries of the nineteenth century, the prisoner was expected to be reformed through inner reflection and moral guidance. In the control units of the 1970s, prisoners were expected to modify their behaviour through manipulation of their environment and the use of positive and negative reinforcements. In supermax prisons, 'change' is expected to occur through isolation, deprivation and the prisoner's automatic compliance with rules and regulations, a form of 'operant conditioning' (Skinner 1953). Thus, while the psychological narrative of 'people changing' is mostly not part of the discourses around supermax prisons, the idea that isolation in stark, highly controlled environments would result in some change in prisoners is implicit in official narratives. A senior supermax administrator captured this tension:

> You know, there are various schools of thought, well, okay, do you make this a place where you drive people to learn new behaviours, or do you make [it] a place where they don't want to be? And I think that [we've] kind of tried to be a little bit of each and I'm not sure that we've done either one real well.

The use of solitary confinement in other contexts and for different official aims, including its use as an interrogation technique, a means of reaching a 'higher' spiritual place in various religious practices, and a means of simulating extreme environments in scientific experiments, illustrates that isolation is known to, intends to, and *does* create certain mental states. Thus, although the extreme design and tightly controlled operation of supermax prisons are justified primarily in terms of managerial needs, throughout interviews with prison designers and penal professionals there was an underlying narrative of 'people changing'. When asked whether he thought that supermax confinement was a form of brainwashing, one senior administrator replied that it was a resocialisation tool:

> I think if people regard behaviour modification as brainwashing, then we pretty much have to accept the fact that we've all been brainwashed through our process of just growing up, by being told what's acceptable in society and what's not acceptable in society if you want to ... be a part of society. And when I talk of behaviour modification, I'm talking, generally speaking, of giving people access to the same tools that the rest of us not only had access to, but we took advantage of when we were growing up ... and a lot of these people did not accept them. They accepted an alternate lifestyle that was either stealing or hurting people and they disregarded some of the social evolutionary processes that the majority of people took. So I think it's an opportunity to tell people when they get into prison that there's still some social values that you're going to have to accept, and if you choose to be violent then there's some consequences to that and one of the consequences is that you're not going to be living in comfort for this period of time, but if you decide that you don't want to do that then we're going to give you an opportunity to go through an evolution, to go through a learning process to give yourself access to some skills that will give you alternatives to violence ... *and if you want to call it 'brainwashing' that's okay. But if it enables people to modify their behaviour so that they don't feel that they need to resort to violence, then I think it's something that we need to do.* [interviewee's emphasis].

It should be noted, and I return to this issue throughout the following chapters, that supermaxes do not offer any 'alternative to violence'. On the contrary, they are themselves highly violent places. But the people-changing narrative is present in current discourses, even if almost apologetically. Further, one can again trace a blurring between the 'dangerous individual' who threatens society at large and the 'disruptive prisoner' who threatens prison order.

Rational choice/wilful behaviour

A recurring claim made by prison officials and related professionals is that prisoners have 'earned their way' into a supermax unit.

> Nobody is here for not having done something. They've done something to earn their way here. [prison officer]

> Inmates that are assigned to [the unit] ... have entered this agency at a lower custody status and have, in most cases, refused to comply and adjust to the agency's policy and procedures. *Thus, because of their personal intent to disobey or to not follow directions*, comes the management problem, and they can get here because of disciplinary issues, they can also be housed here because of their aggressive and assaultive behaviour ... so the type of inmate that is housed at this facility is *those that cannot be controlled or do not want to be controlled* in the other type of facility *and pretty much they're predators* that are housed at this facility. [administrator; my emphasis]

> the problem is that the vast majority of those guys already made their decision when they had access to programmes that they didn't want, they wanted to do this other stuff – the other stuff was dealing drugs, smuggling drugs, preying on other inmates out there, being violent – and so ... you gave them access at one point, they made this decision so now we're not going to give them access to that and we're going to put them over here. [prison officer]

Since prisoners have made a rational choice to misbehave and thus earned their way into a supermax, it follows that any treatment meted out to them is 'their own fault'.

Progression

A different but related claim is that supermax prisons offer prisoners a progressive programme. Prisoners, it is claimed, are not incarcerated in the supermax indefinitely, but can gradually work their way out of it. Just as they 'earned their way in', most of them can 'earn their way out' of supermax prisons:

They have earned their way into here. There are some that can earn their way out by adjusting and complying with established policy and procedure. [prison officer]

The claim that prisoners can progress out of supermax units usually has limited grounding in reality, however.

There are some that can't earn their way out because they are here and this is where they belong and this is where they'll stay until they are released from the agency. [administrator]

Where some gradual system which allows prisoners to progress out of the unit is in place, it is typically one which mainly uses negative reinforcements, giving prisoners little incentive to comply with its requirements. Furthermore, the initial time that a prisoner has to spend in solitary confinement with basic provisions is typically quite long. In short, where supermax prisons operate some form of a gradual progression programme, it is typically one that is based on crude 'carrot-and-stick' principles, but mainly uses the 'stick'.

To sum up, managerial objectives (maintaining prison order and discipline) are predominant in official discourses about the roles of supermax confinement. These include 'classic' penological objectives of deterrence and incapacitation, but notions of retribution and punishment are also implicit. The 'operational' goals of supermax prisons are largely articulated in utilitarian terms through their system-wide managerial benefits – namely that by selective incapacitation and the isolation of troublemakers, and through situational controls, the entire prison system operates in a more orderly and secure way.

Although the managerial narrative prevails over any other in official discourse, and in that sense supermax prisons may be said to be a feature of the 'new penology' (Feeley and Simon 1992), the actual practice of solitary confinement has remained extraordinarily similar throughout the decades of its use. Deeper narratives about the nature of prisoners destined to supermax confinement also have their roots in the 'old' as much as they do in the 'new'. In the first two historical 'waves' of its use, solitary confinement had an official 'people-changing' role; that is, it was intended to result in internalised change in those subjected to it. In supermax prisons, solitary confinement has no official 'people-changing' role, but rather a containment/control function. Nonetheless and although the stated purpose of isolation in current-day prisons is not reforming, resocialising or otherwise changing individuals, there is little doubt that, intended or not, the experience does change the individual involved. Isolating prisoners in present-day supermaxes performs similar functions as in the past; that is, stripping prisoners of previous habits, thought processes and influences, but with an important difference: this time, there is no official effort to 'engrave' anything on the *tabula rasa*, the blank slate, which the prisoner becomes. As a former prisoner put it, 'They strip you of everything but they replace it with nothing.' Thus, if supermax prisons have any 'people-changing' aspirations, they are to create docile and more obedient prisoners, and to prepare them for prison life (or life in prison). Rather than deterring free citizens from committing crime or deterring prisoners from misbehaving in prison, supermax confinement is so extreme that it may make the prospect of life as free citizens intimidating for prisoners, thus deterring them from living a free life.

In the following chapters, I examine how these general concepts, justifications, objectives and claims are translated into practices and routines in supermax prisons. First, I examine, in the following chapter, how and which prisoners are selected into the category of 'dangerous and disruptive'.

Notes

1 Marion prisoner Ray Luc Levasseur, in Burton-Rose *et al.* (1998: 202).
2 Well-known examples outside the USA include Nelson Mandela and other members of the African National Congress in South Africa, Václav Havel in the former Czechoslovakia, 'enemies of the state' in the former USSR, and members of the Tupac Amaru Revolutionary Movement in Peru (Article 20 of the Penal Law in Peru requires that all prisoners whose sentence is linked with terrorism be isolated during the first year of their incarceration), Mordechi Vaanunu in Israel, and, more recently, 'enemy combatants' apprehended by the USA and held at Guantánamo Bay, Cuba.
3 Colorado Department of Corrections spokeswoman, regarding the Colorado's State Penitentiary, which operates a 23 hour a day solitary regime, cited in Prendergast 1995.
4 Pelican Bay State Prison SHU Mission Statement, Pelican Bay Public Information Office, n.d.
5 This claim had been discredited many years ago, as observers noted that, while in times of relative stability in the prison system, isolating prisoners may work as a deterrent, under conditions of instability and tension, occupants of such units may be considered as heroes by the

prison community at large (McCleery 1961: 260–1). See also Ward and Schmidt (1981: 65) on the ineffectiveness of Alcatraz as a deterrent.

6 National Institute of Corrections (1991: 9). The authors note, however, that 'a gang may not be as closely controlled by its leadership or as cohesive as it seems'. I return to an evaluation of this strategy in the concluding chapter.

7 Haney and Lynch (1997: 493). For a discussion and description of life in one such 'special unit', see Cohen and Taylor ([1972] 1981).

Chapter 5

The bureaucratisation of control: prisoner classification and placement in supermax prisons

The magic wand of classification has long been held out as the key to a successful system.... All that has changed over the last century is the basis of the binary classification. It used to be 'moral character'; sometimes it was 'treatability' or 'security risk', now it tends to be 'dangerousness'. (Cohen 1985: 194–5)

Once prisoners are sentenced by the court to a custodial sentence, the 'administration of their penalty' is handed over to prison authorities: 'Although the principle of penalty was certainly a legal decision, its administration, its quality and its rigours must belong to an autonomous mechanism that supervises the effects of punishment within the very apparatus that produces them' (Foucault 1977: 246). Prisoner classification and placement are the main mechanisms through which the 'quality and rigour' of prisoners' confinement are determined: once prisoners are classified to a certain security category, their institutional placement, entitlement to privileges, access to programmes, and entire experience of the prison system are predetermined to a very large extent. If prison architecture, discussed in the following chapter, is the main 'hardware' of prison systems, classification is the 'software' of their make-up.

This chapter examines how the justifications for supermax prisons discussed in the previous chapter, namely that they are designated for the 'worst of the worst', prisoners who supposedly cannot be controlled in less restrictive environments, are translated into operational bureaucratic principles.

The roles of classification in the prison setting

Contemporary classification instruments have a dual role in prisons: to categorise and distribute prisoners across the limited prison estate, and to distribute system resources (manpower, security arrangements, educational and vocational programmes) to prisons.

In their role of categorising prisoners, classification instruments arrange prisoners in groupings which are based on many factors including age and gender, as well as personality/behavioural characteristics (e.g. 'aggressive' or 'submissive') assessed by psychological examination or statistical techniques.[1] Groupings are also based on the nature of prisoners' crimes (e.g. violence/property/drugs) as stipulated in the court's judgement, their institutional characteristics (e.g. first time/repeat offender) found in data on the prisoner drawn from within the criminal justice system, and socio-economic factors (e.g. education and employment). The role of these groupings, in current prison classification systems, is to predict prisoners' behaviour in prison and the risk they pose to public safety and/or institutional security, as well as to identify prisoners with 'special needs', such as mentally ill prisoners.

In its role as the distributor of resources, classification is charged with constructing the 'fit' between categories of prisoners and categories of prisons, and the distribution of resources to each category. The higher the security category of a prison, the more expensive it is to house prisoners in it. The outcome of prisoner classification, namely the number of prisoners allocated to each security category, plays a major role in budgetary projections and estimates of future need for prison beds in each security category. These estimates are also used in long-term projections of the prison system's future construction needs. Since these projections are based on classificatory assignments, classification can be described as a circular process with built-in mechanisms for reinforcing its own predictions and setting in stone administrative decisions and policies.

The weights assigned to classification criteria and the declared purposes of creating classificatory groupings have changed throughout the history of the modern prison to correspond with shifts in correctional philosophies and practices. Initially, newly developed classification systems of the late eighteenth century classified sentenced prisoners into primary categories including age and gender. With time, classification systems became increasingly complex and included a growing number of categories, or 'classes' of prisoners. The main shifts in the role of prisoner classification can crudely be divided into three waves, which are roughly parallel to those identified earlier: the early nineteenth century, the late 1950s to the 1970s, and the mid- to late 1980s to the present day. In the early nineteenth century, classifying prisoners was a means to prevent the spread of the 'disease' of criminality in prisons, where all prisoners were mixed together, 'the old and the young, the confirmed villain and the novice in crime, the thoughtless youth who has fallen into the guilt or suspicion only of one solitary offence, as well as the most hardened and brutal wretch' (Kingsmill 1854: 96). The definitive solution to this contagious mix was solitary confinement, for 'solitude was in a way the most perfect form of classification ... the ultimate in classification was to set every prisoner apart from every other, each in their own category' (Evans 1982: 325). By the late nineteenth to early twentieth century, the 'separate system' had largely disintegrated, and most prisoners were held together with others, no longer 'each in their own category'.

In the 'medical model of corrections' classification, instruments took on a diagnostic role, a tool to determine the cause of the individual prisoner's problem and allocate him to a facility where the appropriate treatment could be administered (MacKenzie 1989: 165). Clinicians became increasingly involved in the process, both through devising new classificatory instruments that included psychological predictors and through playing a central role in classification hearings.

In the mid- to late 1970s, the 'justice model of corrections' came to the fore, pressing for increased rationality and accountability in penal systems. Simultaneously, an increase in prison overcrowding meant that fewer resources were available for long, personal classification interviews. Further, the reliance on clinicians using subjective criteria was increasingly criticised by the courts and prison reform groups, leading to increased pressures for objective, standardised classification systems and an engagement with actuarial risk predictions (California Department of Finance 1996: 37). Classification instruments continued to include some psychological assessment, but the emphasis on the clinical judgement of the individual's 'treatability' gave way to statistical risk predictions. The engagement with actuarial risk predictions is one of the central features of what Feeley and Simon (1992) term the 'new penology', where 'moral or clinical description of the individual [is replaced] with an actuarial language of probabilistic calculations and statistical distributions applied to populations.'[2] It is useful to note, however, that even at the height of the 'treatment era' when psychological/therapeutic discourses were relatively strong, security rather than treatment was usually the overriding consideration in classifying prisoners:

> Probably most classification committees base their decisions on considerations of custody, convenience, discipline and treatment, in that order. Thus, it may be decided that a particular inmate must be handled as a maximum-security risk and if, for example, psychiatric services are not available to maximum security prisoners, then that decision will mean that the psychiatric help will not be available to the inmate in question, no matter what his treatment needs. (Sutherland and Cressey 1970: 540)

In what follows, I examine how groups of prisoners are identified as requiring supermax confinement, and how the category of 'dangerousness' is constructed in this context. I also look at how and which prisoners are selected to be included in this category and how, and when, they can be deselected from it. Although my analysis is relevant to the American prison system as a whole, I will be using the California Department of Corrections and Rehabilitation[3] (hereafter 'CDCR' or 'CDC') classification system and the Pelican Bay Security Housing Unit (hereafter 'SHU') as my primary examples. I begin with a short overview of the CDCR and California's prison population, and the hierarchy of classification decision makers in California.

Who is in California's prisons?

CDCR operates one of the largest prison systems in the world. In late 2008, CDCR held some 172,008 adult prisoners in its custody – over twice as many as the total prisoner population of England and Wales in the same year, and employed 52,982 people in its institutions.[4] Its operating budget was $9.7 billion, around 7 per cent of California's state budget (2007–8 figures). To accommodate a rapidly growing prisoner population, in the early 1980s California embarked on large-scale prison construction. Between 1982 and 2001 alone, California's legislature authorised the construction of 27 new prisons at a cost of more than $5.6 billion. The department now operates 33 state prisons, 40 minimum-security fire and conservation camps, 12 community correctional facilities, and five prisoner mother facilities (CDCR Facts and Figures, *ibid.*) Yet, California's prisons are still severely overcrowded. In early 2007, around 10 per cent of California's prison population were housed in gyms, dayrooms, holding cells and hallways (California LAO 2007). The problem of overcrowding in

California's prisons remains so acute, that in February 2009 a panel of three federal judges ordered the CDCR to reduce its prisoner population by a third within three years (Moore 2009).

As many as 47.2 per cent of prisoners held in CDCR's custody in 2008 were incarcerated for non-violent offences, including drug and property offences. Another 34 per cent were parolees returned to prison for violation of their parole terms (9 per cent), or were committed by the courts for a new offence (25 per cent).[5] Another large group among California's prisoners are 'second' and 'third strikers' sentenced under its 'three strikes' laws. In 2008, 32,680 (or 20 per cent) of California's prisoners were 'second strikers', and 8,409 (just under 5 per cent) 'third strikers'. Finally, another characteristic of California's prison population is its racial make-up. African-Americans make up less than 7 per cent of California's population, yet they make up 29 per cent of its prison population. Hispanics and Latinos make up 19 per cent of California's population but 38.9 per cent of its prison population.

Classification decision makers in California

The hierarchy of classificatory decision making in California includes:

Reception Center Personnel: determine prisoners' initial classification score.

Unit Classification Committee (UCC): conducts routine classification hearings, work, education and privilege assignments, and annual reviews. Composition: Unit Captain (chair), Correctional Councillor III, Correctional Councillor II or I, Programme Lieutenant, Educational/Vocational Program representative, other staff as required.

Institutional Classification Committee (ICC): oversees transfers (including transfers to segregation units and SHU facilities), programme participation, supervision, housing and all cases involving increases to the prisoner's score. Composition: Warden or Chief Deputy Warden (chair), psychiatrist or physician, Captain, Correctional Councillor III or II; Assignment lieutenant; Educational or Vocational Program representative; other staff as required.

Classification Services Unit (CSU): CDCR Headquarters level; examines difficult cases referred to them by the different ICCs.

Departmental Review Board (DRB): provides the 'Director's final review' of classification issues referred to it. The DRB decision is final and cannot be appealed against. It 'concludes the inmate/parolee's departmental administrative remedy of such issues' (Title 15 Section 3377). Composition: Deputy Director or an Assistant Deputy Director of the Institutions Division (chair), Deputy Director or Assistant Deputy Director of the Parole and Community Services Division, Chief of Classification Services, Chief of Health Services (when required).

The initial classification of prisoners

> [In] fabricating delinquency, it [prison] gave the criminal justice a unitary field of objects, authenticated by the 'sciences', and thus enables it to function on a general horizon of 'truth'. (Foucault 1977: 256)

The initial determination of prisoners' 'security' or 'custody' level aims to reflect the risk that prisoners pose to public or institutional security and, by extension, the degree of surveillance that they will require in custody.[6] This is done by separating prisoners into open, minimum, medium or maximum security groups.[7] Supermax prisons or SHUs, as they are called in California, constitute a separate security level, outside the main categories.[8] The prison estate is also categorised in similar groupings based on physical security arrangements and the types of prisoners which may safely be held in each category. The broad objectives of the prisoner classification process are to

> separate the sophisticated from the uninitiated, the violent from the non-violent and the passive from the aggressive inmates. In addition, the classification system should: assist in identifying security risks; address any special physical or mental health needs; safeguard those requiring protective custody and those who may become victims to assertive and assaultive inmates; and identify those eligible for facility programs. (California Board of Corrections 2001: 2)

Once the level of risk posed by the prisoner is identified, correctly or incorrectly, the prisoner has to be 'managed' in accordance with his risk level. There are two possible approaches to risk management: 'At the one extreme, given unlimited resources and a conservative philosophy, all inmates could be placed in maximum security.... At the other extreme, given limited resources and a liberal philosophy, all the prisoners could be placed in minimum security' (Alexander and Austin 1992: 26). Many departments of corrections declare their policy to be the latter, and claim that they strive to place prisoners in the lowest security category possible. California is one such example. The policy goals of its current classification system are set out in the CDCR's Department Operations Manual and include:[9]

- Placement of inmates in the lowest custody level consistent with case factors and public safety
- Place inmates according to their classification score based on objective information and criteria unless case factors or departmental requirements indicate otherwise
- Application of the classification process uniformly for all inmates in similar situations
- Provision for centralised control over the classification process
- Maintenance of an ongoing classification system information data base for departmental research and evaluation.

Administrative guidelines give a clue as to some of the perceived advantages of objective classification instruments:

> The potential for violence, staff/inmate confrontations and subsequent lawsuits is reduced and security is enhanced. The expense of planning and administrating a classification system is more than returned to the facility by the creation of an improved environment, a lower ratio of injuries to staff and inmates, lower medical costs and a reduction in time spent in defending the facility in court.[10]

The concern with future litigation reflects the department's past experience with legal challenges to its classification system in general and the process of allocating prisoners to segregation units in particular. More elaborate systems based on 'objective', detailed, measurable criteria and laden with procedural requirements make classification decisions more difficult to challenge in the courts, as 'objective' criteria applied 'uniformly' are quantifiable and measurable. The policy goals cited above also reflect the lack of concern for the personal attributes and needs of the individual prisoner and a preoccupation with risk management. Despite the official insistence on scientifically measurable objectivity, the processes of classification, allocation and review of prisoners' security categories are essentially administrative, governed by internal guidelines and regulations. Prison staff decide how prisoners will be classified and who will be allocated to which prison. Further, when classification personnel do not agree with findings of the 'objective' criteria, they can exercise administrative discretion to override them.

In California, the initial classification of new prisoners typically takes place in one of the 12 special reception or diagnostic centres operated by CDCR. Prisoners arrive from the court with an 'abstract of judgement', a summary of their case facts, and the court's sentence. Firstly, prisoners are 'processed' by reception centre personnel. They are fingerprinted, photographed, issued with a prisoner number, and given a copy of CDCR's rules and regulations (for which they are asked to sign a receipt, which will be placed in their personal file). Prisoners then undergo medical and dental examinations, and an 'initial custodial interview' with a correctional counsellor. Prisoners who complain of mental health problems, or have been identified as mentally ill in their personal file or by the counsellor's interview, may (but are not entitled to) also be referred for a psychological examination. The system of observation, evaluation and decision making is accompanied by many forms that record every detail of the process. These are later fed into a centralised database to be stored indefinitely on the prisoner's personal file. As in most other states in the USA, CDCR operates a computerised database, the offender information system, which allows criminal justice officials statewide easy access to information about the prisoner's current term, past custody assignments, institutional behaviour and criminal history.

The detailed classification procedures, necessary documentation, and list of components of the 'classification score' and how it should be calculated are set out in Article 10 of Title 15 of California's Code of Regulations (hereafter Title 15).[11] Prisoners are given a classification score based on a points system. Each of the score's components is given a specific numerical weight, and the total calculation of these weights determines the prisoner's security classification. The higher the score, the higher the prisoner's security level and the higher are the security level of the prison where he will be placed.

For all the complexity of the scoring system, however, the main factor determining the number of points is the length of the prisoner's sentence. This reflects an assumption that the length of sentence provides an indication of the degree to which prisoners pose a risk of violence, an assumption that is inherently flawed in the context of sentencing policies such as 'three strikes and you're out'. There also remains significant administrative discretion in the scoring system, which allows for 'administrative determinates', marked out with a three-letter code (27 in all) to override the prisoner's point-based score in determining his placement. Some of these relate directly to violent or disruptive prisoners, and may be used to recommend allocation to an SHU, pending an appearance before an institutional classification committee (ICC) and endorsement by CDCR head-quarters, immediately from the reception centre. Administrative determinates include:

> *AGE*: Inmate's youthfulness, immaturity or advanced age
> *DIS*: Inmate's disciplinary record indicates a history of serious problems or threatens the security of the facility
> *ESC*: Unusual circumstances suggest the inmate is a much greater escape risk than indicated by their classification score; e.g. the inmate verbalised intent to escape
> *GAN*: Documentation establishes that the inmate's gang membership or association requires special attention or placement consideration
> *PUB*: High notoriety of an inmate has caused public interest in the case and requires special placement
> *TIM*: Inmate time to serve is long, requiring placement in a facility with a higher security classification level than indicated by their classification score
> *VIO*: Inmate has a current or prior conviction for a violent felony

In addition, special suffixes are applied to identify prisoners with particular housing restrictions or designations. For example, 'R' suffixes are used to identify sex offenders and 'S' suffixes to identify inmates requiring single-cell housing. These suffixes remain attached to prisoners throughout their incarceration.

The 'special security' category: avenues into a supermax

> The decision to segregate or compulsorily transfer a long-term maximum security prisoner can be an especially fateful one for all concerned. With the exception of the death penalty, it stands at perhaps the furthest point of repertoire of sanctions and compulsions available to a liberal democratic state outside time of war. (Sparks *et al.* 1996: 30)

Supermax prisons are by far the most powerful weapon in the arsenal of penalties and control measures available to prison administrators. In theory, the tool of supermax is only used for those who have been identified as dangerous and predatory by objective classification criteria. In practice, definitions of 'predatory' and 'dangerous' are wide and potentially all-encompassing. That is illustrated by the significant variation between states in the percentage of prisoners classified as requiring special security. California holds just under 2 per cent of its prisoners in supermax prisons (or SHUs) and an additional 5 per cent of its prisoners in Administrative Segregation Units (ASUs). A US Department of Justice national survey of supermax custody found that Florida and Iowa classified 3 per cent of their prisoners as requiring supermax custody; Louisiana and Washington held 6 per cent of their prisoner population in supermax facilities; Ohio, Wyoming, Maryland and Michigan required supermax housing for 1 per cent of their adult male population; and Mississippi held as many as 20 per cent of its male, adult prisoners in a supermax (National Institute of Corrections 1997: 4–6). This diversity, from one to 20 per cent, raises interesting questions: does Mississippi, for example, really have twenty times more dangerous prisoners than Ohio or Maryland, or is the diversity a result of how the category of 'special security' is constructed in different states and how individual prisoners are selected for it?

The specific composition of groups of 'difficult to control' prisoners accordingly differs slightly from one jurisdiction to another, but most states house in their supermax prisons a combination of violent and dangerous (i.e. high-risk) prisoners, mentally ill prisoners, confirmed and alleged gang members, and death-row prisoners. Arizona, Colorado, Oklahoma, Utah and Maryland, among others, hold their death-row prisoners in supermax prisons regardless of their disciplinary record, while California holds them in segregation wings in high-security prisons, but not in supermax facilities. Some states, including Oklahoma, Indiana, Ohio, Texas and Illinois, also hold mentally ill offenders in their supermax prisons, though the courts increasingly intervene in the practice and have ordered departments of corrections to remove such prisoners to specialist units.[12]

As in other states, prisoners from racial minorities are over-represented in California's supermax units compared to general population prisons. At Pelican Bay SHU, around 17 per cent of prisoners are white, 12 per cent are African-American, and 68 per cent are Hispanic. It is beyond the scope of this discussion to examine the relationship between race and allocation to supermax prisons, but in the context of racial prejudice and discrimination, which are fundamental features of the American criminal justice system in its entirety, the high percentage of prisoners from racial minorities in supermaxes should not come as a surprise. Research indicated that prisoners from racial minorities may be over-represented in high-security prisons not as a result of their actual behaviour, but as a result of the design of classification instruments. Poole and Regoli (1980), for example, found that although African-Americans and whites were as likely to be involved in prison rule-breaking, African-Americans were more likely to be reported officially, mainly as a result of a 'cumulative labelling effect'; that is, closer surveillance of labelled prisoners, resulting in 'more frequent detection of infractions'.[13] Silberman (1995) similarly commented that classification systems, such as the Adult Internal Management System (AIMS), which rely on socio-economic factors such as education and employment, reproduce and reinforce societal biases against prisoners from disadvantaged racial minorities. Like Poole and Regoli's (1980) earlier study, Silberman (1995: 95–105) found that the higher assault rate among those classified as 'heavies' can be partly explained by the fact that they were subjected to closer supervision because of their label and thus more likely to be reported.

The general categories of prisoners who may be placed in an SHU are listed in CDCR's Operations Manual (section 62050.13.2), which stipulates that an inmate shall be placed in an SHU if:

- The inmate has requested segregation for their own protection and the need can be substantiated by appropriate staff.

- The inmate is newly arrived at the institution and more information is needed to determine whether the inmate may be incompatible with any element of the general population. No inmate shall be involuntarily segregated for this reason for more than 10 days.

- The inmate has been found guilty of a disciplinary offence sufficiently serious to warrant confinement for a fixed term in segregation and the term is fixed in conformance with the SHU Assessment Chart.

- The inmate's continued presence in general population would severely endanger lives of inmates or staff, the security of the institution or the integrity of an investigation into suspected criminal activity.

These broad criteria, particularly the last one, are couched in terms that can be applied to almost any prisoner. Prisoners who fit the first criterion, and request to be segregated for their own protection (known as OPs), are not, usually, held in an SHU facility, but in special segregation wings of 'general population' prisons or in a Protective Housing Unit (PHU). The second criterion applies mainly to newly arrived prisoners who were classified as gang members in the initial classification, and the third to those who committed a 'serious rule violation' while in prison. The fourth criterion applies to anyone who is deemed dangerous by prison authorities but does not fall under any of the other categories. Pelican Bay SHU mainly holds alleged gang members or gang affiliates (two-thirds of SHU prisoners), 'serious rule violators', and a small group of prisoners who have committed crimes of high notoriety. It also holds prisoners who paroled from the SHU and returned to custody following a violation of their parole terms, or to serve a new prison sentence. The categories of rule violators and gang members are governed by different administrative regulations, although once at the SHU, prisoners from both categories are subjected to the same conditions of confinement.

Prison rule violators

A prisoner who is found by a disciplinary hearing to be guilty of a serious prison rule violation may be referred to the ICC to be reclassified and assigned to a SHU for a determinate time. The length of 'SHU term' is regulated by administrative rules and regulations, and calculated according to the 'SHU term assessment chart',[14] which lays out the minimum and maximum SHU time that may be given for listed offences. The maximum determinate SHU term is 60 months. A rule violation is classified as 'serious' if it involves one or more of the following: the use of force or violence against another person; a breach of or hazard to facility security; a serious disruption of facility operations; the introduction or possession of a controlled substance; or, an attempt or threat to commit any of the above, coupled with the ability to carry out the threat. A non-exhaustive list of 24 'serious rule violations' includes some of the following offences (Title 15, section 3315):

> [B] Theft, destruction, misuse, alteration, damage, unauthorised acquisition or exchange of personal or state property amounting to more than $50; [D] Tattooing or possession of tattoo paraphernalia;

[G] Possession of $5 or more without authorisation; [H] Acts of disobedience or disrespect which by reason of their intensity or context create potential for violence or mass disruptive conduct; [J] Refusal to perform work or participate in a programme as ordered or assigned; [O] Harassment of another person, group or entity either directly or indirectly through the use of the mail or other means; [P] Throwing any liquid or solid substance on a non-prisoner; [T] Participation in gambling; [U] Unauthorised possession of materials or substances which have been diverted or altered from the original manufactured state or purpose with the potential to be made into a weapon, explosive, poison, caustic substance, any destructive device; (W) Self mutilation or attempted suicide for the purpose of manipulation; and (X) *Involvement in a conspiracy or attempt to do any of the above.* [my emphasis]

Although the SHU term assessment chart sets out the range of typical terms for 20 listed offences, and prescribes maximum and minimum terms, this still leaves classification staff with wide discretion. The SHU term for homicide, for example, ranges from 36 to 60 months. Assaults result in varying terms, depending on the nature of the assault, and on whether it was committed against a prisoner or against a 'non-inmate'. Throwing a 'caustic substance' on a non-inmate, for example, carries an SHU term of two to four months. The same offence against a prisoner does not carry any SHU term. An assault on a prisoner with a weapon or physical force capable of causing mortal or serious injury, results in an SHU term of 6–24 months. The same offence against a non-prisoner results in an SHU term of 9–48 months. Proven *attempts* to commit listed offences result in half of the specified term. An inmate who *conspires* to commit any of these offences will be placed in the SHU for the full specified SHU term. As the wording of section 3315 suggests, not only actual acts but also attempts, threats, and even alleged *intentions* to break prison rules are sufficient grounds for allocation to one of the most restrictive environments within CDCR.

This practice of 'isolating risk' (Riveland 1999) is widespread across the USA. Recalling the language of justifications for the use of supermax prisons and the emphasis on prisoners' dangerousness, the list of serious rule violations appears somewhat insubstantial. Moreover, some of the listed offences are specific to prison environments and have come to be defined as 'serious' as a result of internal pressures and the bargaining power of prison staff and their representatives, and not necessarily because they are serious as such. Take item (P) ('throwing liquid or solid substance'), for example. 'Gassing', as it is termed internally, is defined in Title 15 as 'serious' if it involves a non-inmate. Since the introduction of supermax confinement, gassing has become the subject of much uproar among prison staff. An entry on CCPOA's website reads:

> On average, nine correctional officers are assaulted by inmates every day inside California prisons.... A common assault is 'gassing,' in which inmates throw a mixture of urine and feces in officers' faces, exposing the officers and their families to AIDS, hepatitis, tuberculosis and other deadly diseases common in prison. (CCPOA website, February 2009)

California's penal code dedicates an entire section to it and in 1998 reclassified gassing as aggravated battery, punishable by two to five years in segregation. The actual number and nature of gassing incidents are not matched by the official preoccupation with it. A study carried out by the California Board of Corrections (2000) between 1998 and 1999 found that gassing incidents were 'not substantial in number, nor do they appear to pose a health threat to staff'. Interestingly, all the gassing incidents (28) which occurred during that period took place in special housing units. Elsewhere, I discuss some of the issues regarding gassing, and question what motivates a prisoner to throw his own urine or faeces at another person. For the purpose of the discussion here, however, the redefinition of gassing demonstrates how classification instruments and definitions of 'dangerous acts' at times come to reflect the exaggerated concerns of prison staff, rather than legitimate safety concerns. 'Gassing' is a good example of how, as Becker (1963) put it, 'social groups create deviance by making the rules whose infraction constitutes deviance, and by applying these rules to particular people and labelling them as outsiders ... the deviant is one to whom the label was successfully applied; deviant behaviour is behaviour that people so label' (Becker 1963: 9). Also disturbing is the official differentiation between inmate and 'non-inmate' victims of assaults, and the heavier penalties on assaults on the latter.

Serious rule violators serving determined SHU terms constitute around a third of prisoners at Pelican Bay SHU.

Gang members and affiliates

The largest group at Pelican Bay SHU are gang members (alleged and confirmed), who constitute roughly two-thirds of prisoners in the unit. Elsewhere, gang members, or 'security threat groups' as they are known in some jurisdictions, are also typically held in supermaxes, though their proportion may be smaller than in California. Title 15 (subsection 3000) defines a gang as:

> Any ongoing formal or informal organization, association or group of three or more persons which has a common name or identifying sign or symbol whose members and/or associates, individually or collectively, engage or have engaged, on behalf of that organization, association or group, in two or more acts which include, planning, organizing threatening, financing, soliciting, or committing unlawful acts or acts of misconduct classified as serious pursuant to section 3315.

A prison gang is defined as any gang which originated and has its roots within the department or any other prison system. Identifying prisons as independent entities which require protection, Title 15 further states that 'Gangs present a serious threat to the safety and security of California prisons' (subsection 3023). To tackle the problem, special 'gang investigation units' now operate in most of California's maximum-security prisons, charged with collecting information on gangs and gang activities and validating allegations of gang membership or association, as defined in Title 15:

> A *gang member* is an inmate/parolee who has been accepted into membership by a gang. An *associate* is an inmate/parolee who is involved periodically or regularly with members or associates of a gang. Both identifications require at least three independent sources of documentation indicative of actual membership/association. (Title 15, subsection 3378(c))

The process of validating gang membership was described by one supermax official as 'extensive' and 'in-depth', though, when asked to elaborate, he did not reveal much beyond formalistic procedural stages:

> The validation is done on a points system, and there are also several groups of criteria that they have to meet. It's not as

simple as saying that you're a gang member so we're going to assign you to [the unit].... There are also several criteria they have to meet, which means if they have a specific tattoo that identifies them as a gang member, which most of the prison gang members have – it's called a 'patch', self-proclamation – there's various other avenues that we must go through in order to ensure that it's done as proper as it possibly can be so that it isn't just okay, you know, you're doing something wrong so we're going to say you're a prison gang member. There's a very in-depth procedure for them to be validated. Once they fit the criteria, a packet is made on them ... intelligence is gathered on them until there is either a conclusion that they're not a member and there's not enough here to do anything with them, or the decision is made there is enough to go before a committee. The information that is gathered is researched by the committee and reviewed.... If it's termed to be factual, they are validated. They have an appeal process. Once all avenues are exhausted, if they remain validated they come to this unit.

The list of criteria for determining gang membership or association is long and includes:

Self admission; Tattoos and symbols ('body markings, hand signs, distinctive clothing, graffiti and so on, which have been identified by gang coordinators/investigators as being used by and distinctive to specific gangs'); Written materials (membership or enemy lists, organisational structures, codes, training material) of specific gangs; Photographs; Staff information; Information from other agencies; Association ('information related to the inmate/parolee's association with validated gang affiliates'); Informants; Visitors ('visits from persons who are documented as gang "runners" or community affiliates, or members of an organization which associates with a gang'); Communications ('documentation of telephone conversations, mail, notes, or other communication, including coded messages evidencing gang activity'); Debriefing reports. (Title 15, subsection 3378)

The all-encompassing nature of the criteria means that almost anyone can be defined as a gang member.[15] Prisoners testified that talking to a gang member in the exercise yard or being reported as a gang member by another prisoner who had a personal 'score' to settle with them constituted enough evidence to validate them as gang associates. One can easily envisage a situation where a newly arrived prisoner speaks to someone they know from their school or neighbourhood and, as a result, is labelled as a gang affiliate. In fact, by these criteria, it may be difficult for prisoners from certain socio-economic and racial backgrounds *not* to be labelled as gang members.

Parole violators

The third group of prisoners placed in supermaxes are those paroled from a supermax that have either violated the terms of their parole or were returned to prison with a new prison term. In California, such prisoners are automatically returned to the SHU as soon as they are incarcerated, regardless of the nature of their original or new offence. Space does not permit a detailed discussion of some of the issues related to parole, but suffice it to say that rates of parole violations are very high (as noted earlier, more than 34 per cent of prisoners in CDCR's custody are parolees who violated the terms of their parole or returned with a new prison term). It should also be noted that violating parole terms does not require much more than missing an appointment with one's parole officer. Returning parolees who were paroled from the SHU will be brought before the ICC directly from the reception centre.

Once at the SHU, all three categories of prisoners are subjected to the same conditions and provisions, detailed in the following section.

Assignment to custody, programme and privilege groups

In the first instance, newly admitted prisoners who were classified as requiring 'maximum security' at the reception centre will be sent to general population units at the Pelican Bay prison or to one of the other maximum-security (Level IV) prisons operated by CDCR, and may be subsequently sent to a SHU. Parole violators who were paroled from a SHU will be sent directly back to it upon their return to prison. Internal regulations require that new arrivals be assessed by the ICC within 14 days of their placement. The ICC determines prisoners' housing placement and programme assignment. Theoretically, programme assignment should be tailored to prisoners' individual needs, and not based on their housing assignment. In practice, prisoners' housing assignment largely predetermines their access to vocational, recreational and educational programmes.

Some states have developed separate 'internal classification' measurements to determine prisoners' housing, work, and programme assignment once they have been placed in the designated facility. Among those who opted for such separate measures, many use AIMS, which was developed specifically for internal classification (Quay 1983). AIMS relies on two inventories to classify prisoners: analysis of life history records, and a 'correctional adjustment checklist', to differentiate between prisoners who are aggressive and independent ('heavies'), prisoners who are passive and dependent ('lights'), and prisoners who fall into neither category ('moderates'). Another internal classification instrument is the Personality-Based Adult Internal Classification System, which uses clinical predictors (designed so they can be assessed by classification staff rather than clinicians) to identify and separate prisoners and determine housing placements and access to educational and vocational programmes. CDCR operates 'integrated classification instruments' (i.e. the same measurements are used for both external and internal classification) to determine custody level and institutional assignment, and then, at the assigned prison, to determine housing unit and programme assignments.

Custody designations

Housing placements or 'custody designations' are stipulated in Title 15. There are seven custody levels, ranging from the highest in the spectrum, maximum custody, to the lowest, minimum B. Maximum custody (i.e. segregation), is specifically designed for inmates who require the most restrictive housing in Segregated Program Housing Units which include PHUs, SHUs, ASUs and Psychiatric Services Units. Placement and release from these units require further approval by a Classification Staff Representative. The physical security arrangements required for maximum custody prisoners include:[16]

- Housing shall be in cells in an approved segregated program housing unit.
- Assignments and activities shall be within the confines of the approved segregated program housing unit.
- Inmates shall be under the direct supervision and control of custody staff.

The physical arrangements at the SHU are discussed in detail in the following chapter.

Work, training and 'good time credit' group assignment

Once the ICC has made its decision regarding the prisoner's housing placement, it assigns the prisoner to education, vocational, or other institutional programmes, arranged in eight categories. Each grouping entails certain good time credit earning, as well as privileges. As noted earlier, although this segment of the classification process is supposed to be individually tailored and separate from the 'security classification', prisoners' housing assignment will in practice determine their access to work and privileges. Prisoners who are assigned to a SHU are automatically classified as work group D-1 or D-2. Prisoners serving indeterminate SHU terms (mainly prisoners charged with gang membership or affiliation) will be assigned to work group D-1 and will be entitled to one-day credit towards parole for each two days served. Those serving determinate SHU terms (prisoners assigned to the SHU for a disciplinary offence) will be placed in work group D-2 and will not be entitled to any good time credits.[17] The rationale is that:

> Conforming behaviour in SHU is not equivalent to conforming behaviour in a general population setting ... periods in SHU or other segregated housing are typically at maximum custody. Thus, periods spent by the inmate in maximum custody do not provide the same type of freedom and risks presented in periods of close custody.... Moreover, a SHU term is established in response to a serious and specific disciplinary violation or to a validated involvement in a prison gang which compromises correctional safety and security. The purposes of SHU are the protection of staff and other inmates and the security of the facility. SHU is not intended to provide an opportunity to observe inmate success in good behaviour and programming. (Explanatory Note to Title 15, Feb. 2000 amendments)

In other words, since there are few opportunities to offend in the SHU, prisoners cannot demonstrate good behaviour that would earn them good time credits and therefore should not be entitled to any. The explanatory note also reiterates that prisoners have been allocated to the SHU for serious, well-validated reasons, and should not be rewarded. This Alice in Wonderland logic leaves SHU prisoners with little to lose, and prison administrations with even more control over all aspects of prisoners' lives than is usual in the prison setting.

With the exception of an in-cell pre-release video programme, SHU prisoners have no access to vocational, educational or recreational activities. In other jurisdictions, where supermax prisoners are allowed access to additional programmes, these are also provided in-cell through a television set.

Privilege and incentive groups

Privileges are defined in Title 15 as 'administratively authorised activities or benefits ... governed by an inmate's behaviour, custody classification and assignment'. Privileges constitute an administrative tool which can be, and originally was, used as an incentive for prisoners to demonstrate good behaviour. But alongside the wider shift in the 1980s towards the managerial approach to corrections and the growing emphasis on standardisation, administrative discretion in the use of privileges was gradually reduced, and regulations regarding their distribution established. Currently, all prisoners assigned to an SHU are entitled only to a minimal level of privileges, as required by law and by court orders, and are automatically placed in work group D. SHU prisoners' entitlement to privileges, then, is based on their security category, not on their actual behaviour. Privileges for SHU prisoners include:

- One fourth of the maximum monthly canteen draw
- Telephone calls on an emergency basis only
- Limited yard access; no access to any other recreational or entertainment activities
- One annual package
- One off special purchase of a TV/radio.

All prisoners assigned to the SHU (and similarly other supermax units), then, are automatically excluded from association with other prisoners, from participation in programmes which might enhance their personal development or earn them credits towards parole, and from receiving any privileges beyond a basic minimum required by law. They also 'earn' a label that cannot be easily removed later, as the housing assignment is noted in the prisoner's file and will follow him for the rest of time in the criminal justice system.

Once at the SHU, no distinction is made between the various types of prisoners and the background to their confinement in the SHU. Commentators note that the lack of internal differentiation between the groups of prisoners and the 'one size fits all' attitude neglects to address differences in the level of risk posed by individual prisoners and their programming needs. Some prison staff agree with this logic, if for different reasons:

> I think we're probably going to be doing, as time goes by, a better and better job at distinguishing between these types of inmates and finding programmes that will provide better control over the predators and the inmates who just can't get along with others, and try to find a way to provide the most normal prison programming for those inmates who just have a long time to serve. [administrator]

Nonetheless, no such differentiation is currently made. Prison planners and administrators continue to push for fewer prisoner privileges and more control. For example, California's Department of Corrections 2001–2 budget proposal suggested reducing privileges for SHU prisoners to the basic levels of care mandated by law and making all SHU terms indeterminate.[18] Hinting at problems of legitimacy and the possible consequences of increased control and reduced privileges, California's Legislative Analyst's Office (LAO) rejected the proposed plan, on the grounds that it may lead to

> unintended consequences and result in increased costs: the proposal includes two significant policy changes to the operation of the SHU units which could potentially increase the level of inmate violence. It is possible that a further reduction in privileges could have no change or even increase violent inmate behaviour in these restrictive housing units, resulting in a need for additional security resources in the future.... In addition, the conversion of terms for inmates in SHU from determinate to indeterminate time frames could cause inmates to be housed at a higher security level for longer than necessary, thereby adding to the existing shortage of SHU housing. (California Legislative Analyst Office, 2001–02 Budget Bill Analysis, section 5240)

Such proposals, with some modifications and adjustments, are nonetheless likely to return to the agenda, further reducing privileges and increasing control of supermax prisoners, albeit always within the letter of the law. Indeed, where departments of corrections do offer some form of progressive programming for their supermax populations (including, for example, those of Washington, New Mexico and the Federal Bureau of Prisons), these typically start with the very basic level of provisions (essentially showers and exercise), and prisoners need to 'work their way' towards increased privileges previously provided as a matter of course, such as televisions and family visits. Classification, as the administrative tool for identifying specific groups or categories of prisoners for these regimes, thus carries enormous practical consequences.

Reclassification/exit criteria: snitch, parole or die

If the initial classification is a crude way of dividing prisoners into security groups, the reclassification or review process is theoretically intended to re-evaluate and fine-tune initial decisions according to the prisoner's actual (rather than predicted) behaviour at the assigned prison. Classification, according to official directives, 'shall be an ongoing process of evaluating the inmate's needs, interests and desires, keeping in mind individual, security and public safety'.[19] As we shall see, however, the process is essentially formalistic, pays little attention to individual needs, and focuses mainly on issues of institutional security.

In California, the body charged with reviewing prisoners' classification score is the unit classification committee (UCC). Title 15 requires that prisoners serving determinate SHU terms will appear before a UCC at least once a year, whereas those serving indeterminate SHU terms are reviewed by the UCC at least once every 180 days. Parole and classification board hearings are held in centralised rooms in the SHU. The area is zoned-off from the housing units by long corridors, and several security doors and grill gates, which are operated from the wing control rooms. The area includes several committee rooms, a row of individual holding cells, and an area for searching prisoners. Holding cells are equipped with handcuffing slots and view panels for placing and removing handcuffs. Before their scheduled hearing, prisoners are strip searched in their cells, escorted to the designated area, and placed in the holding cells until their classification/parole hearing commences. Hearings are held in committee rooms containing a large table and chairs. During the hearing, the prisoner sits facing the back of his chair, with his hands cuffed in front.[20] Up to 10 people, all of whom are SHU staff members, participate in reclassification hearings. In addition to re-evaluating prisoners' initial classification score, hearings also provide, according to one unit manager, an opportunity to evaluate the facility's operation:

It's a good way for me to check and make sure that the people working with me are doing their jobs. Are the mental health professionals seeing them? Has this man been seen for medical care? Is the counsellor asking these questions? It is part of a check and balance system that we have, to ensure that all the processes are working. When I get a man in Committee that's very angry and frustrated, I know that perhaps something in our system isn't working. He's not getting answers or he's not getting some needs met.

But even at these hearings, the only official platform for him to present his case, the 'truth' about the prisoner is gained from staff reports, not from the prisoner himself:

The officer who works the building every day can often times give me more insight to that inmate than the inmate himself. Also, the inmate can't lie to me. If the inmate starts to tell me a story, they will bring him into check and say, 'Now just a minute, that's not the way that's happening,' and give me some good information. [unit manager]

First, the prisoner's 'favourable' and 'unfavourable' behaviour since the last classification hearing is computed with numerical scores including some of the following (Title 15, section 3375.4):

(a) *Unfavourable behaviour* 1) serious rule violation during a 6 months period (between 8 and 4 points for each violation of one or more of 55 listed offenses, depending on the seriousness of the offense); 2) battery or attempted battery on a non-prisoner (8 points); 3) battery on an inmate (4 points); 4) distribution of drugs (4 points); 5) possession of a deadly weapon (15 points); 6) inciting a disturbance (4 points); 7) battery causing serious injury (16 points).

(b) *Favourable behaviour* since last review (no serious disciplinary violation, 2 credits for each 6 months period).

Prisoners are confronted with a long list of penalties (note also the greater penalties for 'misbehaviour' directed against prison staff) and one single 'favourable' factor – the lack of *any* misconduct – meagrely awarded. Reclassification hearings are essentially procedural, providing little, if any, opportunity or incentive for prisoners.

Average hearings last between 5 and 25 minutes and an internal audit report found that up to 60 per cent of annual reviews result in no change to the prisoner's programme assignment or custody level.[21] As 'good conduct' is only rewarded with two credits and 'misconduct' is widely defined and heavily penalised, prisoners have few avenues for leaving the SHU before their minimum eligibility release date. Indeed, prisoners are more likely than not to commit minor breaches of the strict rules and regulations that govern their lives, thus reaffirming their label and feeding into the classification system's self-fulfilling prophecies.[22]

Prisoners who are allocated to the SHU for a determinate time undergo a fairly straightforward process. Unless they have breached SHU rules and regulations or exhibited violent behaviour (in which case they will receive an additional SHU term), they will remain in the SHU until they have finished serving their SHU term. Prisoners who are placed in the SHU on gang-related grounds will remain there for an indeterminate time. The only avenues they have for leaving the SHU are limited to what is colloquially known as 'snitching, paroling, or dying'. Death and parole are self-explanatory. 'Snitching', or 'debriefing' in official language, involves the prisoner providing prison authorities with a detailed report of his gang-related activities, names of other people involved, and any other pertinent information (a 'biography' as prisoners call it). The process of debriefing brings to mind the Catholic practice of confession, but its function is perhaps closer to brainwashing techniques used in communist Russia and China with political dissenters, where, following a period in isolation, the prisoner 'was forced to prove his sincerity by making irrevocable behavioural commitments, such as denouncing and implicating his friends and relatives in his own newly recognised crimes. Once he had done this, he became further alienated from his former self, even in his own eyes' (Schein 1960: 155). According to officials, all the prisoner has to do is decide to change his ways:

> If an inmate chooses not to continue as a gang member ... they can renounce their membership within that specific Security Threat Group. What that entails is the inmate goes before some investigators, some intelligence personnel, and they have a debriefing. And they must discuss specific information. And ... that information must also be validated and proven. Once it's determined that it's factual, the inmate can renounce his membership and he may leave this unit and go to another unit for the inmates that have renounced. [administrator]

Renouncing a gang, however, is not a simple or an easy option for prisoners. One officer referred to prisoners as rational actors who can exercise free choice, and said that around 80 per cent of prisoners are 'not willing to take the steps to get themselves out of the unit'. When asked why she thought this was the case, she acknowledged the complexities of renouncing a gang:

> Sometimes inmates are not willing to take the steps to get themselves out of [the unit] because they're so socialised into the gang. For them, the gang is their whole life; it's their family, it's their relationships, it is how they live, and for them to go against those mores is just too difficult. It's all they know.

One prisoner, who at the time was serving his tenth year in a supermax unit, confirmed this view and said that he thought that debriefing was 'dishonourable':

> Why betray friends, people who you, who you grow up with … but you do not spend time with, just for a chance of going to the mainline. I don't see no honour in that. I think it's dishonourable.

In the prison setting, gang membership provides prisoners with protection, a sense of belonging, and sometimes simply a group of familiar faces. As a senior administrator put it, for many prisoners, the 'gang' is synonymous with 'family':

> Most of these guys didn't just come to prison and decide, 'Gee, I think I'm going to be a gang member' and they go out and join a gang. Most of them had been associated with gang activities, many of them, since pre-teen. For many of them it was a family lifestyle – their fathers, their mothers, their brothers, sisters, aunts, and uncles – the whole family network was associated with gang activity.

This understanding of the dynamics of inner-city poor and racially segregated communities is not an empathetic one, but part of the social distancing between 'us' and 'them' that I discussed previously. Such statements are also deterministic in the sense that they imply that supermax prisoners cannot change.

Prisoners who do wish to debrief have to complete a detailed debriefing report (see above), which is sent to Department of

Corrections (DOC) headquarters for evaluation. If the prisoner provides what gang investigators consider to be an 'unreliable' or 'insufficient' amount of information, the debriefing report may be rejected, and the prisoner will retain his status as a gang member/affiliate. If the report is accepted, the prisoner will appear before the ICC to be reclassified and allocated to a Transitional Housing Unit (THU), where he will be housed with others who have debriefed. This time, the purpose of the 'special placement' in a THU is to protect the prisoner, and to test his good faith and willingness to disassociate himself from gang activity. Prior to 1995, when the *Madrid* court ordered the CDC to introduce a THU for prisoners who debriefed, these prisoners were still housed in a SHU, but required to participate for six months in an integrated yard programme in association with others. These 'others' included former enemies from opposing gangs, and the idea was for prisoners to demonstrate that 'they could now get along with people who were former enemies and because now they're dropouts they don't consider them enemies anymore'.

> We thought there was something missing in that process and if you took a gangster who dropped out of a gang and they debriefed, and even though they went through a six month trial period within an Integrated Yard, they didn't magically gain the skills in social interaction that they never learned through their association with the gang.... And so what we consider typical social skills of settling a dispute without resorting to physical violence, without killing somebody, what we regard as just having an ability to make day to day decisions without resorting to violence – a lot of these people never learned. They got their self-esteem through the gang – that was their esteem: 'I'm a member of the Mexican Mafia, I'm, you know a joker from this neighbourhood.' ... So part of the Transitional Housing Unit concept was based on trying to get these people back their self-esteem through individualised education programming and through a variety of self help programmes; significant group counselling, anger management, parenting programmes – a lot of these people became parents and don't have a clue what that means. [senior administrator]

At the THU, members of opposing gangs are expected to demonstrate their sincere intentions by getting along with each other. Prisoners may be put two to a cell and asked to sign a 'marriage contract', as it is colloquially known, vowing not to engage in any hostile acts towards each other. The senior administrator (above) stated, rather cautiously, that the THU aims to prepare former gang members so that 'maybe eventually, and a lot of them have gone back out to the street on parole, on discharge, have some social skills that will enable them to maybe not come back.' Recidivism rates and prisoners' reports of their time at the THU are not encouraging as to its success. Furthermore, prisoners who debrief are under a real threat of retaliation by members of their former gang, and once they leave the THU and move to general population units or are released from prison, no one can guarantee their safety.

Some of the prisoners labelled as gang members/affiliates reject the label, contest any affiliation with gang activities, and say that they cannot debrief, since they have no knowledge of gang activities. These individuals find themselves in an impossible situation: they will not be released from the unit unless they debrief, but since they are not gang members, they cannot provide any information on gang activities and therefore are unable to debrief. One supermax administrator referred to such situations as 'catch 22s' and stated, rather unsympathetically, that

> I think that there are some interesting glitches or Catch 22s in the system … the inevitable guy who is not a member, is not an associate, but is validated as a member or an associate, and in order for him to get out of the unit he has to debrief, but he keeps saying, 'Well I don't know anything therefore I can't debrief so I guess I'm just here forever' and it seems like the person is caught in a Catch 22.

Another group of prisoners who find themselves in a difficult position are those who were gang members when they were first placed in the supermax, but have been isolated for so long that any information they might have had in the past is outdated and irrelevant. Following court interventions in matters of prisoner classification and a growing demand for SHU beds, in April 2000, over a decade after Pelican Bay SHU was opened, the CDC introduced a new category, 'inactive gang members'. This new category was designed as an alternative to 'debriefing' for prisoners who have not been involved in gang activity for a minimum of six years.[23] The new category was created because

We have a lot of men that have been up here a long time and we recognise that now they probably don't all need the strict controls we have on them.... We are [now] evaluating each man for what we call Inactive Status, and that gives them a way out where they don't have to come forward and debrief or drop out officially from the gang. It, if you will, for lack of a better way to describe it, it gives them a label they can live with. We still identify them as a participant in some sort of a gang activity, yet we're calling them 'inactive' so not as dangerous and able to go out to a mainline prison to function. [unit manager]

The process is highly subjective and discretionary. Prisoners may (but do not have a right to) be reclassified by the Departmental Review Board (DRB) as inactive gang members. Regulations stipulate that the decision made by the DRB will be reviewed *no more* than once every two years. Inactive gang members who are selected by the DRB for release from the SHU have to 'pass' another test. They are allocated to the general population of a Level IV facility (maximum security) for a 'period of observation', which may last up to 12 months, and upon its completion they are housed in a facility consistent with their (initial) classification score. It is sufficient for one 'reliable source item' to identify the prisoner as being involved in gang activity during this period for the prisoner to be returned to the SHU. The DRB may also decide that although a prisoner is an inactive gang member he should be retained in the SHU. The procedures are couched in, the by now familiar, open-ended language which gives the DRB almost absolute discretion:

The DRB is authorised to retain an inactive gang member or associate in a SHU based on the inmate's past or present level of influence in the gang, history of misconduct, history of criminal activity, or other factors indicating that the inmate poses a threat to other inmates or institutional security. (Title 15, section 3341.4[c])

In short, the number of prisoners that can be included in the 'inactive' category is very small to begin with, and the CDCR retains complete discretion in releasing or retaining these prisoners in the SHU. As the *Madrid* (1995) court recognised, on the whole, the processes of validation, classification, review and debriefing remain highly problematic,

> Not only is the risk of false information high, but the consequences of an improper validation – confinement in the SHU for an indeterminate term, with all its attendant restrictions and adverse impacts on parole – are severe. Moreover, inmates improperly validated as gang members have little chance of rectifying such an error or otherwise obtaining release from the SHU. (*Madrid* 1995: 1274)

I have spent some time discussing gang-related issues, since gang members constitute the main body of Pelican Bay SHU prisoners, and because the process of classifying and validating gang membership is typical of the entire enterprise of classification: all-embracing categories, highly subjective procedures, and a general reluctance to make any change to prisoners' status or to encourage them to improve their behaviour. Although the process for leaving the SHU is more straightforward for 'rule violators', we saw that the design of reclassification scores is geared towards punishment rather than self-improvement. Misconduct is severely punished, but there is little emphasis on, or scope for, rewarding good conduct.

The power to classify in the context of supermax prisons

> The real significance of classification lies in the form, not the content, the enterprise itself and not its end-results. The power to classify is the purest of all deposits of professionalism. (Cohen 1985: 246)

Prisoner classification and placement play a pivotal role in determining the 'quality and rigours' (Foucault 1977: 246) of prisoners' confinement. Prisoner classification dictates the physical conditions in which prisoners are held, and their access to vocational, educational and recreational programmes and other 'privileges' that encompass most aspects of prisoners' daily lives. Through the use of classification factors in parole hearings designed to assess prisoners' risk to the community, and through the administration of good time credits, classification also affects prisoners' chances of parole. The process of classification is circular, as prison systems use their own definitions, regulations and database of prior institutional behaviour to reinforce their own predictions, creating self-fulfilling prophecies as to the 'nature' of prisoners. These self-fulfilling prophecies become set in stone, quite literally, since projections of future prison construction needs are based on current classification groupings. Since the early 1990s, these have consisted of growing numbers of maximum and special security prisoners.

The process of prisoner security classification may be described as a junction of power and knowledge – different forms of knowledge and the power to punish (Foucault 1977). Classification is the tool through which judicial, professional and administrative knowledge is used to distribute control (power) in accordance with penal policies and administrative directives, in ways that are intended to minimise risk and maximise resources. The knowledge which feeds into prisoner classification is processed through 'objective' tools and statistical measures borrowed from the positivistic sciences to produce an outcome (decision or label) which then feeds back into the system both physically, through the construction of prisons, and by feeding into a database later used to reinforce the label on the individual. For prisoners categorised as 'special security', this may mean the beginning of a vicious circle from which few are able to emerge. 'Power' and 'knowledge' thus have very concrete consequences in this instance. The 'power' to classify is an exercise of the power to punish, and in the case of supermax confinement, it is the power to exclude, isolate and deprive. As confinement to a supermax has very serious implications for prisoners, in practice it constitutes a substantial addition in severity to the sentence given to the prisoner by a court of justice. Further, once they are placed in a supermax unit, no distinction is made between different types of prisoners. As a senior prison administrator conceded,

> I think that ultimately what we as a department are going to have to do, is we're going to have to rethink a little bit our approach to controlling the gangs per se and how we are locking people up – now when I say lock up people, I mean putting them in a supermax unit – people both label driven, and when I say label driven I mean by validating them, and we lock up people based on their behaviour, and they may not have a label. And I think that ultimately where we're going to have to shift our emphasis more to the behaviour driven issues to get people locked up, as opposed to the label driven issues that are getting people locked up.

Despite its serious implications for prisoners, a relatively low-level body (in California, the ICC) is charged with allocating prisoners to supermax, or SHU, units. A US national survey of supermax confinement similarly found that of the 34 departments of corrections that responded and operated a supermax facility at the time, half reported that placement and removal of prisoners from supermax is made at the institutional level, while the other half reported that the decision is made at central office level, by the DOC director or deputy director. None of the jurisdictions had mechanisms for external scrutiny of allocation and release processes (NIC 1997: 3). Definitions of 'serious rule violations' that may lead to allocation to a supermax unit are very wide and all-encompassing. Some of the factors that count as disruptive, dangerous or violent behaviours and constitute sufficient grounds for allocation to a supermax are both minor in themselves and specific to the prison environment. Furthermore, prisoners may be allocated to a supermax not only for offences which were actually committed, as minor as they may be, but also to prevent the risk, possibility, or perceived likelihood of such offending.

Above and beyond the methodological flaws and biases which influence the design and application of classification instruments, there is a problem with the very concept of managing risk through classification. As King and McDermott (1995) put it,

> Attempts to predict 'troublesome inmates' (through risk profiles and the like) will always be imperfect, for the research evidence is clear that 'troublesomeness' and similar concepts are not just naturally occurring phenomena, carried around by individuals as a set of characteristics, identifiable in advance and just waiting to erupt. (King and McDermott 1995: 453)

None of these issues appear to threaten seriously prison officials' view that classification instruments work well in identifying prisoners and allocating them to a supermax.

> I think that we operate very smoothly here. I think that it [classification] is one of the things that we are very good at. It's not perfect. We do make mistakes. But because we have so many checks and balances in our system, we catch them. If somebody is improperly classified, the inmate may catch it and bring it to our attention so we can correct it, the supervisors in a chain of command reviewing the actions we're taking sometimes may catch an error. Just like any other system with checks and balances, we police ourselves fairly well. [unit manager]

In practice, however, there is no real 'chain of command' reviewing classification decisions, especially not once a prisoner has been classified as requiring 'special security'. The entire setting of review hearings discourages individualised and positive interaction with the prisoner, and indeed any proactive attitudes by staff. In California, the body charged with making the final decision in the case of disputes, the DRB, only reviews decisions that are referred to it by the ICC, an internal body whose decision was challenged in the first place, and whose main consideration is 'institutional security' as represented by staff reports.

Current trends do not indicate a reduction in the number of prisoners assigned to high-security categories and segregated. Most prison systems in the USA are, in fact, seeing an increase in the number of prisoners categorised as requiring supermax confinement. As previously noted, the increase in the use of segregation (punitive, protective and administrative) outpaced that of the growth in prison populations (40 and 28 per cent respectively) between 1995 and 2000 (Commission on Safety and Abuse 2006). Inside supermax prisons, we see the creation of subcategories of 'dangerousness' for prisoners who are claimed to require even more control. The threshold of 'dangerousness' is lowered as a new subcategory is created among those classified as the 'most dangerous' – the most dangerous among the most dangerous. Adopting such tactics, some supermax units now have special sections for holding prisoners who commit violent offences while in isolation. Prisoners who 'gas' guards have their cell doors covered with Plexiglas, further isolating them. Repeat 'gassers' will be identified as such on their personal file, and will not be able to leave the unit since gassing is classified as a serious offence. This process brings to mind what Messinger (1969) termed the 'complicated Chinese box effect' when, in the 1960s, California developed special segregation units within existing segregation units as a tool for managing 'difficult' prisoners who were already segregated. This resulted in 'inmates in the innermost box ideally required to traverse each enclosing one on the way to relative freedom'.[24] The layers of isolation surrounding prisoners in high-security categories enclose them from within, separating them from the prison community, as well as from free society.

If the goal of classification in the context of supermax confinement is to identify dangerous and disruptive prisoners and isolate them in order to reduce the level of violence within the entire prison estate, then, in California at least, it cannot be seen as a success, since prison violence there is constantly increasing. This may be the case because there is something wrong with the 'technical' side of classification; for example, that it does not recognise the targeted individuals correctly. It is also possible that the problem is not with the classification instruments themselves, but with the way they are applied by staff, for example by excessive use of administrative overrides.

If success is defined as incapacitating certain categories of prisoners, however, and allocation to a supermax prison acts as a tool to control defined segments of the prisoner population, not necessarily dangerous individuals, then classification may not, in fact, be a failure at all. Currently, targeted groups appear to include those from racial minorities and small-time repeat offenders, but the definition of the category of special security is flexible enough to include in it anyone whom prison authorities wish to include, according to either penal policies or administrative convenience. The so-called objective nature of classification instruments and processes, and the rules and procedures guiding their application, are flagged by officials as 'proof' of the authenticity of the results of the process, making it difficult for prisoners to challenge classificatory decisions in the courts. Thus, 'What appears to be no more than an administrative concern to produce standardisation and homogeneity does in fact carry a heavy penological and ideological significance' (Garland 1985: 12).

Those less familiar with the ins and outs of prison systems are satisfied by official narratives regarding the assignment of prisoners to supermax confinement, and are reassured by the promise that it keeps the most dangerous predators securely under lock and key. Those more familiar with prisoner classification repeatedly comment on the components and structure of the classification process, but few have taken the more radical step of questioning its utility in principle. As Cohen (1985) observed, 'the "failure" of a classification system rarely evokes troublesome ideological questions and never threatens professional interests. It simply calls for more and better classification, an agenda which can be followed with total agreement from everyone' (Cohen 1985: 193).

In addition to being a convenient policy and administrative tool, classification in and by itself may also have another, more subtle role: by objectifying prisoners and their characteristics through the use of 'objective', 'scientific' measures, and by defining (and thinking of) prisoners as categories rather than individuals with all that is implied by each category (e.g. dangerousness), classification strengthens the psychological barriers between prisoners and guards. Through making more of the 'category' and less of the 'human' in the prisoner, the task of guarding him may be easier to perform. I return to this issue later. First, in the next chapter, I examine the 'hardware' of supermax prisons: their architectural design and the surveillance and control devices used in them.

Notes

1 For example, the Minnesota Multiphasic Personality Inventory (MMPI) (Megargee and Bohn 1979), and Quay's (1983) Behavioural Classification.

2 Feeley and Simon (1992: 453). We should note that while it is true that since the 1980s there has been a growing reliance on actuarial risk predictions, some prison systems developed risk-based prisoner security classification systems much earlier. The prisoner security classification system used in England and Wales, for example, was adopted in 1967 following a series of prison escapes and the findings of the Mountbatten Committee of Inquiry (1966) into these escapes. The Committee recommended putting prisoners into four categories, A to D, in descending order of the risk they pose to prison security, and placing them under a regime appropriate to their security category.

3 In July 2005, the California Department of Corrections (CDC) was reorganised and renamed the California Department of Corrections and Rehabilitation (CDCR). The department is called 'CDC' in references to documents, statements and publications predating the reorganisation, and 'CDCR' in references to later documents throughout this book.

4 CDCR Facts and Figures (2008).

5 Administrative parole violation occurs when the parolee violates a condition of parole that may not constitute a violation of law or is unlikely to be prosecuted by local officials, such as missing an appointment with one's parole officer.

6 The term 'security' is used to encompass both public and institutional order, although the two are in fact different, and public security can be addressed by preventing escapes through fortified exterior and perimeter security devices.

7 Although different jurisdictions use different names for their security categories, these are the basic categories used by most states in the USA, and indeed in many other countries.

8 Some states in the USA have now adopted new classification systems that include a separate category for supermax prisons.

9 CDCR Department Operations Manual, Chapter 6, Article 5: Classification Process Section 62010.1, effective 25 October 1989 (updated through 31 December 2006).

10 California's Board of Corrections Programs and Procedures Guidelines, Article 5: Classification and Segregation, section 1050, 2001 Revisions.

11 (Section 3375.3). The categories, language and numbering in this section are as they appear in Title 15, updated through September 2007.

12 This was the case with Pelican Bay SHU, when CDC was ordered by the *Madrid* court (1995) to remove all mentally ill prisoners from the SHU. Virginia's department of corrections, similarly, lost an ongoing court case challenging its practice of holding mentally ill prisoners in its two supermax facilities (Human Rights Watch 1997, 2000), as did Wisconsin, where the court ordered the department to remove mentally ill prisoners from its supermax facility (*Jones'El* 2001).

13 Poole and Regoli 1980: 943, cited in Bottoms 1999: 224.

14 The chart, guidelines for the ICC, mitigating factors, etc., are set out in Subsection 3341.5 of Title 15.

15 Space does not permit an in-depth discussion of prison gangs, nor their growth in prisons across the USA and their role in prison society, but see, for example, Irwin (1980) and Jacobs (1977). For discussion of legal issues regarding the segregation of alleged gang members, see Tachiki (1995).

16 Title 15, Section 3377.1(a) 23 February 2000 amendments. Previously, there were nine custody designations, which included a distinction between maximum A and maximum B. This distinction was eliminated, since 'in reality, there is little difference in the security needs at the two steps, and it is difficult to classify cases to that fine a degree' (accompanying notes to February Amendments, *ibid.*).

17 Title 15, Section 3044. Further, 'An inmate's status in work group D-2 may be extended, in up to 6-month increments, in unusual cases where no credit qualifying programme can be assigned [to] the inmate without causing a substantial risk of physical harm to staff or others' (*ibid.*).

18 California LAO (2001–02 Budget Bill Analysis, section 5240). The proposals suggest, for example, that SHU prisoners will not be entitled to have television sets and radios in their cells nor make canteen purchases, thus taking away the few privileges they currently have.

19 CDCR Operations Manual, Chapter 6, section 62010.4.

20 Holding classification and parole hearings in such an institutionalised setting and keeping the prisoner in physical restraints may also give rise to issues of due process and the right to a fair hearing.

21 California Department of Finance (1996: 48). The authors commented, 'Whilst most hearings last only a few minutes counsellors report that much of their time is spent in hearings ... even a few minutes per inmate for seven or eight persons, make the hearings a major activity of everyone's week' (at p. 51).

22 Whether or not one accepts this view of the interaction between initial labelling and subsequent offending, we must question the practice, in California and other states, of subjecting those identified as 'high risk' prisoners to conditions of confinement that are known to be conducive to violent behaviour. I return to this issue later.

23 Title 15 section 3378(e) 27 April 2000 revisions.
24 Messinger, S. (1969) *Strategies of Control*. Centre for the Study of Law and Society, University of California, Berkeley, Cited in Cohen and Taylor (1981: 201).

Chapter 6

Technologies of control: the architectural design, physical fixtures and security arrangements in supermax prisons

> There is no mute architecture. All architects, all buildings 'tell stories' with varying degrees of consciousness. Architecture is permeated with narratives because it is constituted within a field of discourses and economies (formal, psychological, and ideological) to any one aspect of which it cannot be reduced, from any one of which it cannot be removed. (Rakatansky 1991: 1)

Prison design reflects penal ideologies, managerial tactics, political discourses, economic considerations, and cultural and social sensitivities, sentiments and insecurities. These discourses 'enter into construction and ... in consequence buildings or planned environments become statements' (Hirst 1985: 175). The design, in turn, affects discourses and shapes practices: the 'hardware' of a prison building, including building materials, colour schemes and surveillance mechanisms, has great impact on the way in which the prison is managed, on the daily experiences of prisoners and prison staff, and on the relationship and interactions between them. In the case of supermax prisons, which are designed to isolate prisoners, the design itself dictates the reality of life to a particularly large extent.

This chapter examines the 'hardware' of supermax prisons, using Pelican Bay Security Housing Unit (SHU) in California and Special Management Unit II (SMU) in Arizona to illustrate design features, considerations and discourses. I enquire whether any one of the discourses identified above (managerial, economic, social, cultural) dominated the design process and considerations, and, if so, how it affected the architectural outcome. It illustrates how the interdependencies between social life and territory, the 'socio-spatial dialectic' (Wolch and Dear 1989: 4), are manifested in supermax prisons by reconstructing a dual narrative: the silent yet powerful narrative presented by the building itself, and the verbal professional narratives accompanying it.

Prison architecture

> Architecture is a social art; it provides structure for human activity, influences patterns, enriches the sensible world, and provides expression and continuity to social values. (Moyer 1975: 53)

Most prison buildings share some general design principles and characteristics. In Goffman's standard definition, prisons are total, closed institutions, whose main feature is a breakdown of 'one of the basic social arrangements in modern society ... that the individual tends to sleep, play, and work in different places, with different co-participants, under different authorities and without an over-all rational plan' (Goffman 1961: 6). The design of prison buildings has to enable these different activities within a limited, closed physical space. 'Space', however, is more than a physical element, and its organisation is a 'purposeful social product' that cannot be regarded as a 'separable structure with rules of construction and transformation independent of social practice' (Wolch and Dear 1989: 6). In prisons, as in other closed total institutions, space is a fundamental ingredient in the exercise of power. Since the arrangement of space is within architecture's domain, prison architecture sustains great power in regulating lives, dictating movement across time and space, and shaping human experiences. In prisons, perhaps more than any other building, the apparently passive building becomes an active, powerful force in shaping the daily lives of those who inhabit it.

Prison buildings share these general principles, but they vary in their design and space arrangement, which reflect, among other factors, the prison's mission, its security assignment, its staffing levels, and its budget. Additionally, 'the type of facility created is driven as much by the treatment tradition and culture of the state as it is by the public and political perception of crimes within the state' (American Institute of Architects 1999a: 5). Within these constraints and discourses, architecture has room for manoeuvre and can manipulate the prison's environment to a considerable extent. The building should be a tool:

> The main question is 'does it [the building] work for that institution make up and that inmate make up'? We have graduated levels of housing, and we have housing for similar descriptions of inmates, all behaviour driven. As we have situations, our designers respond. (Chadbourne 1998)

Despite more than two centuries of experience with prison design, however, the relationship between the prison environment and prisoner behaviour has not been studied with the same rigour as the relationship between crime and the environment.[1] The result is sparse literature and few empirical studies, which reaffirm the fairly obvious: 'the design of the prison environment is crucial to its operation and to the impact it has on the achievement of correctional goals for inmates, staff and public users.'[2]

Below, I briefly examine the impact of specific prison design factors on prisoners and staff. As shorthand, I will describe those impacts as 'negative' and 'positive' to indicate their documented effects on well-being and behaviour. 'Positive' design features are those that contribute to lessen the institutionalised atmosphere in prisons; reduce stress, aggression, and violence; and generally increase prisoners' well-being. 'Negative' features are those that foster and increase the above. Prison architecture has an important role in five general areas.[3]

Organising relationships between people

On the macro-scale, the location of a prison facility influences the possibility of family visits, reintegrative, community-based pro-grammes, specialised services and so on (Moyer 1975: 58–60. See also Fairweather 2000: 34). On the micro-scale, the design of the facility 'encompasses a complex series of internal spatial organisations ... of the frequency and character of human interaction within the building' (Moyer, *ibid.*). Generally, a 'positive' design encourages interactions and individualised treatment, and a 'negative' design discourages and makes such interactions more difficult.

Enabling adaptability, flexibility and mobility

Prison environments typically present 'formidable obstacles to the introduction of any other form of habitation or utilisation than that which is currently conducted within them' (Moyer, *ibid.*). Positive architecture allows adaptability to future change. Planning can anticipate, and the design should include, the possibility of future alteration of internal spatial divisions, external additions or subtractions, and 'functional flexibility'. New prefabricated technologies make facility mobility possible, so that a facility can move in whole or in part to new areas of service delivery.

Communication

Architecture communicates to prisoners how society perceives them, and reinforces this perception for society. It is a '24-hour communicator' that should be used as 'part of the treatment process' and communicate positive values and attitudes to prisoners (Moyer, *ibid.*).

Arranging space

Utilising space for structured and unstructured activities, where 'personal territories ... and identity' can be developed, is an 'enabling power of architecture'. The lack of such space, and 'deprivations which stem from sterile, routinized and mechanical characteristics of the physical environment ... constitute a significant constraint on any programme endeavour' (Moyer, *ibid.*). There also has to be an appropriate balance between the requirements of security and the adverse consequences of an over-oppressive atmosphere, which can lead to hostile reactions from prisoners and to a negative response from the public (Fairweather 2000: 47).

Determining supervision style

The prison's supervision style is determined by both its management style and its architectural layout, and is cited as one of the most important factors in affecting behaviour. There are two basic layouts: direct supervision and indirect supervision. In prisons with indirect supervision, staff and prisoners occupy separate territories. Supervision and control are remote and characterised by reliance on distant visual surveillance from guards' secure stations, and on patrolling corridors and landings. Prisons with indirect supervision are styled in radial or cruciform layouts, with variations such as courtyards, and 'T', 'H' and 'L' configurations. The indirect supervision style 'lends itself to reactive management style because it encourages staff to respond to problems rather than facilitating their ability to anticipate and prevent them' (Buchanan *et al.* 1988: 52). An additional problem associated with indirect supervision is that 'a sense of alienation is evident … leading to the development of inmate cultures and hierarchies that officers may find difficult to understand and control. On the staff side, there may be a tendency to stereotype and a failure to treat the prisoners as individuals' (Fairweather 2000: 35). Direct supervision prisons have larger association areas, and staff areas are located inside the housing units, so that staff have greater face to face contact with prisoners. These prisons are proactive in nature, as the presence of staff lessens opportunities for prisoner misconduct. Many prison researchers assert that direct supervision results in a dramatic reduction in prison violence and 'increased positive relationships, allowing more effective surveillance and better security'.[4] Direct supervision has also been endorsed by professional bodies, as well as the US National Institute of Corrections, as the best method for managing prisoners, including disruptive populations (Dewitt 1997: iv).

In addition to these general principles, one can find in literature on prison design assertions about the effects of specific design and environmental factors on prisoners' behaviour. Privacy for example, is cited as an important factor:

> [Privacy provides] an emotional haven; it allows the opportunity for self-evaluation, permits limited communication and establishes a psychological distance from others. It provides personal autonomy and sense of individuality and control over one's situation.… The manipulation of distance or barriers in the environment is a critical mechanism in achieving privacy. A barred cell provides physical separation but little visual or auditory isolation … an inability to achieve socially accepted norms for bodily functions has a dehumanising effects – an exposed toilet, for example, shows little respect for privacy or dignity of the inmates … and may further blunt or debase sensibilities … lack of privacy fosters considerable stress and aggression.[5]

Other factors cited as positively influencing behaviour include thermal comfort, low noise levels, natural light, colourful environment and the use of 'soft materials' for cell furnishings. Through these and other design features, prison architecture has the power to influence the environment and directly affect behaviour (in a 'positive' or 'negative' way). On a more general level, the appearance and impression of the prison communicates to prisoners how they are expected to behave

(Wener 2000: 52). These factors and principles are relevant to all prison design and perhaps take on a special importance in the design of supermax prisons. In what follows, I examine the main architectural features of modern supermax prisons and the environment fostered by their design.

The architecture of control: 'new-generation' supermax prisons

> Morals reformed – health preserved – industry invigorated – instruction diffused – public burdens lightened – Economy seated, as it were, upon a rock – the Gordian knot of the Poor-Laws are not cut, but untied – all by a simple idea in Architecture! (Bentham 1791: i–ii)

In the early 1980s, a new concept emerged in prison architecture: 'new-generation' prisons. New-generation prisons were conceived of as a design and a managerial concept, reflecting the interdependence of the architectural design (environmental factors) and the management style (organisational and social factors) of prisons. These prisons are constituted of small housing units ('pods'), which are arranged around a communal area where most activities take place. Prisoners are directly supervised by guards who mingle with them in the communal area. The small unit design enables the provision of specific environments for defined groups of prisoners, while maintaining close and direct staff supervision. The architecture of new-generation prisons 'seeks to incorporate desirable features of situational crime prevention into prison design' (Bottoms 1999: 242); that is, reducing the opportunities for crime and increasing the risk of getting caught. In design terms, this is achieved by making prisoner areas visible and eliminating 'blind spots' where violence can occur, by using tamper-proof building materials and furniture, and by enabling direct staff supervision. The 'new-generation' concept also emphasises 'deliberate manipulation of symbolic features of the environment so that the reduced opportunity physical design does not feel oppressive to inmates' (Bottoms 1999: 243).

The concept of small-pod design combined with direct supervision was endorsed in 1984 by the US National Institute of Corrections, the American Correctional Association, the American Jail Association, and the Architecture for Justice Committee of the American Institute of Architects (Dewitt 1997: iv). More recently, new-generation prisons have been praised for their success in reducing violence levels: 'these facilities have had an impressive record of success ... [they] have been remarkably free of violent behaviour, as verified by many anecdotal commentaries and a number of formal evaluation studies' (Wener 2000: 49). The problems of sealed air quality and monotonous atmosphere, which are associated with new-generation design, are considered to be negligible in view of the advantages described above.

Supermax prisons typically utilise some of these new design principles, but not quite for the purpose for which they were intended. Instead of direct staff supervision and increased contact between staff and prisoners, the small unit layout and new technologies are used to reduce staff numbers, to support total separation of staff and prisoners, and to enable a regime based on remote surveillance and command. As previously discussed, supermaxes are designed as 'end of the line' institutions, 'prisons within prisons', used to accommodate the 'worst of the worst', prisoners who need to be removed from the general prison population and subjected to the highest degree of control.[6] The chosen method for managing these prisoners is solitary confinement, coupled with restricted movement under tight control and enhanced security measures. Prisoners are individually 'secured' by layers upon layers of physical controls, maximising isolation and immobilisation. In supermax prisons, architecture's power is demonstrated with rare bluntness: every detail of the design, materials and colours is carefully and, quite overtly, calculated to achieve maximum control of prisoners.

The key elements in his brief, according to one architect who designs supermax prisons, are

> First of all to isolate ... particular inmates from the rest of the population, to try to cut off as much as possible the communication that they have with that population or with the outside world, and to put them in an environment where it's both safe for staff and the other inmates that are around them to live ... an environment that allows you to manage them without taking away their rights that they have.

This vision represents a sharp break with traditional segregation units, where isolation was a short-term punishment, to a carefully designed system of prolonged isolation as a tool of long-term prisoner management. In designing supermax prisons, architects aim to maximise the available space to contain the greatest number of prisoners (typically 500–1100) strictly isolated from each other and from staff, under the highest level of control, while providing the basic conditions required by law, and to do so at the lowest possible cost. The discourse of prisoners' 'rights' enters the design considerations to prevent future prisoner litigation rather than as an expression of concern with prisoners' civil and human rights.

The core architectural feature of supermax prisons is their design as self-contained units with isolation cells. Prison designs using similar principles to enable long-term isolation of entire prison populations were used extensively in especially designed prisons in the early nineteenth century on both sides of the Atlantic. The fundamental aim of these prisons, as previously discussed, was to reform prisoners, and architecture was to act directly upon the prisoner's moral character.

> Prison architecture was developed quite consciously as a means to this end. Increasing technical sophistication was a consequence of successive failures to achieve reformation, which were frequently seen as failures of performance in the prison building. The critical link, then, was the link between reformation of character, which held out a possibility, and the technology of prison through which that possibility was to be realised. (Evans 1982: 363)

By the mid-nineteenth century, the notion that the prison could reform prisoners had 'evaporated from penal theory with astonishing speed ... but the change was a change of opinion with no significant correlative change in practice.... Doctrine and practice, architecture and reform, were now uncoupled' (Evans 1982: 388). When systematic isolation returned to the penal scene in the late twentieth century, the coupling was between architecture and control. New technologies, building materials and accumulated professional knowledge now made it possible to raise isolation, surveillance and control to levels that had not been feasible in the past.

The key design requirements in supermax prisons are isolation and physical control, and their goals are 'obvious: control behaviour and violence' (Cambra 1997). The subdivision of space reflects these requirements, and enables the regime to function as intended. The regime and the design are intertwined: the planned regime of isolation and restricted movement serves as a guideline for the architectural design, and the architectural design makes the regime possible by interior division and organisation of space, and by the control of movement across time and space.

Most newly built supermax prisons adopt the compact small housing unit ('pod') design, with remote supervision from a circular control booth.[7] Cell areas are separated into small groupings to allow maximum control and observation by a single guard. Housing units include provisions for delivering food and services to the cell front, a solitary recreational yard and a single shower cell. Each housing unit is separately secured with its own controls, gates, and 'zoning-off' areas. Then, there are separate cell-block, wing, and facility controls. These are brick and mortar, physical objects, ensuring that movements within the facility are restricted, monitored and controlled. Prisoners are secured behind all these and other enclosures and layers of isolation as illustrated in Figure 6.1.[8]

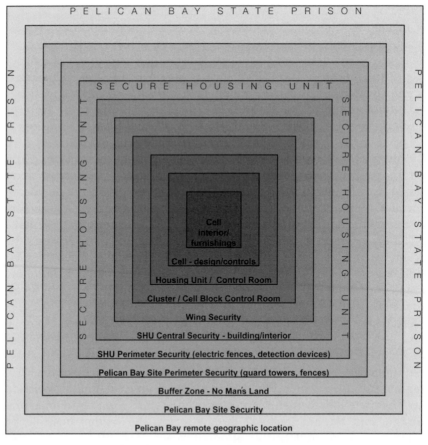

Figure 6.1 Layers of enclosures and isolation in a supermax

In this design, the cell is the real 'prison within prison', as prisoners spend a minimum of 22.5 hours a day inside it, and only leave their cell for 1 hour of solitary exercise four times weekly and a 15-minute shower three times weekly. Prisoner provisions including food, canteen goods, books, post, and religious services are delivered to the cell front. Housing units and cells thus need to be designed and equipped in a way that allows for all these activities to take place, while ensuring that prisoners are separated from each other and from prison staff and do not have access to 'unauthorised objects'. On the rare occasions that a prisoner leaves the pod area, all these arrangements are deemed to be insufficient, and an additional layer of control in the form of body restraints, including hand, leg and body chains, is applied to him. To the controls which are part of the design and regime *inside* the building, are added controls fitted into the exterior of the building itself, which is fortified with additional security measures, as is the entire prison site. The geographically remote location of many supermax prisons provides another layer of isolation. In short, the individual prisoner is secured behind layers upon layers of enclosures and isolation, as illustrated in the following section using the Security Housing Unit (SHU) at Pelican Bay State Prison as a primary example.

Layers of isolation in a supermax

Pelican Bay SHU was built as part of the massive prison construction plan that the California Department of Corrections (CDC), as it was then known, embarked on in the early 1980s.[9] The plan included the construction of high-security prisons, reflecting lessons learnt from the wave of prison riots that struck prisons across the USA, including California, in the 1970s. In design terms, this meant utilising principles of situational crime prevention: reducing the opportunities and tools to commit violent acts, and increasing the chances of getting caught through close prisoner surveillance and supervision.

> [The design of these] hi-tech prisons would reduce, if not eliminate, the blind spots where inmates could hide to kill other inmates. It would reduce tremendously inmate access to materials to make weapons. It would give staff a tremendous advantage in control. You could control smaller groups of inmates. [administrator]

The site

Supermax prisons are typically hidden from public view, away from main roads and public life, and many are located in remote rural areas. Once the CDC took the initial decision to construct a high-tech, super-maximum-security prison, it embarked on the process of selecting an appropriate site that would fit this criterion. The site selection process included, as one official described it, 'consideration for a remote, somewhat isolated area in order to adversely impact gang members' ability to communicate throughout the prison system. It was felt that by isolating these predatory gang leaders in a remote area their ability to control inmate behaviour outside of the SHU would be severely limited.'[10] In 1986, a disused logging site located 7.4 miles from Crescent City, a small economically depressed town in northern California, was selected and approved. Weather conditions in this geographically remote area isolate it further, since the constant mist and fog coming from the ocean often lead to cancellation of flights to Crescent City and road closures, cutting off traffic to the area. Located in the heart of the lush Redwood area, the prison site is grey and barren, completely cut off from its surroundings. The site covers 460 acres, of which 260 acres were later built-up. It cannot be seen from the main road, and apart from a single road sign marked 'Pelican Bay State Prison' at the entrance to Crescent City, there are no apparent indications of its existence. Isolation, in this case, begins with the site (Figure 6.2).

Once the site was decided upon and the main prison in the process of being built, the next stage was choosing the architectural design that would best fit the mission statement of the planned new special secure unit.[11] In late 1986, a group consisting of a CDC Assistant Deputy Director, the Pelican Bay State Prison Programme Director, an architect, and former prison guards, captains and wardens toured new maximum-security facilities across the USA in search of the design that would best suit their needs. The unit they 'liked best', as one member of the team put it, was Special Management Unit (SMU) I in Florence, Arizona, designed by an Arizona-based architectural firm:

> We contacted them and ended up arranging to have them be a partner with the architects and engineers who were building the rest of the prison for us, and decided what could we do that would make that basic design a little bit better and better stand up and, to be honest, given our past with litigation

Figure 6.2 Pelican Bay State Prison site and surroundings (Image courtesy of the California Department of Corrections and Rehabilitation)

particularly here in California, we wanted to make sure that we were building something that would stand court scrutiny. [administrator]

A promotional leaflet by the architectural firm further lays out the tension between the architecture and management of supermax units and prisoners' constitutional rights: 'since inmates (in secure units) will have less privileges than general population inmates, attention must be given to required standards, so that an inmate cannot fault the facility and defeat the goals and purpose of the unit'.[12] The caution in designing the SHU so that it complies with legal requirements was prescient. In a class-action lawsuit brought by SHU prisoners shortly after it opened (*Madrid v. Gomez 1995*), the legality of the SHU's design and its impact on prisoners were the core issues, and CDC narrowly escaped a court order to shut down the unit altogether. It is important to note that prisons may present one of the only instances in which the *constitutionality* of a physical building is so closely scrutinised.

Following the initial planning stages, the architectural firm started developing the actual design of the SHU, using SMU I as a model. Over a period of 2 months, they worked closely with prison staff, held detailed consultations, and heard about their needs, concerns and desires. The architectural team took time to explain how things were going to work within the unit, and to build models of the design. In order for SHU staff to 'feel really comfortable', a full-scale model of one-quarter of a cell-block control room was constructed. The model was so precise that it enabled staff to 'actually open the sliding doors and put their weapons out into the space and see that they actually worked and they had all the gun coverage they were looking for' [prison architect]. Prison guards and administrators loved the design which offered them clear sight-lines, minimal contact with prisoners, and maximum control over them.

The partnership between architects and penal officials did not include the end-users of the facility, prisoners. While lessons from the past regarding security weaknesses and prisoner litigation were taken into account in the design of the facility, lessons regarding the adverse health effects of isolation and their impact on behaviour were not. Input from psychologists, prison activists or bodies concerned with prisoners' welfare was not sought during the design stage, nor was any effort made to determine whether, within the time, money and security constraints, anything could be done to make confinement in the SHU more tolerable for prisoners. As we shall see, the prevalence of 'security' considerations is apparent in each detail of the design and regime in supermax prisons. The construction of the SHU took 18 months and cost \$74,000 per bed and around \$48 million in total.[13] The SHU received its first prisoners on 1 December, 1989.

Perimeter security

The main function of perimeter security is to place barriers between the prison and the outside world to prevent escapes, and to prevent unauthorised people and materials from reaching those inside. When prisoner security classification systems began to evolve (see previous chapter), the main design response was corresponding perimeter security arrangements, reflecting the prison's security level. The SHU is part of Pelican Bay State Prison, which is a maximum-security (Level IV) prison. As such, it was designed with 'state of the art' security coverage. The entire complex is surrounded by straight-line double-fencing with razor ribbon, monitored by a dual electronic detection system. Pelican Bay perimeter security also includes microwave detection, coaxial cable detection, and systems that set off an alarm if the fence is tampered with. Additionally, the site has elevated guard towers situated at 700-foot intervals, which provide unobstructed sight lines of the security perimeters and the surrounding roads and properties. Originally, 11 such towers were built, but over time an

Figure 6.3 Pelican Bay Guard Tower (Image courtesy of the California Department of Corrections and Rehabilitation)

electric fence was added between the two existing fences, allowing the deactivation of all but three guard towers (Figure 6.3).

SHU exterior

A prison's exterior design plays a dual role: functional and symbolic. Returning to Goffman's (1961) definition of prisons as total, closed institutions, a prison's 'encompassing or total character is symbolised by the barrier to social intercourse with the outside and to departure that is often built right into the physical plant, such as locked doors, high walls, barbed wire, cliffs, water, forests, or moors' (Goffman 1961: 4). In the past, the symbolic role of prisons was expressed through their design as fortresses surrounded by high, intimidating stone walls, even when these were not required for functional reasons. Prison exteriors in the nineteenth century were designed to 'serve needs of security, containment, and anonymity ... [but] these muted, functional buildings nevertheless project an eloquent and well-understood symbolism, which speaks of unshakeable authority, of stored-up power, and of a silent, brooding capacity to control intransigence' (Garland 1990: 260). The facade of Eastern State Penitentiary, for example, was designed as a fortress with high walls to imply physical punishment, in contrast to its interior design, which had high ceilings, skylights and arches, reflecting the strategy of effecting internal change in the prisoner.

The external design of supermax prisons is not intended as a means to communicate a message of deterrence to the outside world, because the outside world, as noted above, has no view of the prison site. Rather, it is a functional design which aims to control those within. The entire prison site is covered with gravel, for the stated purpose that should a prisoner attempt to escape from the facility (virtually impossible) the sound of his running on the gravel would alert guards. The grey gravel blends well with the prison's buildings, which are made of grey concrete, resulting in an entirely grey and dull site, with no vegetation or other beautifying features. The contrast between the lush surrounding views and the stark greyness of the prison site is striking. When asked about the bareness of the site, one administrator explained that for security reasons, visibility on the site had to be clear and unobstructed by trees. When asked about the choice of building materials and colours for the prison itself, he spelled out the set of priorities:

> You want concrete to last. Up here we've sealed the concrete with probably more than you would in an area that doesn't get the eighty to ninety inches of rain a year that we get up here and ... if you don't want to be making it look bad from year to year, you want a nice neutral colour and so we've got a nice neutral colour. Concrete by its nature is somewhat severe.

There is no view from the outside into the SHU, and there is little movement in and out of it. It has a total footage of 16,356 square feet, and is separated from other parts of the prison by a secure fence. Its exterior layout is X-shaped, a version of the telephone-pole design first introduced in the USA in 1914[14] (Figure 6.4).

Interior design and central security

Supermax prisons, as implied by their name, are designed to maximise security: 'Safety, security knowledge, just the overall logistics of this

Figure 6.4 SMU II exterior (Photograph by Jason Oddy©)

building, the entire layout is built strictly for staff safety, public safety and the control of inmates' [administrator]. Although 'public safety' was thrown into this statement for good measure, in fact supermax prisons have very little direct bearing on the public's safety. Escapes, hostage taking, or any other acts that may involve members of the public, are highly improbable, given the fortified perimeter security described above. What is really meant by 'security' in supermax terms is *internal control* of prisoners.

> When you're planning a [supermax] unit ... security is the highest priority. You want to make sure that the inmates don't have an opportunity to assault each other or assault staff. [administrator]

> Logistically, the structure of this facility, everything is done inside. The inmates, once they arrived at this unit, do not, for all intents and purposes, have any movement outside. [prison officer]

The extreme application of situational crime-prevention principles entails isolating prisoners, minimising any movement within the units and contact between prisoners and staff, eliminating physical contact between prisoners, choosing tamperproof building materials and furnishings, and other pre-emptive measures which aim to reduce significantly the risk of an incident. The reduction of risk, however, comes at a price.

No single design is used by all supermax prisons, but certain designs predominate. A popular design is the one used in SMU I in Arizona, which served as the prototype for self-contained facilities later used, with minor modifications, at Pelican Bay SHU, SMU II in Arizona, and other purpose-built facilities (King 1999: 172; Riveland 1999). Prisoners are housed in small pods, or housing units, which radiate around their own circular control room and are remotely supervised from it. This design, which allows constant observation and supervision of prisoners without the associated increase in staff numbers, is an attractive option in resource terms. The internal layout is a mezzanine design, with straight corridors and sight lines. Space is divided into sections and subsections which can be secured separately, with the single cell as the core unit. The geometrical subdivision of space at Pelican Bay SHU is as follows:

Eight cells (arranged in two tiers) constitute a *pod* or *housing unit*;
Six pods (48 cells) make up a *cell block* or *cluster*;
A group of cell blocks makes up a *wing* or *facility*.

Pelican Bay SHU has two wings: C Wing has 12 cell blocks (576 cells), and D Wing has 10 cell blocks (480 cells), totalling 1,056 cells. Eighty per cent of these cells hold single prisoners, and the remaining 20 per cent, which house prisoners nearing their parole date, hold two prisoners each. One cell block is a dedicated Violence Control Unit and one cell block is a dedicated Transitional Housing Unit (THU). Each wing has its own control room, whose primary function is monitoring, observing and controlling staff and prisoner corridor traffic throughout the wing. Wing control rooms contain CCTV monitors and an intercom system for communication throughout the wing with each officer and the cell-block control rooms. Access doors between the housing and service areas, which are located at the centre of the SHU complex, are also operated from the wing control room. Both control rooms (C Wing and D Wing) have a view to, and control of, the main entrance to the SHU building. A central control

Figure 6.5 SHU secure wing corridor (Image courtesy of the California Department of Corrections and Rehabilitation)

room monitors movement in and out of the building, and movement in the secure main corridors (Figure 6.5).

Cell-block supervision and surveillance

Each cell block, or six pods (48 cells), is monitored and supervised by a security control room, staffed by a single officer armed with a Ruger Mini-14 carbine in a standby position and a 37 mm federal gas gun ready for use. The design of the control room resembles the control tower in Bentham's Panopticon: the pods radiate around a raised central control room, surrounded by glass walls. Unlike Bentham's 360 degrees design, SHU control rooms have a '180 design' – living pods fall within a field of view of 180 degrees of the control room guard, so there always is good visibility of all the pods, and the guard always faces the cell area. CCTV cameras mounted in each corridor face the cells and allow guards to look into any cell at any time. The pods are separated from the control area by electronically controlled metal gates, and each pod can be sealed off separately in case of an emergency.

The cell-block control room guard controls the operation of doors and gates (cells, shower, exercise yard and pods), pod and cell lighting, and the length of showers through an electronic control panel. The panel is fitted with a system that does not allow two doors within the pod area to be open at the same time, so two prisoners cannot be outside their cells at the same time, and will never have physical contact with each other. The system enables daily activities that require movement of prisoners from their cells (shower and exercise) to be carried out without direct staff contact with the prisoners. All communication with prisoners is conducted through an intercom system. At SMU I, the early prototype for the SHU and SMU II, the control board was manually operated. When Pelican Bay SHU and later SMU II were designed, the manual control board was replaced with an electronic touch-screen system. Newer technologies may take controlling the pods a step further and make them 'almost like the use of your cellular telephone, where control positions will be mobile; where an officer ... working in a unit, will be able to communicate from anywhere and maybe even be able to control doors from anywhere using a handheld telephone, basically a mobile control panel' [prison architect]. Below and around the control room is the housing unit's administration area where guards keep charts, lists of prisoners, daily timetables and so on (Figure 6.6).

Each cell block also contains two 'holding cells' which are located at the cell-block entrance. These are small cells containing a concrete bench used for holding prisoners awaiting escort to or from the pod area. The cell block is secured by an electronic gate which opens into a grey corridor, where 'cell extraction' gear, including helmets, knee pads, protective plastic suits, stretchers, and non-lethal weapons, is stored for easy access.

Housing units: tiny and claustrophobic

The configuration of the housing units is based on the 'new-generation', small-pod concept, allowing for all daily routines to take place within the pod. Each pod contains eight single cells arranged in two tiers (Figure 6.7). When the prototype for the SHU was developed at SMU I, the exact size of the cell grouping was carefully calculated around prisoners' daily routine.

> The eight-person pod development came from analysis of the daily movement of inmates, their daily operational procedures, and we determined at that time that eight was about the

Figure 6.6 SMU II cell block control room (Photograph by Jason Oddy©)

maximum number of inmates that you could have in one area
so that they could get through their daily routine without having
to have two inmates in the same space and to have to have staff
escorting them throughout the facility. [prison architect]

When SMU II was designed in 1996, the number of cells in each pod
was increased from 8 to 10, an architectural solution motivated by
financial considerations:

By then, we had a great record on what their daily procedures
were, what the staffing implications were, and we determined
that we could increase the pod size from eight to ten, and in
doing that we were able to cut out four housing units, which
is a tremendous staff saving ... we saved over twenty-five staff
positions, and the annual salary rates add up very quickly as a
large cost saving. [prison architect]

The overall area taken up by the pods was not increased to correspond
with the growth in cell numbers, so, for prisoners at SMU II, the

Figure 6.7 A pod at SMU II (Photograph by Jason Oddy©)

result of this architectural money-saving change was an environment that is even more claustrophobic than that of Pelican Bay SHU and SMU I.

Pods are arranged in two tiers. Each pod has one exercise yard attached to it, and each tier has an individual shower cell attached to it. Photo ID cards of all the prisoners who are confined in the pod hang on the wall outside the pod's gate. The design of the housing unit is such that for the duration of his confinement, a prisoner will only see (very briefly) the three other prisoners on his tier when they leave their cells for their solitary exercise or shower, and when they are escorted out for a medical examination, classification hearing or a family visit. The only view that prisoners have from their cells is a narrow corridor, blocked off by a brick wall with a CCTV mounted on it.

Colours, windows and natural light

Supermax prisons are stark and monotonous. The main colours are typically beige or grey, dark blue or brown, and white. This dull colour scheme is intentional, reflecting managerial discourses on the nature of prisoners for whom the units are designed:

> The colour schemes that we used were... I'd call a joint effort on the part of the Department of corrections and ourselves. Yes, the goal of the facility is to try to reduce the privileges, the advantages of being in the normal population ... I think it's a philosophy that the units are a little more stark and a little more grey than average. [prison architect]

In other words, the colour scheme is stark since being in a colourful environment is a privilege that prisoners in supermax prisons have lost.

Windows are considered as a 'weak spot' in terms of security: they present a possible escape route, they can be broken down into materials that could be made into weapons, and they offer the possibility of interaction or communication between the prisoner and the outside world. Legal and professional standards, however, require that prisoners have a certain amount of natural light in their cells. The architectural solution: windowless cells, and 4-foot-wide by 20-foot-long skylights in the pod corridors. A promotional leaflet by an architectural firm which designs supermaxes boasts that in their designs,

> Windows, a constant target of attack by inmates, are virtually eliminated. The alternative: windowless cells with good natural light. Lynn Arrington created a cell front which allows light from sky-lighted day spaces to penetrate the cells, meeting ACA standard 2-4130 and virtually eliminating security concerns relating to windows. (Arrington Watkins Architects, Arizona, n.d.)

The 'day space' referred to in the leaflet is no more than a narrow corridor, blocked-off by a brick wall (see figure 6.7 above). The perforated cell front is an innovation, but the skylights are a design concept that has been used in the past,

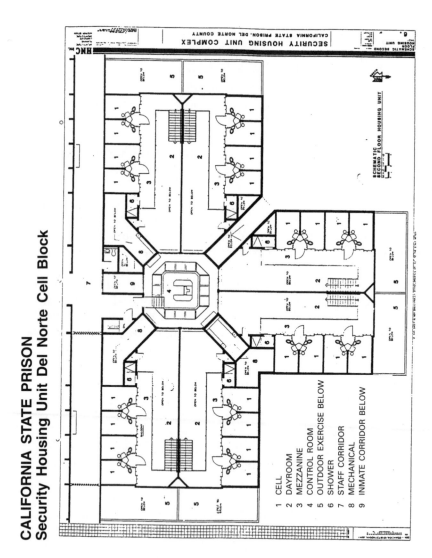

Figure 6.8 Pelican Bay SHU cell-block plan (upper tier)

In all correctional facilities, there's a requirement to have natural light. We took maybe a step – I wouldn't call it backwards – but a step back to what they would do in a lot of country jail facilities where providing natural light to the inmate doesn't necessarily mean that it has to come through a window. [prison architect]

Skylights were also used in the 'separate' penitentiaries of the nineteenth century, but in these prisons they were an addition to, not a substitute for, cell windows. At Eastern State Penitentiary, for example, cells had windows and skylights, and prisoners also had access to an individual outdoor exercise yard, where they could have access to natural light and fresh air. In the design of contemporary supermax prisons, however, the overriding considerations are those of security, cost and adherence to the letter of the law, and in that context the skylight has a number of advantages over windows:

it meets the requirements that they need for natural light, but again it takes away that ability to look out on the yard, communicate with somebody out on the outside. It also allowed us to bring the facility together in a very compact configuration reducing the overall size of the facility, and reducing the construction cost. So that one approach to using sky-lighted day-rooms created a tremendous cost savings for the taxpayers and the department. [prison architect]

It is illuminating that nowhere in the architectural line of reasoning is prisoners' well-being mentioned, even though eliminating windows has a huge impact on their daily lives. A former supermax prisoner described his cell being 'like living in a dungeon, like in a cave, like in a place ... where no sun hits. There are no windows, no windows at all, so you don't see the sun.' A prisoner at Pelican Bay SHU, testifying before the *Madrid* court, described the SHU as 'a space capsule where one is shot into space and left in isolation' (*Madrid* 1995: 1262). This analogy is familiar from studies of other high-security units, such as the maximum-security wing at Durham Prison in the UK in the late 1960s, which was likened by one of its prisoners to living in a submarine, and by the authors of the study as having the 'claustrophobia of a tomb' (Cohen and Taylor, [1972]1981: 70). When asked whether he thought that supermax environments were a form of sensory deprivation, a prison architect replied that,

Well, we always have the natural light that comes in and there's a lot of colour associated with the natural light in all of these units, so I don't know that they're deprived of any colour sensory sort of things that they should receive and probably get as much, or more than they would in a normal environment. But they don't have windows, you know, they're not let out of the units and that's all a part of, again, you've got your rights but you don't have your privileges. And so, it's up to the inmates to, to learn to change.

This is an intriguing claim. On the one hand, the lack of windows and views of the outside does not constitute a form of sensory deprivation, and supermax prisoners receive the legally required amount of natural light. On the other hand, the lack of windows is intended to 'teach prisoners to change', or modify their behaviour. In other words, the environment is used as a tool for reforming prisoners, an aim which, at the time, was officially abandoned. Asked whether she thought that prisoners were held in conditions of sensory deprivation, one supermax officer denied that the lack of windows poses any problem, as

[Cells] face into the centre of the housing unit where they can see the other cell fronts and they can see the staff walking by and they can see the Correctional Officer working up in the Control Booth. I haven't experienced the sensory deprivation issue ... and I work in an office with no window.

By equating her own office with a cell, she diminished the notion of isolation and dismissed it.

Cells: the innermost prison

Cells are made of concrete and painted in white or beige. They measure 80 square feet, the standard minimum requirement when a prisoner is held in his cell for more than 10 hours a day (ACA Standard 3-4136). Concrete has qualities which make it appealing: it is cheap, durable and indestructible. It also has qualities which make it a poor choice in terms of prisoners' comfort:

You're in a cement cell where everything is cement, your bed's a cement slab, you know. In the morning I used to get my milk and wrap it with toilet paper and keep it on the bottom because that was the coldest area, and by noon time my milk was still cold, you know.... You try to wear as much clothing as you can that they give you, and it ain't much, and you keep your blanket around you to keep warm because cement stays cold. And with the yard being at the back of the pod, underneath the door you have a pretty good gap where the wind comes in and brings all the cold in. [former prisoner]

The cell door is made of perforated stainless steel, and painted in dark brown or dark blue. The only view a prisoner has through it is that of a concrete or brick wall. A slot in the upper part of the door is used for feeding prisoners, for delivering post, medication and canteen goods to them, and for handcuffing them prior to escorting them out of the cell. In contrast to most other features of the prison, which lack sensory stimulation, the perforated metal with its small holes creates a sensory overload. Its design has an additional drawback for prisoners: the perforation obstructs their view to the outside, but at the same time allows no privacy in the cells. It also allows in noise,[15] draughts and smells, as a former prisoner described:

Your cell is made up really of three walls, three cement walls and one where your door's at, that's one wall. It's like a screen, like a real thick metal screen that is made up with hundreds and hundreds of little holes, like they just got a metal slab and poked, hundreds and hundreds of holes. So you can hear every noise that your neighbour makes, you know, the noises from the shower, the noises from anywhere, like the noise from the light... it's just a bunch of millions of little holes but it keeps you inside the cell, you know, that way you don't come out. But it's just like that there is nothing there. You feel everything, the cold, the wind, when inmates walk by.

The main design consideration in choosing perforated cell doors, however, was to improve surveillance of prisoners:

The doors that we built are stainless steel doors, and they have perforations in them at regular intervals ... the idea was to maximise the amount of natural light coming in and the thought was that it will allow us good vision into the cell, much better than solid doors with a window. [administrator]

Although in general, as the officer put it, the 'design keeps inmates from acting out in a violent and bloody way against staff', some prisoners require further measures of control.

Inmates were still going to have grievances either with an individual staff or with the system in general, and their acting out way became to 'gas' staff with bodily fluids. And in order to find a way around that, what we chose, and again in order to maintain the natural light, is a Plexiglas cover for a about one-sixth of the cells.

The Plexiglas cover insulates the cell from sound, air, and vision. At Pelican Bay, 17 per cent of the cells are permanently covered with Plexiglas, and a Plexiglas cover may be fitted on to other cell doors as and when needed. In other supermax units, notably some of the newer facilities, cells are designed with solid steel doors as a standard, cutting off vision and sound almost completely.

Cells contain a stainless steel toilet/sink unit, a white concrete double bunk, concrete table and chair, and lockers which are holes in the concrete of the lower bunk. These are built-in features, prefabricated as integral elements of the cell. Security considerations again determine the choice of materials for cell furnishings, and the main aim is to prevent opportunities for prisoners to create weapons:

> The way the cells themselves were built means that inmates have a much reduced chance of getting weapon stock. In a typical cell ... you're going to find 'soft metal', steel, but not stainless steel, and inmates know how to cut up regular steel. They'll use either toothpowder or dental floss or whatever they can get their hands on, and they've got plenty of time, and they'll work their way through [it]. In order to avoid that, we constructed the unit out of concrete... The only remaining metal is the door front and the toilet/sink that's made out of stainless steel, which, while nothing is tamper proof, is incredibly tamper resistant [administrator].

The toilet/sink unit is located at the cell front, offering prisoners no privacy, and the 'table', which is no more than a small concrete slab, is located right next to it so that when the prisoner sits by the table, he has full view of the open toilet (Figure 6.9).

I return to other features of the cells in the following chapter, and discuss in detail the types and amount of personal property that prisoners may keep in them.

Exercise yard: the 'dog run'

Prisoners are entitled by law to a minimum amount of outdoor

Figure 6.9 SMU II cell (Photograph by Jason Oddy©)

exercise a week. In supermax prisons, security requirements and the principle of isolation preclude the option of a congregated exercise yard. Once again, architecture provided a solution that adheres to legal requirements while maintaining isolation: solitary exercise yards, located within the pods.[16] Each pod (8 or 10 cells) has a narrow and barren concrete exercise yard attached to it. The yard measures 26 by 10 feet and is surrounded by 20-foot high walls. The yard's top is covered partly by a thick mesh screen, and partly by a Plexiglas cover. It contains no recreational equipment (Figure 6.10). A CCTV camera is mounted at the top corner of the yard, allowing the control room guard to monitor the prisoner's movements. An intercom system allows communication between the prisoner and the control room guard.[17]

Figure 6.10 Exercise yard at Pelican Bay SHU (Image courtesy of the California Department of Corrections and Rehabilitation)

> You're going into what they call the 'dog run', and the dog run is … just straight four walls, nothing there, no nothing to play with. All you could do is run around, you know, the same thing you could do in your cell but they say it's the yard. You can't see the sky very well because you have your Plexiglas and then you got the fence over it. [former prisoner]

Support facilities

All the support facilities, including kitchen, laundry, staff offices, law library, medical clinic and attorney/family visiting areas, are located within the SHU/SMU building. This allows movements and interactions between supermax prisoners and other areas of the prison to be further minimised. Each services area can be sealed off separately if necessary. I discussed the setting for classification hearings in the previous chapter. Below, I examine the design features and technologies used in the medical clinic, the law library, and the family visits area.

Medical clinic

The SHU has its own medical and dental clinics, located in the centre of the building complex. Most common medical problems can be treated at the facility. More specialist treatment is provided in hospitals in the area, the nearest being an hour and a half drive away. The transfer of prisoners outside the SHU is done almost Hollywood style, in a very costly exercise involving an inmate transport van, a lead car, a chase car and a minimum of four correctional officers (Rosen 2000). In exceptional cases, medical experts are brought to the facility, usually from Sacramento, 350 miles away from Crescent City.

New technologies step in again to resolve financial and potential security issues. Telemedicine allows medical examinations and consultations to be conducted through a video conferencing link between the prison and medical centres. All of California's prisons are now equipped with telemedicine equipment, though not all of them use it. Nationwide, slightly over half of state correctional institutions and 39 per cent of federal institutions use some sort of telemedicine applications (Larsen *et al.* 2004). Psychiatric examinations, alongside 10 other medical specialities, can be conducted through video cameras and monitors without direct contact between the prisoner and the medical professional. Telemedicine may be cheaper than transporting prisoners to outside medical facilities, but it further isolates prisoners and distances them from human contact. It is also questionable whether a camera can capture all the details that face-to-face interaction does. A 10-minute telemedicine session requires around 2 hours of related activities. Prisoners are strip searched before and after each visit, and are escorted to the telemedicine clinic by two guards, who remain with them throughout the examination.

These procedures frustrate and anger prisoners, as one telemedicine staff member observed in an interview for an industry magazine: 'If inmates weren't angry when they left for treatment, they were angry by the time they arrived' (Rosen 2000). Many departments of corrections are nonetheless happy with the new technology, and would like to see it extended. Medical professionals, too, adopt the language and considerations of control and costs, justified with a token reference to public safety. In an interview for the same industry magazine, the health deputy director for CDC explained the advantages of telemedicine:

> What I have seen so far is extremely encouraging in terms of cost avoidance. The specialists and psychiatrists can see more patients ... above and beyond the cost saving is the public safety question. Every time you take an inmate out of an institution, there are issues of public safety that occur. (in Rosen 2000)

Cost avoidance, efficiency and 'public safety': the familiar utilitarian justifications which make no mention of prisoner needs or welfare.

Law library and special programmes

The design of Pelican Bay SHU is so 'tight' that when it was ordered by a court of law to provide prisoners with access to a law library, the only available space was one that was originally designed as an additional visiting area. Since, it was reasoned, prisoners receive very few family visits (see below), the space was redundant as a visiting area and suitable for conversion. In design terms, the 'conversion' meant little more than equipping the space with bookshelves and books. The prisoner area remained as it was: a row of holding cells, with a glass partition, equipped with a small concrete bench and a raised surface used as a table. Soon after the law library started serving prisoners, staff felt uncomfortable being watched by prisoners in the cells through the glass partition. The glass was then tinted on one side, so prisoners could not look out, but staff could look in.

Most jurisdictions do not offer out-of-cell educational or vocational programmes in their supermax prisons. Where some form of programming is legally required, architecture, technology, and prison management team together to provide solutions. For example, according to the law, prisoners who are minors are eligible for educational programmes in line with the national curriculum. One of Arizona's supermax prisons, Special Management Unit II, holds minors, who are entitled to education but are considered by the correctional system to be too disruptive to interact with each other. The solution: a 'classroom' made of a row of single holding cells, each furnished with a small concrete stool and table, and a grilled door. Before lessons, prisoners are handcuffed and escorted individually to the classroom cell. The teacher stands in the centre of the classroom in front of a video camera that transmits the lesson to the minors through TV monitors which are placed in front of their cells (Figure 6.11). Almost a regular classroom, but not quite.

Once the prisoner reaches his eighteenth birthday, his education ceases, even if he expresses a wish to keep it up.

> If they want to continue their education, they have the opportunity to [do so] in a lesser custody where they have earned the right to be able to have that privilege. That privilege ceases to exist here because of their behaviour. [prison officer]

Again, the official discourse regarding supermax prisoners is entirely devoid of any narratives of rehabilitation or the betterment of prisoners, even if only as lip service. Within the wider system of punishments and rewards, the main function of supermax prisons is to punish.

Figure 6.11   Classroom at SMU II (Photograph by Jason Oddy©)

Family visits area

The visiting area is adjacent to the SHU and has its own control room. As noted above, the SHU was originally designed with two large visiting areas, one of which was later converted into a law library. The area and its adjoining corridors are overlooked by CCTV cameras. It has small cubicles, 5 feet wide and 8 feet long, divided by a glass partition. Both the prisoner and his visitor(s) sit on a small stool facing the glass area, and communicate through a telephone receiver.[18] There is no physical contact between the prisoner and the visitor at any time.

Some jurisdictions now use 'video visitation' in their jails and prisons as a replacement for family visits. Video visitation is another form of videoconferencing, similar to that used for telemedicine. Family members can go to a local computer services centre equipped for videoconferencing and at a prearranged time 'meet' with the prisoner, who is in the prison's teleconferencing room, through video cameras and monitors. So far, however, family members have proved less enthusiastic than officials had hoped about video visitation, and some states discontinued its use (Missouri, for example). This technology has far-reaching implications. It is cheaper, quicker and more secure to conduct family visits through teleconferencing. It also, however, further isolates prisoners from 'normal' human interactions, and this is all the more worrying in the case of prisoners who are held in prolonged social isolation. I discuss family visits in more detail in the following chapter.

Architecture as an agent of penal control

> The Separate system maintained isolation with the passive instrument of the prison building itself. The administrative advantages of this were of less consequence than the fact of passive control – a form of constraint transcending the need for human intervention and thereby avoiding violence. (Evans 1982: 323)

Designing prisons, which in themselves present a web of contradictory aims and purposes (e.g. punishment and rehabilitation), is inherently problematic. Contemporary prison architects are influenced by managerial discourses and are inclined to repeat past mistakes:

> These architects are influenced by prison wardens, administrators, clients and politicians with traditional mindsets.... When

prisons are designed, the basic needs of privacy or of a safe
and therapeutic environment are a relatively low priority ...
as a result of such facility planning, the serious mistakes of
the past are repeated, and the violence associated with such
environments is magnified. (Braswell *et al.* 1985: vii)

In supermax prisons, as this chapter has demonstrated, discourses
promoting normalisation of prison environments have no voice. It is
as if the debate on the desired nature of prison environments, which
led to some attempts to make prison environments more 'normal' or
'therapeutic' in the period following World War II and up to the 1960s,
had never happened.[19] Supermax prisons are designed not to resemble
a 'normal' environment, nor even a 'normal' prison environment.
Professional knowledge of design and environmental issues is utilised
to produce an effect diametrically opposed to principles of 'positive
architecture'. The use of the new-generation, small-pod design,
coupled with indirect, rather than direct, supervision as originally
intended, illustrates this point well. The problematic aspects of the
relationship between architecture and the penal system are intensified
in the design of supermax prisons. The role of the design, as a
prison architect plainly put it, is 'operational rather than aesthetic',
and the architect's duty is to design functional and secure prison
units that will comply with legal standards. In contrast to traditional
architectural aspirations of beauty and aesthetics, the atmosphere
and 'feel' of supermax prisons are designed to be ones of stark, grey,
non-stimulating dullness. Supermax prisoners have not only lost the
privilege of living in regular prison conditions, but they have also
earned the burden of living in a harsh and punitive environment.
Repeating managerial narratives and identifying prison architects as
part of the penal system, an architect who designs supermax units
connected the 'feel' of the units with their purposes:

We've always had the challenges within every facility as to
decide colour schemes and how a facility should feel. I think
that the States agree that [these] facilities are not supposed to be
the nicest place you can go – it's a place that you go, that you
can work your way out of.

When asked how prisoners can 'work their way out' of supermax
units, their architect adopted the official rhetoric of progression,
asserting that the length of confinement in a supermax is dependent
on the prisoner himself:

> It's not the goal to isolate people here and to leave them there. It's to put them in there and give them an opportunity to understand what it's like to have all their privileges taken away but not their rights taken away, and work their way back into general population and hopefully do some change to their lifestyle.

This assertion, however, is incorrect, since supermax prisoners mostly cannot 'work their way out' and there are few incentives or mechanisms for rewarding good behaviour. Rather, supermax prisons operate on the principles of the retribution-oriented, punishment model, where punishment is increased in cases of further misconduct, but good behaviour does not decrease it.

In designing supermaxes, architects are commissioned to create an environment that will reflect the policy that disruptive prisoners should be contained in stark surroundings that will act as a deterrent, effect behavioural change, and comply with minimum legal standards to avoid future litigation. One attorney who had been involved in prison litigation identified in an interview an ongoing tension between the penal team (architects and administrators) and the legal and judicial systems. When new supermax prisons are constructed, 'prison builders and prison administrators desire to get as far along the spectrum in terms of constructing a supermax like environment as they can, and stay within the boundaries that were set by the constitution of this country.' Pushing the boundaries with each new facility, the design is slightly modified and 'improved'. As the sequence of design changes from SMU I to Pelican Bay SHU and the later SMU II demonstrates, 'improvements' mean further enhancement of security measures, which increase prisoners' isolation and limit the radius of space of their activities even more.

The architectural principles of isolation, surveillance and control in contemporary supermax prisons remain surprisingly similar to those of the 'separate' and 'silent' penitentiaries of the early nineteenth century. Supermax prisons also borrow some design and surveillance principles from Bentham's Panopticon, described by Foucault (1977: 205) as a 'type of location of bodies in space, of distribution of individuals in relation to one another, of hierarchical organisation, of disposition of centres and channels of power, of definition of the instruments and modes of intervention of power ... [A] diagram of power reduced to its ideal form'. The principles and functioning of the Panopticon operate in supermax prisons in a very real way. The Panopticon, as Foucault put it, acts directly on individuals without any 'physical instrument other than architecture and geometry ... the panoptic schema makes any apparatus of power more intense; it assures its efficacy by its preventative character, its continuous functioning and its automatic mechanisms' (1977: 206). The operation of supermax prisons corresponds with this description. When asked about the similarity between the supermax units he designed and the isolation prisons of the nineteenth century, however, a prison architect reacted angrily and chose to refer to 'the hole' (interestingly, since the hole was overtly a place of punishment), while offering yet again a narrative of progression, emphasising that there is a reason for this treatment:

> There've been comparisons made of supermax units to the old term the 'Hole' – the isolation, the dungeon as some people call it. Actually, there isn't very much similar between [them]. They both had the purpose of isolating an inmate for cause – either disruptive or threatening a group or maybe killing a staff member or another inmate – but they were, in the olden days, just that ... a hole; no light, no utilities, not a good situation. These facilities are designed to, as I said earlier, to give the inmates the access to the things that they have the right to have access to – light, water, good sanitation,[20] legal library, all of the things that they're entitled to – but to take away the privileges that they have, and that's the ability to exercise with other people, to go to dining rooms, to go to libraries and participate in classes and all those sort of things. It's a far cry from the Hole, but it's a very specialised unit that tightens an inmate's day up considerably and gives the Department a lot of control over what they do.

This view resembles attitudes to the penitentiaries and insane asylums of the nineteenth century, which were viewed as 'a machine – a tool, an instrument – which had to be properly constructed, maintained and operated' (Philo 1989: 270). The architect's role in the nineteenth century was to construct the 'tool' so it would 'assist the medical officers in their vital and onerous task of curing the insane' (*ibid.*) The earlier proclaimed aim of curing the insane now has a different role, controlling danger, but contemporary penal architects, too, view their role as 'helping the helpers' do their job safely. The prison architect whom I interviewed is proud of his work, and expresses no ambiguity as to where his loyalties lie. Supermax units are built first and foremost with a view to ensuring staff safety:

I have a lot of respect for the Correctional Officers and the staff, people that work in these facilities and the job that they do, and we'll do everything we can to make their working environment safe.

Beyond the respect and the altruistic desire to create safe working environments for prison staff, there are additional motivations. The correctional system and its officials are the architect's clients, the ones who control budgets. Their satisfaction will guarantee more contracts, generating more income for architectural firms. And according to the same architect, prison staff are very happy with the design:

We know from our interviews with staff in the design of the multiple facilities that, that they feel pretty comfortable working inside these facilities, and as far as I'm concerned, the staff and the safety of staff is a number one priority.

Once the association had been made, the road to creating extreme environments is clear, and prison architects and prison administrators work as a team. This unholy alliance is reflected in professional jargon, which refers to prison architects as 'justice' or 'corrections' architects.[21] Prisoners are not part of this team, and the process of penal design is such that architects rarely encounter them:

[The architect] functions as the agent of the owner or the client ... consistent with standard relations between an architect and his client, the definition of needs comprises the client's responsibility while the architect is expected to provide for their translation in environmental equivalents.... The professional architect seldom becomes involved in evaluative study which could provide significant feedback to the problem definition phases. Equally seldom does the professional architect become involved in the earliest phases of problem and resource assessment in their broadest terms. (Moyer 1975: 58)

In other words, prison administrations define the need, and architecture provides the 'know-how'. The architect whom I interviewed was fluent in the language of the correctional world. He was comfortable inside the system, repeating the ideological 'party line' without having any apparent qualms about the harshness of the living conditions he carefully designs. Instead, he reduced the debate to issues of functionality alone: functional for prison staff, the department of corrections, public opinion and security considerations, not functional as a positive living environment for prisoners.

Architects are not alone, but are part of a growing group of 'professional penal agents [who] tend to represent themselves in a positive, utilitarian way, as offering a particular service, or carrying out a useful social task, as a way of avoiding bad conscience and cultural infamy' (Garland 1990: 182). In the case of supermax prisons, architects' 'useful social task' is containing danger and enabling the management of those who were rejected not only by society, but also by the prison system. As I have demonstrated, the discourse of dangerousness prevails throughout the system, and is articulated with bluntness and without any apologetic tones. Professionals value security considerations above the accepted discourses of their own professions.[22] Other narratives, including prisoners' needs, welfare or personal betterment are not part of the discourse, not even as lip service. The partnership between prison designers and penal officials in creating supermax prisons compelled one observer to comment that

Architecture and technology have recently joined with prison policy in the United States to build a series of Supermax prisons that raise the level of punishment close to that of psychological torture ... prisoners are more isolated, observed and controlled, afforded less human contact and suffer more sensory deprivation than in earlier dungeons. To the staff, prisoners become more dehumanised, and the temptation is strong to treat them less than another human being. It is the same process that we bring to bear in wartime – the enemy, soldier and civilian alike, are demonised, and whatever happens to them is of little concern. (Morris 2000: 98–107)

Another commentator, a psychologist and long-standing prison researcher, also emphasised the partnership between architects and prison officials in creating supermax prisons: 'Architects and corrections officials have created living environments that are devoid of social stimulation. The atmosphere is antiseptic and sterile; you search in vain for humanising touches or physical traces that human activity takes place there' (Haney 1994: 3). Since architects are removed from the main inhabitants of the building they design, they are more prone to espousing official ideologies and media representations of crime and punishment. They may choose to remain as ill-informed as the public about what actually happens within the prison walls, even though they are the ones who designed them. When asked if he has ever spent any time inside a cell in one of the supermax units which he designed, the prison architect said that he had, and acknowledged that the units felt 'eerie', but then reverted to the discourse of prisoners' free choice:

> During the process of designing it, we did spend a considerable amount of time in existing facilities, and being in the environment that the inmates are in.... It's ... it's a little bit of an eerie feeling to spend time in there, but the departments are using these facilities to give the inmate a chance to decide whether they want to stay there or not, and I think that's key to the success of a [supermax] is that the inmates now decide their destiny.

A situation which allows a professional architect to design admittedly 'eerie' environments raises the question of professional ethics. Turning to professional bodies like the American Institute of Architects for guidance, one finds that those in the business of 'justice architecture' are given elaborate guidelines on self-promotion, project presentation, planning and so on, but no ethical guidelines regarding the nature of the environments they design. Other bodies, like the American Institute of Corrections, also provide guidelines that set minimum design requirements (cell size, amount of natural light and access to sanitation) but offer no ethical guidance for prison designers. Appealing to architecture's 'higher purpose', one commentator called upon architects who design supermax prisons to 'insist on being advised of the necessity of every element of isolation that is being sought, and should advise on every possibility of allowing the prisoner in solitary confinement to communicate with staff, family and friends without negating the justified purposes of isolation' (Morris 2000: 108). Another commentator stated that

> There can be no justification for deliberately designing unwhole-some accommodation or choosing dowdy colours, dim lighting and excessively harsh materials.... This form of institutional brutality only brutalises society as a whole. It also has a severely detrimental effect on the working conditions of officers, and restricts the formation of any effective relationship between them and the prisoners.... Oppression and ugliness can only lead to alienation and aggression. (Fairweather 2000: 41)

These appeals to the higher cause of architecture largely fall on deaf ears. The promise of big design contracts, it would seem, has more resonance with 'justice' architects. The design of supermax prisons assumes that prisoners' disposition is to act violently, an assumption that is reflected in each and every design detail. It is an inflexible, harsh and extreme design, which aims to pre-empt administratively defined dangerousness. The architectural design not only reflects the discourse of dangerousness, but also realises it. The architect whom I interviewed was a perfectly nice man, a caring individual. Yet, he creates very extreme environments that are 'home' to thousands of prisoners, using professional knowledge to make them barren, artificial, clinical and highly controlled.[23] In contrast to architects of the nineteenth century, however, contemporary architects cannot claim lack of knowledge of the adverse effects of isolation and life in highly controlled environments. Not only do they have the knowledge, but they use it to create its documented effect.

Isolation, enhanced security and special control measures entail certain unique design features, which make the construction of a supermax prison a costly affair. In an era when prison systems are severely overcrowded, budgets over-stretched and expenditure closely monitored, supermax prisons with their single cells and advanced technology seem incongruous. Correctional departments throughout the USA, nonetheless, willingly spend billions of dollars on the construction of new, bigger and securer supermax prisons, justified in the name of security and prisoners' dangerousness. Current trends, as previously discussed, confirm that supermax confinement shows few signs of slowing down. It is likely that architectural firms across the USA will continue to be called upon to come up with design solutions that will further prisoners' isolation and control. As a former supermax prisoner observed, however, very few further deprivations can be inflicted:

> They say they want to make a stronger, tougher, a harder prison ... how harder can they get? Maybe putting us in a cell the size of a coffin and you just lay there, with no light. I mean I can't see it getting much worse than it is now ... maybe total darkness.

The design features of supermax prisons: positive or negative architecture?

In the beginning of this chapter, I examined some design principles and environmental features and their documented effect on behaviour in prisons. The bulk of this chapter dealt, in detail, with the specific design features and considerations of a typical supermax. Table 6.1 revisits some of the recommended 'positive architecture' (Buchanan *et al.* 1988) design features and summarises their application in a typical supermax facility.

When we look at these criteria and their application in the design of supermaxes, it is almost as if architects designing these prisons took principles of 'positive architecture', reversed them, and used the reverse as a blueprint for their design. The architectural design of supermax prisons, then, can only be described as 'negative architecture': that is, a design which has negative effects on prisoners' (and prison staff) well-being and behaviour. It is an extreme design that disregards at best, and utilises at worst, professional knowledge about the effects of various factors on prisoners' behaviour, by creating stark, monotonous, sterile and highly controlled environments. Put more simply, based on existing knowledge, it would seem that the design of supermax is more likely to induce violence than to reduce it. The role of architecture in this process is crucial, for it translates managerial ideologies of control into physical features and measures that then become their own *de facto* justification.

Table 6.1 Recommended prison design features

Design feature	Application in supermax
Location	No
Communication	No
Supervision	No
Thermal comfort	No
Noise	No
Light	Partial
Sensory stimulation	No
Colour	No
Furniture	No
Single-cell occupancy	Yes
Privacy	No
Facility adaptability	No

Once a building has been constructed, changing its design or modifying its use is no simple task. This is particularly true for buildings, such as supermax prisons, with strict geometry and built-in control mechanisms. Recognising this factor, the author of a USA-wide study of supermax prisons urges correctional agencies planning to build a supermax facility to avoid designs that are so 'tight' that they restrict additions or changes to the facility in the future.

> [Although] an agency may choose to provide few programmes … consideration should be given to including programme delivery capabilities in the design and construction to accommodate necessary modifications in future years based on changing needs, court decisions or policy revisions. (Riveland 1999: 20)

Such recommendations are largely ignored. When supermax prisons are designed, no additional space is allocated to accommodate future modifications because (a) no such modifications are planned and (b) space equals money:

> We designed the unit as a single purpose unit. We didn't build in extra space for say to bring in education classes because it was not and is not our intention to bring these inmates into a joint co-working setting. And it's been our practice not to build more than you think that you're going to need for the foreseeable future because it costs the taxpayers additional money. [administrator]

The design of supermax prisons sets in stone very extreme conditions of confinement. It is a compact and inflexible design, which may have far-reaching implications for the future. In highly overcrowded prison systems, such as those of most states across the USA, the likelihood of prisons being demolished is slim. Since the design of supermax prisons cannot be modified, it can be assumed that even if the official need for high-security housing for 'problem prisoners' were to drop dramatically, prisoners would still be housed in existing prisons, regardless of the threat they pose to security. Further, even if there was a political will to make confinement in supermax prisons less harsh and isolated, the design would make changes very difficult, if not impossible, to implement.

In the following chapters, I go deeper into the world of supermax, and examine how those who inhabit it, both prisoners and staff, are affected by life in a highly controlled environment that is devoid of 'normal' human interactions.

Notes

1 From the early days of the Chicago School (Park 1925) to more recent studies; see Bottoms and Wiles (1997).
2 Fairweather 2000: 47. The sparseness of literature is due to methodological difficulties in separating variables (e.g. management styles and personal characteristics), access problems, lack of interest among researchers, as well as a feeling that 'the results of their research are not always welcome by the authorities' (Fairweather 2000: 31).
3 The discussion here largely draws on Moyer (1975). Other sources include Fairweather (1975, 2000) and Buchanan et al. (1988).
4 Fairweather 2000: 35. See also Bottoms 1999: 243–5 and Buchanan et al. 1988: 51–54.
5 Fairweather 2000: 38. See also Goffman's (1961) classic study of total institutions and Buchanan et al. 1988: 93; Wener 2000: 52–3.
6 The prisoner security classification system has direct bearing on prison architecture, since each security level requires certain design and security features. In California, for example, prisons of the highest security level (Level IV) are required to have a secure perimeter and internal and external armed coverage, and cells must not be adjacent to exterior walls.
7 Including Pelican Bay SHU in California, SMU I and II in Arizona, and supermax units in Indiana, Texas, Virginia, West Virginia and Wisconsin, among other states.
8 The illustration is a development of the concept of 'hierarchy of security needs' introduced in Buchanan et al. 1988: 96.
9 Between the summer of 1984 and the end of 1988 alone, CDC constructed more than 23,000 new prison beds (CDC Public Information Office). This massive expansion was due to severe overcrowding, tougher laws, longer sentences and other factors discussed in Chapter 3.
10 Cambra (1997). Arizona's supermax units (SMUs) are also located in a remote area, deep in the desert between Tucson and Phoenix. Most supermax prisons across the USA are similarly located in remote areas.
11 The main Pelican Bay State Prison facility has 1,024 cells for general population maximum security (Level IV) prisoners, and 200 cells for minimum aecurity (Level I) prisoners located outside the secured perimeter, along with centralised services such as administration, warehousing and maintenance. The Security Housing Unit (SHU) is located in a separate building, and has 1,056 cells.
12 Arrington Watkins Architects Leaflet, undated, at p. 3.
13 Pelican Bay State Prison Public Information Office, n.d. By the time that SMU II was built in Arizona (1996), the construction took only 6 months

and cost $27 million. The smaller size of SMU II (720 cells) accounts for some of the savings, but these were mainly due to the accumulated knowledge and experience that allowed some modifications: the number of cells in each housing unit was increased from 8 to 10, and the basic structure was made of precast concrete tees, columns and beams, rather than the steel structure that was used at SMU I and Pelican Bay SHU (this change alone is estimated to have saved at least 6 months during the construction stage).

14 For illustrations and discussion of both designs, see Johnston 2000.

15 A study carried out in a hospital found that hearing sounds without having a visual view 'often generates disturbing or even frightening thoughts and experiences' (Rice 2003: 4).

16 In many of the 'separate' penitentiaries of the nineteenth century, each cell had a small outdoor area attached to it, so the idea of solitary exercise yards is not entirely new.

17 Some prisoners complained that once in the yard, they have to stay there for the full duration of their exercise time, even in bad weather, and even if they ask the control room guard to allow them back in.

18 Up to three visitors are allowed in the 'cubbies' at any one time. By the time SMU II in Arizona was designed, its architects came up with another innovation: visiting room partitions now made of perforated metal, which enables communication without using telephones. Prisoners and their visitors complain that they have to raise their voices in order to be heard, and therefore lack any sense of privacy.

19 See Rothman 1995: 170–73 and Brodie et al. 1999.

20 Those promoting the separate penitentiaries of the nineteenth century also emphasised how they were an improvement over older prisons. Eastern State Penitentiary officials, for example, had boasted about having the most advanced sanitation and heating systems of the time, and having flush-toilets and central heating installed before the White House.

21 The term 'justice architects' is used, for example, in the American Institute of Architecture Committee on Justice Architecture Reports (1997, 1999a, 1999b). The term 'corrections architects' appears in industry magazines, such as the 'Corrections Connection' online magazine.

22 Not only architects but also, as discussed in the following chapter, prison librarians, health professionals, teachers and food services personnel all cite 'security' as the main consideration of their work in supermaxes.

23 I enquire what mechanisms allow the professional to take over the compassionate human, and how such actions are justified (Sykes and Matza 1957; Cohen 1993, 2001), in Chapter 8.

Chapter 7

Inside a supermax: daily routines and prisoner provisions

In the prison world, however, there is still another degree of extreme constraint – a corner in which the steel, the concrete, and the shadows converge into a massive and gloomy cell block. Its walls are thicker, its bars more closely spaced, and its regimentation more exacting. This most heavily guarded section is the incorrigible unit. Confined in individual cells within that unit are rows of men removed from contact with free society and the prison community by every device available to the management of the institution. For months or, in some case, even years, these isolated men live in a perceptual universe which consists of the steel walls of their cells and the more barren wall beyond the grated cell door. The stark simplicity of life in the incorrigible unit combines the qualities of a nightmare with those of an extremely rational, and artificial, logic. In the ordered squares of steel, restriction and denial of individuality reach an extreme that cannot be extended, even in one's imagination. The governing of men within this unit becomes in part a prototype and in part a fantastic caricature of the authoritarian situation. (McCleery 1961: 264)

McCleery's description of the regimented, highly controlled and heavily guarded isolation cells of Oahu Prison's incorrigible unit in Hawaii in the late 1950s immediately brings to mind the design and operation of supermax units as described so far. His assumption that the extremity of the incorrigible units could not be extended further, however, is disproved with the construction of each newer, starker and more tightly controlled supermax. Viewed on a continuum, present-day supermax prisons use the old strategy of solitary confinement as devised in the separate penitentiaries of the early nineteenth century, enhanced by professional knowledge and experience that have accumulated over time, as well as by the most advanced measures of control and surveillance offered by modern technology.

Following the 'layers of control' concept introduced in the previous chapter, here I focus on the innermost layer of control, the cell, and on the objects of this control: prisoners. In addition to setting out the daily routines and control measures applied to prisoners' bodies, provisions and possessions, this chapter aims to describe something which is difficult to glean from official guidelines and procedures: the atmosphere inside a supermax housing unit.

'Inside, no one can hear you scream'[1]

One of the most noticeable things about supermax prisons is their lifeless quietness. Both of the supermax prisons which I visited were very quiet and extremely clean, almost antiseptic. Apart from the occasional harsh sound of clanging metal gates in the secure corridors and the infrequent call 'Escort!' indicating that guards are escorting a prisoner through them, there are very few sounds and signs of life inside these prisons. Given that each prison houses several hundred prisoners, the quietness is eerie. Walking along the straight-lined, narrow corridors, passing through several automated metal gates, and entering a housing unit is somewhat shocking. Standing in the centralised control room of a housing unit, 'home' to those confined within, one cannot but stare into the barren concrete cells and the prisoners confined in them, unprotected from prying eyes. Privacy is non-existent, as cell doors are made of perforated metal that allows a view into the cell, and regulations prohibit prisoners from obstructing this view. A prisoner who hangs a towel or a shirt over his perforated cell door in an effort to gain some privacy will be charged with a disciplinary offence, resulting in a possible extension of his time in the unit. Prisoners have to conduct all activities under the constant view of the control room guard.

Guards wear army combat uniforms, and prisoners are dressed in yellow or orange overalls. As standard procedure, anyone entering the housing units is required to wear goggles and knife/bulletproof vests, depending on whether or not firearms may be used inside the prison. Where staff do carry arms, the vest is bulletproof, to protect those who may be caught in the line of fire should prison staff fire one of the many arms at their disposal.[2] The goggles are intended to protect the eyes from 'bodily fluids' that prisoners may throw from their cells, and from makeshift 'spears'. These accessories place immediate barriers, physical as well as symbolic, between prison staff and prisoners, portraying the latter as unpredictable and dangerous animals awaiting the chance to harm others. During my visits, these barriers between us and the prisoners were accompanied by verbal warnings not to 'fall into a false sense of security' and not to get too close to the cell doors, because *they are capable of anything*. To ensure beyond any doubt that we understood how dangerous prisoners were, we were informed that in accordance with regulations, the Department of Corrections would not be responsible for our safety and will not negotiate our release should we be taken hostage or otherwise harmed by prisoners.

The design, security arrangements, staff attitudes, emphasis on 'security' and 'safety', and constant stream of horror stories about the dangerousness of prisoners in the units create a different sense of reality and an atmosphere of danger lurking behind each cell door and around each corner. They also feel sharply different from places where human beings live and pursue everyday activities. This atmosphere seeps in, and after some time inside a supermax it seemed less obvious to consider rationally the need for a protective vest and goggles, and the realistic likelihood of an assault by a prisoner who is secured inside his cell and watched over by an armed guard. There was no room, in fact, to question why a prisoner would even wish to attack anyone in the first place. As guests of the prison's administration and from their perspective, visitors are assumed to be sharing the view that supermax prisoners are highly dangerous and incapable, indeed not deserving, of 'normal' human contact.

> Do we have an obligation to take care of them? Yes. But do I have an obligation to provide him touching, feeling, contact with another human being? I would say no. He has earned his way to this unit and he's earned just the opposite. He's earned the need for me to keep him apart from other people. [prison officer]

The routine in supermax units reflects this philosophy, in that prisoners' creature needs are met, and little more. Prisoners clean their own cells and have to comply with standards of cleanliness and personal grooming. Prisoners who fail to comply are charged with a disciplinary offence. The few interactions between prisoners and prison staff are carried out in a very efficient, mechanistic way. Food, mail, medication, canteen goods and library books are delivered to prisoners through a slot in their cell door without much conversation or time wasting. Although guards do not have any direct physical contact with prisoners, for ill-defined health and safety reasons, they always wear surgical gloves while performing these duties. The guidelines for guards in carrying their tasks are clear: get in, do what you have to do, and leave immediately. Timetables are accordingly tight and precisely calculated.

Daily routines

A typical daily routine in a supermax unit involves the following:

Food: In cell feeding, twice daily.
Food is distributed through the feeding slot. Prisoners receive a hot breakfast tray and a cold packed lunch at 6 am, and dinner at 4 pm in coordination with staff shifts; food trays are collected immediately after feeding. The prisoner needs to be awake to collect his tray.

Exercise: Solitary exercise four times weekly.
One-hour solitary exercise in a barren concrete yard; prisoner movement to and from the yard is supervised electronically through a control panel without direct staff contact.

Shower: Three times weekly.
Prisoners shower for 15 minutes in the shower cell, located at the end of each pod. Prisoner movement to the shower and back, as well as the length of showers, are supervised by the control room guard.

'Pill call' and *'mail call'*: Daily.
Medication and mail are distributed to prisoners through a slot in their cell door.

Medical Technical Assistant (MTA) visit: Daily.
The MTA[3] stands at the pod gate and prisoners who require care call out to him. The control room guard then electronically opens the prisoner's cell door, and the prisoner walks out to the pod gate and converses with the MTA through it, within the hearing range of other prisoners and prison staff.

The rules are rigid, as is their application by prison staff. Each activity has its related, carefully choreographed rituals, followed to the letter by staff and usually also by prisoners. To illustrate, delivering food to prisoners involves the following routine: when food carts are ready in the 'food services' area (located in a specially designated wing), two officers collect them and deliver them to the housing units. They then take the cart to the front gate of the pod, and wait for the control room guard to open it. They enter the pod, walk to the front of the cell and ensure that the prisoner sits on his concrete bed. They open the feeding slot and place the food tray on it. They step back while the prisoner walks to the cell front, collects his tray, and walks with it back to the farther side of his cell. The officers lock the slot and continue to the neighbouring cell. When the empty food trays are later collected, the same ritual takes place, but in reverse order.

A similarly carefully choreographed ritual takes place when a prisoner is due for a shower or exercise. Prisoners leave their cells individually at a designated time for an hour of solitary exercise. They do not need to be escorted, since the yard is located within the housing unit. The control room guard electronically unlocks the cell door, the prisoner comes out, and the door locks behind him. He walks along the corridor to the yard and stands in front of its gate until the control room guard remotely unlocks it. When the prisoner enters the yard, the door locks behind him, and remains locked for the duration of the exercise period. The process takes a few minutes, and does not require direct staff contact with prisoners. The same procedures apply when prisoners are due for their 15-minute shower three times a week.

At all times there is an atmosphere of imminent danger and the division between prisoners and prison staff is architecturally and procedurally clear.

In-cell provisions

The close control of prisoners' lives and the vigilant surveillance and inspection do not relax when prisoners are safely secured inside their cells (Figures 7.1 and 7.2). When it comes to the 'worst of the worst', isolation is seen as a necessary but insufficient measure. In addition to isolation and extremely restricted movements, prisoner in-cell provisions and their belongings are carefully regulated and subjected to relentless scrutiny and inspection. The following examples, drawn mainly from California's SHU at Pelican Bay, demonstrate the detailed

Figure 7.1 SMU II cell (front) (Photograph by Jason Oddy©)

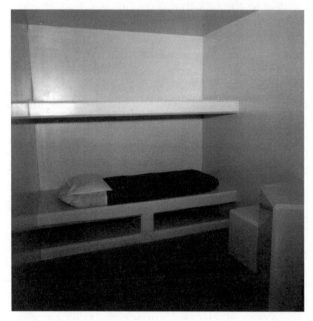

Figure 7.2 SHU cell (far end) (Image courtesy of the California Department of Corrections and Rehabilitation)

attention to security concerns and the way in which daily operations and procedures are pre-planned according to worst-case scenarios.

Food

The quality of food depends on budgets and on the quality of kitchen staff and the facilities available to them, and therefore changes dramatically from one prison and from one state to another. Some state departments of corrections also use food (or the lack of it) as a form of punishment. In Iowa, Michigan, New Mexico, Texas and Washington, for example, prisoners who break prison rules may be fed manufactured 'food-loaves' (or 'nutri-loaves'), a meal which is puréed and baked into a bland loaf.[4] Considerations when feeding supermax prisoners do not revolve around issues of nutrition alone. Food types and their preparation and packaging are carefully adjusted for use by supermax prisoners:

> There are certain foods we cannot give them because of security. On mainline we can give them chicken with bone, but down [here] we can't do that. It'd have to be maybe a chicken breast or something like that. We can't give them any type of fruit with a pip in it due to the fact that they can use that as a weapon.... There's some type of wrapping that we're not allowed to serve. We'd have to actually take that item out of the package and repackage it for them. Some things like plastic, which they can melt down and make weapons out of. All the sack lunches that we send out will be checked by an officer. When we serve a food tray the officers will make sure nothing is missing from the food tray. We have what we call 'paper status' where the officer will say I'm not allowed to give this inmate a plastic tray. I have to give him a paper tray, things like that. In preparing the food ourselves, we have to count all our cans. We count our can lids. We secure them because we don't want them to get out to any inmates to make weapons out of. [Food Services member of staff]

Cooked meals are flavoured but not spicy. Staff say that this is to prevent harm to their eyes should food be spat at them, but some commentators believe that the lack of spices is intended to reduce stimulation, and some even claim that this is a blatant form of punishment directed at Hispanic prisoners, who are accustomed to spicy food. Whichever explanation we adopt, the point here is that food, one of the few creature comforts enjoyed by supermax prisoners, does not escape the regulation and close scrutiny of security concerns as defined by prison administrators. Careful planning further ensures that the steps taken to prevent prisoners from using food for 'prohibited purposes' as described above are not compromised in any way. Food service employees are completely separated from prisoners and may not enter the housing units. Twice a day, before mealtimes, food trays are prepared, heated and placed on carts marked with the name of their destination pod. As a matter of routine practice, a number of individual trays are swapped between the predesignated food carts to prevent their use for hiding messages, drugs and weapons intended for prisoners. Each tray also includes a 'spork', a plastic combination of spoon and fork originally manufactured for use by the army in the World War II, which prisoners must return with the tray at the end of their meal. Food is served in special indestructible containers and trays. These and other food services equipment are manufactured by companies, mostly from the private sector, which specialise in 'correctional products'. One such company, located in California, offers more than 10,000 food service items especially designed for use in prisons in their catalogue (Stockton 2000). Food carts are collected from the kitchen area by guards who then deliver them to the housing units, as described above.

Personal property and prisoner privileges

Personal belongings are considered to be a privilege, not a right. The California Code of Regulations defines privileges as 'administratively authorised activities or benefits required by the director, the statute, case law, governmental regulations or executive orders' (Title 15, subsection 3244(c)). The administration of privileges is discretionary and intended to act as an incentive for prisoners. CDCR regulations stipulate that 'Inmate privileges shall be governed by an inmate's behaviour, custody classification and assignment' (Title 15, subsection 3044(c)). In practice, however, their directives remove most discretionary powers from staff, and set a uniform standard of privileges close to the minimum legal level. These privileges may be withdrawn, but not enhanced, so the possibility of further punishment still exists but there are few mechanisms for rewarding prisoners. Furthermore, as the following examples demonstrate, the few privileges afforded to prisoners are highly regulated and supervised. The privileges for SHU prisoners, as set out in CDCR regulations, include the following:

- One quarter of the monthly canteen draw (up to a total of $35)
- Telephone calls on an emergency basis only as determined by staff
- One 'special package' annually, not exceeding 30 pounds in weight
- A one-off special canteen purchase of one television or one radio or one radio/TV combination unit
- Up to five items of reading materials (magazines and books)
- Unlimited number of personal letters

Although SHU prisoners spend almost all of their days inside their cells, their property allowance is smaller and much more closely regulated than that of prisoners in general population prisons. In total, SHU prisoners may have up to 6 cubic feet of property, including state-issued items (linen and clothing), personal hygiene items (shampoo, toothpaste, etc.) and other personal property (books, photographs, letters, etc.). The exact types and amounts of allowable prisoner property state-wide are listed in the Authorized Personal Property Schedule, defined by security level. For example, some of the following items are not allowed for SHU and ASU (Administrative Segregation Unit) prisoners in Privilege Group D: *clothing*: hats, caps, headbands, sweatshirts, undershirts, slippers; *personal hygiene*: cotton swabs, body powders, hair conditioner, grease or gel, lip balm. Handkerchiefs, calendars, clocks, playing cards and correspondence course materials are also prohibited. The following items are allowed: one ballpoint pen filler, five books and magazines, one address book, five greeting cards, 15 photographs, 15 sheets of writing paper.[5]

Canteen goods

SHU prisoners are entitled to a quarter of the monthly canteen purchase of general population prisoners. Provided they have sufficient funds, prisoners may make a monthly purchase of $35 worth of canteen goods, which include basic toiletries (soap, shampoo, toothpaste and so on) as well as sweets and snacks. Prisoners make their selection in their cell, using a special 'canteen purchase order form'. Before the goods are delivered to prisoners, shampoo and other toiletries are removed from their original packaging and placed in paper cups to prevent prisoners from using the plastic packaging for prohibited purposes.

Annual package

Similar rules and regulations apply to the content of items in the annual package which SHU prisoners may receive from family members (Figure 7.3). The package can weigh up to 30 pounds and may only include approved items. We can only assume that the reasons for permitting only salted crackers, prohibiting cookies with cream, or allowing only three *named* brands of candy bars, are rooted in supposed security considerations similar to those relating to food and canteen goods. In addition to the specificity of the items which may be sent, there are strict rules regarding the weight, size and packaging of the annual package. Failure to comply results in the package being returned to the sender, and the prisoner having to wait an entire year until he is due for his next annual package.

PELICAN BAY STATE PRISON SECURITY HOUSING UNIT
2000 APPROVED INMATE PACKAGE LIST

IF AN ITEM IS NOT ON THIS LIST, DO NOT SEND IT!

1. CANDY BARS: Hershey with or without nuts, Nestle Crunch, Mr. Goodbar, Heathbar or Symphony. These are the only types and brand names authorized *(No Cookies 'n Cream, No bite-size bars less than 3 oz.)*.
2. JELLYBEANS: Only packed in manufacturers sealed containers *(No individual sized packages)*.
3. INSTANT TEA or COFFEE: Instant only *(No individual sized packages)*.
4. INSTANT BOUILLON: Granular only *(No individual sized packages, cubes, or glass containers)*.
5. INSTANT DRINK MIX: *(No individual sized packages, cocoa mix, milk, or dairy products)*.
6. CRACKERS: Saltine, Ritz, Ho-Ho's, and Hits only. Boxed only, salted only *(No individual sized packages or spicy flavors)*.
7. POTATO CHIPS: Salted or plain *(No individual sized packages or spicy flavors)*.
8. CORN CHIPS, TORTILLA CHIPS, or NACHO CHIPS: Plain *(No individual sized packages or picante or spicy flavors)*.
9. COOKIES: *(No individual sized packages, fruit or cream filled, or cookies with candy)*.
10. NUTS and SEEDS: Plain, honey flavor, or salted *(No individual sized packages or shells)*.
11. POPCORN: Plain, cheese, or caramel. Pre-popped only *(No individual sized packages or microwave)*.
12. PRETZELS: Plain *(No individual sized packages)*.
13. DRY CEREAL: Limit 2 boxes *(No individual sized packages, dried fruit, instant cereals, i.e. oatmeal or cream of wheat)*.
14. CUP-O-NOODLES: *(No pepper products / spicy flavors)*.
15. SHAMPOO: Clear, non-medicated products only. Limit 2.
16. DEODORANT: Stick type only. Limit 2 *(No alcohol based, roll-on, or gel types)*.
17. SOAP: Limit 4 bars.
18. DENTURE CREAM: Limit 2.
19. TOOTHPASTE and/or DENTURE CLEANSER: Limit 2 tubes.
20. SHOWER SHOES: Rubber strap only, ½ inch thick sole only *(No stretch rubber or nylon straps)*.
21. ENVELOPES: Limit 40 embossed *(No stamps, or holographic stamps)*.
22. MANILA ENVELOPES: Limit 10 *(No metal closure brackets)*.
23. WRITING PAPER: Limit 3 writing tablets or 200 pages of standard 8 ½ x 11 copy paper only *(No drawing paper or tablets, no paper tablets with spiral metal bindings)*.
24. SHOE LACES: Limit 1 pair, white only *(Not to exceed 54 inches)*.

Figure 7.3 Pelican Bay SHU annual package approved items list

Since 2003, rather than family members sending annual packages to prisoners, packages can only be purchased from, and sent by, vendors approved by the CDCR (15 as of 2009). A note on CDCR's website explains the reasoning behind the changes: 'In an effort to reduce contraband and time-consuming searches of packages destined for inmates, family members cannot send inmate packages ... directly to inmates, who are incarcerated in California State Prison.' The list of annual package approved items above predates this change in policy, but gives a good flavour of the sort of restrictions deemed necessary for SHU prisoners.

Reading and craft materials

The quantity of reading materials (books and magazines) that supermax prisoners may keep in their cells is also limited, though the exact number varies between states. In California, SHU prisoners may have in their cell up to five reading items at any given time, whereas prisoners in New Mexico's Special Control Units may keep in their cells up to five books and six magazines privately purchased, and three books and one magazine from the prison library. Reading materials can only be ordered by prisoners either from the prison library with a special form, or directly from the publisher at great expense. Second-hand or new books sent by friends are prohibited on the grounds that they may be used to conceal drugs or unauthorised communications related to criminal activities. For the same reason, prisoners may not exchange books or magazines with one another. Books and magazines are delivered to prisoners in their cells.

Craft and hobby materials are prohibited in most supermax prisons, as are personal stereo systems, musical instruments and board and card games.

Television

In-cell TV sets are the subject of much controversy and public outrage at the 'luxuries' enjoyed by prisoners, particularly high-security and allegedly dangerous prisoners.[6] Some jurisdictions bow to public and political pressures and prohibit TV sets in their supermax facilities. Where TV sets are permitted, they are often cited as the antidote to prisoners' social isolation and restricted sensory input. It is claimed that supermax prisoners cannot be said to suffer restricted sensory input and stimulation, as the TV provides both. I would argue that while allowing TV may mean that supermax confinement does not constitute sensory deprivation in the traditional sense of the word,

TV sets are nonetheless not a substitute for human interactions, nor can they be said to be an adequate source of stimulation. Whether a sufficient source of stimulation or not, for isolated prisoners TV is the main source of contact with the world outside their tiny, claustrophobic cells. Furthermore, since many prisoners have learning difficulties and craft materials are prohibited, watching TV is often the only thing they can do to pass their time. Some prison officials think that high-security prisoners should not have access to TV sets, but prison staff mostly view TV as a form of a 'babysitter' keeping prisoners docile and therefore easier to control. Yet others think that if TV sets are to be allowed, they should only be used for communicating positive educational messages to prisoners. Proposals made by an internal working group in one state suggested that, since prisoners are literally a captive audience, TV should be used to modify their behaviour. These suggestions for making use of a captive audience to communicate messages of behavioural change brings to mind the behaviour-modification techniques which were experimented with in the 1970s, only on a much larger scale. A senior administrator and a member of the working group described the reasoning behind the proposals:

> It's [supermax] not going to be as comfortable as it was before. It should not be a place where folks want to go. It should be a place where they go and they want to get the heck out of there, where they don't have their personal property, they don't have the packages, they don't have the access to 24 hour a day television that they have right now, that they don't have an environment where they're comfortable ... but in order to get out they have to meet certain criteria where we are going to introduce things like anger management stuff, like behavioural change models that we give them over an in-house television station.

In California's SHUs, prisoners may make a one-off purchase, through the canteen, of an expensive, specially designed, transparent TV set with no speakers, from an approved list. If a prisoner owns a TV, he may watch it as much as he wishes, using headphones. Elsewhere, for example in the Federal Bureau of Prisons' supermax, the ADX, and New Mexico's Special Control Units, TV sets are used to deliver educational programmes to prisoners inside their cells. In New Mexico, the use of TV may be suspended for up to 30 days, and TVs are deactivated after 10 pm. In Washington, where some form of a 'step-down' programme operates in the state's Intensive Management Units, only prisoners who have reached the most progressive stage are eligible for a TV or radio set.

Mail

Prisoners may receive an unlimited number of personal letters. All mail items, incoming and outgoing, are inspected by staff and X-rayed. Stamps are removed to ensure that no drugs or secret messages have been hidden under them. Mail items may also be opened and read with the exception of legal correspondence, which by law is confidential and may be X-rayed but not read. In line with the general trend of tightening control, however, there is mounting pressure by prison officials to change the rules regarding legal correspondence. They claim that prisoners and some legal professionals abuse privileged legal mail to send contraband and communications regarding criminal activities to prisoners. Officials explain how gang leaders smuggle orders and directives to the 'outside' through innovative methods such as using their own urine to write messages 'on the back of an innocent-appearing drawing before sticking it on an envelope ... when the urine dries, the contents of the message remain invisible to the naked eye until the recipient holds the paper to the heat so its secrets can be revealed', or sending 'ghost-writings', messages which are 'lightly embossed with a pointed object on the inside of a manila envelope. The envelope is glued back together, and mailed with other documents to an outside contact who rubs a pencil lead lightly over the markings so the message can be read' (Geniella 2001). Photographic 'proof' is produced to demonstrate the innovative methods used by prisoners despite the close scrutiny they are subjected to, and to support official demands for even more control of prisoners. Mailroom staff in one of the units I visited had a small collection of items allegedly confiscated from mail sent to prisoners, including weapon parts, drugs, and encrypted messages on gang-related and other criminal activities. This collection was compiled in a small booklet used to 'inform other jurisdictions' about methods used by prisoners and lobby the legislature to change rules regarding mail confidentiality.

The design and regime in supermax units make it possible to keep prisoners locked up in their solitary cells for years with very little movement outside their housing units. The careful regulation and constant inspection, monitoring and other controls discussed above are applied to prisoners while they are in their cells. Some activities, nonetheless, necessitate prisoner movement outside the housing unit, and this, as we shall see, leads to the application of additional controls over them.

Non-routine activities

If prisoners only leave their cells for 4 hours weekly of solitary exercise in a barren exercise yard and three 15-minute showers a week, they only leave their pods a few times annually. These rare out-of-pod activities include infrequent prescheduled non-contact family visits, medical or dental appointments, classification or disciplinary hearings, and, if the prisoner has a pending lawsuit, visits to the law library. These activities take place in specially designated areas inside the building complex, to which prisoners are escorted from within the internal corridors of the building: 'the infirmary – everywhere you go, nothing's outside, everything's inside so you ... you never see the sun' [former prisoner]. Other than in medical emergencies which cannot be treated in the prison's medical clinic, prisoners never leave the internal space of the building. In the case of those incarcerated in a supermax for indeterminate periods, this may mean that they will stay inside the building complex for the duration of their prison sentence or natural life.

On the rare occasions that prisoners leave their pods, an additional layer of controls is applied to them, focusing on their bodies. First, they are strip searched. Strip searches involve a ritual whose precise choreography is detailed in official guidelines:

> The inmate shall then completely disrobe. Staff shall inspect and search each item of clothing and visually inspect the inmate's body. The inmate shall face the staff member who shall visually inspect the inmate's hair, ears, mouth, nose, body, armpits, hands, scrotum, genitals, and legs. The inmate shall turn away from staff upon instruction and staff shall then inspect the inmate's back, buttocks, thighs, toes, bottom of the feet and lastly, the anal area by having the inmate bend over, spread the cheeks of their buttocks and cough. (CDCR DOM Chapter 5, Section 52050.18.3, Unclothed Body Search)

When deemed necessary, a 'full body search', which involves an internal examination of the prisoner, may also be performed. Strip searches are officially intended to ensure that nothing is smuggled from or into the unit, but their frequency and rigid application (even when the prisoner is constantly in restraints, does not any have contact with others, and is continually watched by prison staff) anger and humiliate prisoners.

> If you have to go to the infirmary or you have to see the doctor, you know, they strip search you, of course. I mean, they strip search you everywhere you go, and they escort you down the hallways to wherever you're going. [former prisoner]

> The strip searches are degrading and infuriating. They would make me want to hurt somebody because they made no sense. There was no security rationale. Slowly it dawned on me that that's the whole point: they make no sense. Because the key thing to understand about control unit prisons is that they are arbitrary and irrational. The people in charge show you, the prisoner, that they can do anything they want, whenever they want for any reason or for no reason at all. (Berkman 1995)

This degradation ceremony (Goffman 1961) is followed by the application of physical restraints to the prisoner's body, including hand and sometimes also leg restraints. Prisoners are then escorted by two officers to the designated area and placed in a 'holding cell', the size of a telephone box, until their medical appointment, visit to the law library, family visit or classification hearing commences. I discussed the settings and procedures for classification hearings previously. Below I examine some of the procedures related to the other three main occasions on which prisoners leave their pods: medical appointments, visits to the law library and family visits.

Medical and dental appointments

To deter prisoners from requesting 'unnecessary' medical appointments and to cover some of the costs, some departments of corrections charge prisoners for each visit. In California, for example, prisoners are charged $5 per visit. Medical appointments are made unpleasant for prisoners through the accompanying rituals described above. Roughly 2 hours before their scheduled visit to the clinic, prisoners are strip searched, handcuffed and placed in leg irons. They are then escorted by at least two guards to the clinic, where they are put in a holding cell until they can be seen by the doctor, psychologist, or dentist. The careful planning of the building did not take into consideration some basic provisions for prisoners:

You're going to go see the dentist, you're gonna be placed in a holding cell that's about the size of a phone booth, and you will stand there for three to four hours. Now you better hope that you didn't drink coffee that day or drink a lot of water because eventually you're going to have to use the restroom and if you complain that you have to use [it], they'll end up taking you back to your cell and you'll be put back on the three months waiting list to see the doctor. [former prisoner]

When the prisoner is finally seen by the health professional, he may remain handcuffed and guards may stay with him throughout the examination, as 'security' considerations prevail over considerations of medical confidentiality or privacy at all times. Guards' constant presence ensures further control of prisoners and all aspects of their lives as well as providing further information on the prisoner. Their presence is also a physical and psychological reminder to prisoners of where they are, and how they are perceived. In addition to the humiliation of discussing private matters in the presence of guards, the prisoner-patient is less likely to expose delicate psychological matters, fears of breakdown or other personal information that may later be used against him. It should also be noted that medical professionals may be violating principles of medical ethics when examining the prisoner-patient under such conditions as a matter of course.[7] Once the prisoner has been examined, he is escorted back to his cell where he is strip searched again.

Law library visits

Prisoners have to request access to the law library long in advance by filling out a special form, and usually have to wait months for a visit that may last up to 2 hours. Prior to the scheduled visit the prisoner is strip searched, and escorted to the library. He remains in a holding cell while the legal material he has requested is brought to him by the librarian:

The inmates are brought in on chains and they're cuffed. We have officers escort them and they're placed in a holding cell and they're given pen fillers, not pens but pen fillers. They have a request form and a list of all the books and legal forms that we have available. They fill-out the request form and slip it into the cell door. We pick that up and verify that they have their name, their number and their cell number on there. We pull the books that they're requesting and take them back to them. We then date stamp the request form and that is kept in their file. Every inmate who's ever been here has a file where we keep his material requests, his photocopy requests, and that is for our own benefit because a lot of these inmates are very litigious and they ... we have to have verification of everything that we do. [supermax librarian]

It is beyond the scope of this discussion to examine issues of legal confidentiality and due access that these procedures may give rise to, but the point to make here is that, as with other supermax support staff, library personnel concern themselves first and utmost with security issues and share guards' ethos and attitudes to the prisoners. In one supermax, library staff kept what they called a 'gassing chart' listing all the prisoners who threw, or attempted to throw, bodily substances at them, as well as a collection of makeshift weapons made by prisoners. Prisoners who have been involved in 'gassing' or weapon making may be banned from future use of the law library.

Contact with the 'outside': family visits and telephone calls

Typically, supermax prisoners are only permitted prescheduled, no-contact visits with approved visitors. The length and frequency of visits which supermax prisoners are entitled to varies from one jurisdiction to another. Federal Bureau of Prisons regulations allow five visits a month, each lasting up to 3 hours. New Mexico allows four monthly visits, each lasting up to 2.5 hours, and in Washington the length of visits increases as prisoners work their way through a 'step-up' programme – from 1 hour to 3 hours weekly.

In California, SHU prisoners may receive two 2-hour, no-contact family visits at weekends, once a month. If the visitor has travelled over 250 miles, the visit may be extended (extensions must be pre-arranged and approved). Official CDCR directives emphasise the importance of all prisoners maintaining ties with their families and the local community, and the rhetoric remains similar for SHU prisoners. Visits are also viewed by staff as a deterrent against prisoner misconduct:

It's a chance for them to get out of the environment of their housing unit and their yard that they live on. It gives them a chance to talk with someone else that's not with the prison system. They're very careful not to misbehave or act out, knowing that they may have a visit coming. That is a good deterrent in a lot of cases. [visiting area officer]

But there are many obstacles which make family visits difficult in practice. Firstly, as previously noted, the remote location of Pelican Bay SHU isolates its prisoners from their friends and families. Most SHU prisoners come from the Los Angeles area, a 14-hour drive away, a distance which makes the journey expensive and time-consuming for family members. Pelican Bay's location and the allocation of prisoners from Los Angeles County to the SHU thus lead directly to severance of family ties. According to a visiting area officer, on an average weekend day, the total SHU population of over 1,000 prisoners only receive around 50 visits. Then there are bureaucratic obstacles. Prisoners are required to submit a list of their expected guests for approval by the authorities prior to the planned visit. When visitors arrive, they are subjected to special degradation ceremonies reserved for those close to a SHU prisoner. They have to undergo extensive security procedures, which involve a body search, a metal detector, and adherence to a strict dress code suitable for a 'wholesome family atmosphere':

We encourage the visitors not to wear clothing that is in-appropriate as far as being low cut, sleeveless, or short dresses. They must be wholesome in nature. A family atmosphere is what we're trying to create in the visiting rooms. We're pretty stringent upon what they're allowed to wear. They also cannot wear clothing which might resemble what the inmates wear or what staff wears. [visiting area officer]

I observed a visit by a mother whose son had been held in the SHU for over 10 years at the time. She lives 8 hours' drive away and visits her son once a month, but said that other family members had given up, and noted a general decline in family visits received by other SHU prisoners once they have been incarcerated there for some time. She also recounted stories she heard from wives of SHU prisoners who moved to Crescent City to be closer to their jailed husbands, only to be chased out by the local community, which now consists in large part of Pelican Bay prison employees and their families. One staff member to whom I chatted informally remarked that prisoners' families and their children lower the level of teaching in local schools and introduce drug and gang cultures to the otherwise innocent children of Crescent City.

The SHU has a separate 'visitor-processing' area, where visitors register before being driven to the SHU. The area contains a number of tables and chairs for waiting visitors, and a large reception desk manned by two correctional officers. Behind them are big, glass display cabinets, offering visitors of SHU prisoners an opportunity to buy SHU memorabilia including cups, can openers and other gadgets displaying the Pelican Bay logo. One item offered for sale which struck me as particularly tasteless was T-shirts with slogans such as 'PELICAN BAY TIME = HARD TIME' designed to mimic the famous Hard Rock Café logo, with a drawing of a shackled, desperate-looking prisoner.

First, visitors need to fill out a form, and hand it to the officers, who verify that the person is on the approved visitors list. Then they are asked to place their shoes, jewellery, belt, wallet and car keys on a tray which an officer hand searches, wearing white cotton gloves. Visitors who do not adhere to the rules are not allowed to visit their relative. Visitors are then patted-down thoroughly, pass through a metal detector and have their wrist stamped with the letters SHU. They then proceed to a bus which takes them to the visiting area of the SHU building. When they arrive at the visiting area, they are assigned to a booth in the visiting room, where they sit on small stools, facing a thick separating glass.

Meanwhile, the prisoner is 'processed' in his housing unit. He is strip searched, handcuffed and shackled, and escorted by two officers to the visiting area. The entire journey takes place within the building, and at no stage does the prisoner get a glimpse of the outside world. He is taken to the designated visiting booth, which is equipped with a small stool. There is no physical contact between prisoners and their visitors, and communication is done through telephone receivers. During the visit, the constant monitoring and surveillance continue. Staff may randomly listen to conversations, and sometimes record them for future analysis. A conversation on any issue which 'threatens security' can be immediately discontinued by the staff. CCTV cameras cover the cubicles, and some visits are also recorded on videotape:

We have the ability to provide some type of surveillance, whether it's video or audio. We have some cameras and we do videotape some visits if necessary. And we move people around, we don't put them in the same booths all the time. It's just out there as a deterrent and information for us if we need it. [visiting area officer]

The process is frustrating for prisoners and visitors alike, and sometimes even when family members are willing and able to make the long journey to the prison, prisoners are reluctant to receive visits. One prisoner who had not had any visits since being placed in a supermax 10 years earlier, explained that

It's not worth it for them to come driving all the way up here just to visit for an hour and half behind the glass ... it's not worth it ... no.

Another prisoner, who was serving his third year in a supermax at the time, explained that

My family hasn't [visited] here ... they don't got means of transportation to come and visit so I haven't ... and it being behind glass there's no, there is no sense in them coming up, you know, six hours just to come and see me.

Yet when asked what was the worst aspect of his confinement, he replied,

Probably just the fact that I can't see my family. I can't touch my family, you know. That every ... all visits are behind glass and stuff like that, and basically that's about the worst thing I find about being here.

Policies regarding the use of telephones by supermax prisoners vary from one state to another. In California, SHU prisoners may only make or receive telephone calls in case of an emergency. Prisoners held at the Federal Bureau of Prisons' ADX unit may make one telephone call a month, whereas, in New Mexico, supermax prisoners may make four telephone calls a month, each lasting up to 15 minutes.

Yet, even the few, highly controlled and constantly supervised movements of prisoners out of the monotony of the cell are considered by prison officials as risks which should be avoided. New technologies which further eliminate contact between the prisoner and others are readily tried and adopted in supermax prisons. Video visitation, telemedicine, and classification and parole hearings conducted by videoconferencing are a few of the new technologies that are experimented with wherever budgets allow. I have described these technologies in more detail elsewhere, but here we should note that the current trend is a move towards even more separation and less human contact. Prisoners remain in supermax units for years, frustrated, angry and bored, with few avenues to vent their anger and with few opportunities to advance through the system.

Maintaining order and discipline

The threat of force lies close beneath the surface of the custodial institution ... the prison official is a bureaucrat, but he is a bureaucrat with a gun. (Sykes 1958: xv)

To speak about the problems of order and control in prisons today raises questions of power, of unintended consequences, of the impact of modern managerial techniques, and of the relationship between social structure and personal agency that prison studies have not yet confronted adequately, but which are the very stuff of modern social theory. (Sparks *et al.* 1996: 62)

The prison social system has been the focus of many of the early prison sociologies.[8] These identified the workings of the 'prison society' (Clemmer 1940), and described how prisoners engage among themselves and with prison staff, and how processes of ongoing negotiations and accommodations between the two groups contributed to the maintenance of order in prisons. Although prisons were total institutions (Goffman 1961), the power of prison staff was not absolute but constantly negotiated, with staff having to 'buy compliance or obedience in certain areas at the cost of tolerating disobedience elsewhere ... the custodians ... are under strong pressure to compromise with their captives, for it is a paradox that they can ensure their dominance only by allowing it to be corrupted' (Sykes 1958: 57–8). As prisons became more regulated and bureaucratised in the late 1970s and throughout the 1980s, their governance became more akin to Dilulio's (1987) vision, with its emphasis on structured, security-orientated administration that focused on collaboration with external actors, such as the legislature and community groups, rather than with internal actors, the prisoners.

The degree of isolation and near total control of all aspects of prisoners' lives in contemporary supermax prisons, its scope and its duration, were not technically possible or financially viable when the studies cited above were conducted. Hypothesising on the possible effects of strict and continuous isolation on the inmate society, Sykes contended that without association with others, there could be no prison society: 'If men in prison were locked forever in their cells, shut off from all intercourse with each other ... the inmate population would be an aggregate rather than a social group, a mass of isolates rather than a society' (Sykes 1958: 5).

For daily routines to be carried out and order to be maintained on an ongoing basis, nonetheless, some degree of cooperation is necessary with the 'mass of isolates', for even in supermax prisons official power is not absolute. As Sparks *et al.* (1996: 60) rightly noted, 'Members of an organisation (however unbalanced its power relations and however unwillingly some of them are there) confront one another as actors in a dynamic play of conflict, compromise, and mutual influence.' Indeed, despite all the physical and procedural barriers isolating each individual prisoner from his fellow prisoners and from prison staff in supermax prisons, prison staff need prisoners to cooperate to some extent to allow even the minimal daily routines described in this chapter. Imagine, for example, that all prisoners, collectively, were to refuse to collect or return their food trays, decline to obey guards' orders, or engage in a 'dirty protest'. Such situations would make it impossible, in the long run, to continue the routine operation of the prison. As Sykes put it, 'The ability of officials to physically coerce their captives into the paths of compliance is something of an illusion as far as the day-to-day activities of the prison are concerned and may be of doubtful value in moments of crisis' (Sykes 1958: 49).

Segregated prisoners mostly comply with prison rules and regulations because prison officers have near-complete control over the distribution of resources, privileges and punishments, and because non-compliance is swiftly and harshly dealt with. It is largely the environment itself which makes the 'rules of the game' apparent to prisoners:

> I think when they originally get here, it's a macho attitude, you know, 'I can handle this place'. It takes a very short time for an individual that is assigned here to realise that this is not a fun place to be. It's not supposed to be a fun place to be. This is an environment that is very structured, very controlled, very

161

organised. The inmates are told what to do and when to do it and how to do it. So they learn very quickly that their life has changed drastically ... security is paramount and it comes first and foremost above anything else. [prison officer]

The centrality of security in the governance of supermax prisons is reinforced by all available tools and mechanisms, and grounded in administrative rules and regulations. The architectural design puts in place physical and environmental barriers, the classification process provides the 'objective' grounding, and the bureaucratic mechanisms install a regime calculated to minimise points of contact with the prisoner. Prisoners are 'handled' separately from each other in an impersonal, highly utilitarian, strictly timetabled and mechanical way. To a large extent, many of the discretionary powers that prison staff had in the past are taken away from them in the daily running of supermax prisons. There is no system of rewards, only punishments, and these, too, are laid out in detail in administrative regulations.

Guards' combat uniforms, goggles, surgical gloves and the additional physical restraints and weapons they have at their disposal further contribute to expressing and widening the gap, symbolic and physical, between captives and their jailers which exists in any place of confinement (Goffman 1961; Sykes 1958). Official discourses justify these measures by utilitarian security concerns, but they undoubtedly also play an important symbolic role in reproducing the processes of 'role stripping' and 'mortification of the self' (Goffman 1961) and communicating the division between staff and prisoners: the dangerousness of the latter and the no-nonsense preparedness of the former. These arrangements bring to mind Christie's (1992) observation that

With the cold war brought to an end, in a situation with deep economic recession, and where the most important industrial nations have no external enemies to mobilize against, it seems not improbable that the war against the inner enemies will receive top priority according to well established historic precedents. (Christie 1992: 13–14)

The isolation and security measures in supermax prisons reduce the possibilities of and opportunities for both individual and collective acts of disobedience. They also reduce the need for prison officials to engage in dialogue, negotiations and accommodations of prisoners' demands and needs. Social order in supermax prisons is 'reduced ...

to its lowest possible relevance by increasing the level of isolation of the inmate from both other inmates and staff toward the theoretical limit points of total segregation'.[9] While prisoners can find ways of communication even in highly segregated environments, prisoner solidarity in supermax prisons is further weakened by confining to the same pods prisoners who do not necessarily share common ideologies. Staging collective action to increase their bargaining power with prison authorities under such circumstances is almost impossible, because, as one officer put it, 'it takes more than one to have a disturbance':

> It's impossible to have a group disturbance or a work stoppage of any kind because there is only one inmate out at any given time; they are fully restrained, meaning that they are handcuffed, there is a waist restraint on them and that their feet are restrained most of the time, dependent upon the individual. So it takes more than one to have a disturbance. And again the safety precautions that we take to ensure, to the best of our ability, staff safety ... at the minimum there is two staff on each inmate that's escorted.

Weakening the prison society and reducing solidarity among prisoners, then, is not a side effect of supermax confinement, but one of the very central features of its rationale. As Simon (2000: 301) aptly put it, supermax confinement 'acknowledges the presence of the inmate society, but seeks to govern around rather than through it ... to the extent that "super-max" succeeds in breaking up dangerous solidarities within inmate society, it does so by fragmenting that society into individual cells leading in a disturbingly high number of cases to psychosis.' Reduced to individual cells, supermax prisoners are completely dependent on staff for provision of their basic creature needs, and thus have a common interest in the smooth operation of daily routines.[10]

Despite attempts to completely separate prisoners from one another, they find ways to communicate and even maintain some form of clandestine 'prison economy', albeit on a very limited scale.[11] As all cells face a wall, prisoners can verbally communicate by shouting, but they cannot see each other and do not have direct physical contact with one another. The closest contact they can have with each other is through a special 'finger shake', which involves a prisoner on his way to the shower cell or the exercise yard pressing his finger against one of the perforated holes in the cell door of a fellow prisoner, who does the same from the inner side of his cell door. I observed a prisoner about to be released from one unit bid his pod-mates farewell in this way. In this specific case, staff did not intervene, though I am not sure whether that was the result of the presence of outsiders or a regular form of 'accommodation', or informal concession, to prisoners. Sometimes, risking a disciplinary charge, prisoners also 'send' a note, magazine, cookie or a packet of crisps as a gift or in exchange for another item, tied to a long string made of elastic threads from clothing items tied together. The 'sending' prisoner lowers the string through the narrow gap between his cell door and the floor until it reaches the front of the cell on the tier below him, where the 'receiving' prisoner will reach through the gap between his cell door and the floor and slide the item into his cell. I saw items being sent this way. Prisoners wait until the control room guard's attention is focused on the control board or on another pod, and very quickly send their message, gift, or exchange item. Some items fall off the string, and end up on the pod's floor where they will later be collected by staff, who will attempt to determine who sent it and whom it was intended for, so that disciplinary charges can be made against both prisoners. These limited interactions do not involve face-to-face or physical contact, and can be halted at any time or stopped altogether by placing a Plexiglas cover over the perforated cell door. Furthermore, as each pod only has 8–10 cells, these limited interactions can only ever take place among 8–10 prisoners. And so, while prisoners' social isolation is not total, their interactions cannot be said to be 'normal' in any sense of the word.

Whatever small 'accommodations' may or may not take place, these are kept in check by the elimination of all personal interactions between prison staff and prisoners and the highly regimented, strictly timetabled points of contact between them. Mostly, prisoners collect and return their food trays according to regulations, leave their cells to go to the exercise yard or the shower cell at designated times, and return to them quietly without staff intervention. Occasionally, there are individual acts of protest, usually involving a prisoner refusing to return his food tray at the end of a meal or, in more extreme cases, 'gassing' staff. These two forms of 'acting out' are not random: collecting and returning trays from the feeding slot is the main point of contact with staff and, in the highly controlled supermax environment, bodily substances are among the few things which prisoners have some control of.[12] The relationship between these forms of protest and the design and regime in supermax units is clear to those who helped devise them:

By establishing the procedures that we have and by its physical layout ... the inmate-on-inmate violence has dropped to almost nothing and that's a dramatic departure from [supermax unit] of the past in any of the other states we visited. Because of that the inmates have modified their behaviour to find some means of acting out, and the means that they have found to be most prevalent is what we refer to as 'gassing' which is the storing up and throwing of bodily fluids on people that are someone they either want to make mad or irritate in some way, and that can either be another inmate who maybe is on the way back from a shower or it may be a correctional officer or other staff member. [administrator]

Although prison officials may understand the desperate nature of prisoners' attempts to protest or 'act out', this does not in any way modify their reaction to such instances. When prisoners do 'act out', even relatively minor offences such as 'gassing' – admittedly unpleasant but not life-threatening to prison staff – are treated as serious security threats. Guards may have recourse to another layer of control, and may use one of the lethal, non-lethal and chemical weapons they have at their disposal when deemed necessary. These weapons are stored in specially designed containers situated outside the housing units for easy and quick access. The list of 'defense products', as they are officially termed, used inside California's SHUs, for example, includes 'less lethal force' (batons, federal gas gun), 'lethal force' (Ruger Mini-14 carbine, 12-gauge shotgun), 'posted chemical agents' (tear gas, chemical mace, CS agents) and projectiles (grenades, bullets and shells) to use them with, and physical restraints including 'electronic restraints' and 'mechanical restraints' (handcuffs, leg irons, waist chains, lead chains, leather restraints).[13]

Any form of prisoner disobedience, be it 'gassing', verbal insults or infractions of procedural rules, is answered swiftly and harshly by guards. Prisoners are gassed inside their cells, quite literally, with CS gas and other chemical agents. They are beaten up, 'hog-tied' and kept behind Plexiglas doors. These 'reactions' are not spontaneous or unusual. They are stipulated in administrative directives, rules and regulations. Some of these procedures were examined by the court in a class-action lawsuit taken by Pelican Bay SHU prisoners (*Madrid v Gomez* (1995)) and ruled to be highly excessive. These included the use of in-cell 'foetal restraints' (also known as 'hog-tying'), which involves 'handcuffing an inmate's hands at the front of his body, placing him in leg irons and then drawing a chain between the handcuffs and legs until only a few inches separate the bound wrists and ankles [for] anywhere between a few minutes and 24 hours' (*Madrid* 1995: 1168–9); 'caging', which involves holding naked or partially dressed prisoners in outdoor holding cages the size of a telephone box during inclement weather (*Madrid* 1995: 1170); and the extensive use of 'cell extractions', the forcible removal of a prisoner from his cell, described in detail by the court:

> A team of four correctional officers is assembled, wearing special protective gear, including helmets with visors. Each team member carries one of the following: a large Plexiglas shield, a small metal baton, leg irons, or handcuffs. ... The supervising sergeant and/or the lieutenant then typically fire some combination of the following weapons, any one of which can potentially cause serious injury: a 38 millimetre gas gun (which ejects high velocity rounds of rubber blocks), mace (a chemical agent that causes burning sensation and tearing of the eyes) and a taser (which temporarily incapacitates an inmate by way of electrical shock). The four member team then enters the cell. ... Not every weapon described above is used in every cell extraction; however, most ... involved multiple weapons and each weapon was used more than once. It is an undeniably massive combination of weapons and manpower, especially considering that the target is almost always an unarmed inmate already behind cell doors. (*Madrid* 1995: 1174–5)

Cell extractions can be conducted randomly; when a prisoner disobeys an order or does not follow procedures; or, with a targeted cell, if guards suspect that a prisoner has possession of a banned object. When the *Madrid* court revealed that cell extractions at the SHU left many prisoners with broken limbs, the department changed its procedures, and guards now spray pepper gas in the targeted cell before entering it. Because of the design of the units, when a cell is being gassed, neighbouring cells are also affected, and prisoners need to resort to desperate measures:

> The pods are very small, so any cell that they spray into, you know, it's going to affect everybody in the pod ... Our fresh air was our toilet, as we flushed the toilet we stuck our heads in it to get fresh air because the pepper spray makes it very hard to breathe as your eyes burn and your nose runs and you're choking and coughing. [former prisoner]

Figure 7.4 Sign at SMU II (Photograph by Jason Oddy©)

Following the *Madrid* judgement, CDCR also modified other procedures for the use of force at Pelican Bay SHU, but its basic policy of responding to the smallest incidents of prisoner disobedience forcefully remains in place. One change resulting from court interventions is that now, as a matter of course, cell extractions and other use of force incidents are video-recorded and documented in several forms and written reports. The revised policy guidelines on the use of force demonstrate the preoccupation with the bureaucratic aspects of its use: four short paragraphs are dedicated to defining situations when force may be used, while the chain of command and reporting responsibilities of staff are elaborated in 12 pages. Similarly, the mandatory annual staff training programme on the use of force includes six classes on the practical application of force (e.g. training in the use of lethal, non-lethal and chemical agents, and mechanical restraints), three classes on procedures and reporting responsibilities, one class on 'staff ethics and professionalism', and one class on 'dealing with mentally ill inmates'.[14] There are no classes on techniques of negotiation, conflict resolution, or other methods which do not involve the use of force. One can only conclude that departments of corrections sanction guards to use force in response to all acts of prisoner disobedience and provide practical training in its application, but do not concern themselves with root causes or non-violent responses. Importantly, rather than limiting or minimising the use of force, such procedures may contribute to the normalisation of violence. Further, as Bottoms noted in concluding his study of 'order and discipline' in prisons in England and Wales, '[T]o impose additional physical restrictions, especially of a severe character, will almost certainly lead to a legitimacy deficit; and that deficit may well in the end play itself out in enhanced violence' (Bottoms 1999: 263).

Daily routines and 'order and discipline', in short, are maintained in supermax prisons primarily through physical fixtures, procedural arrangements, separation, surveillance, and body controls, which reduce to a minimum both the need for prisoner cooperation and the potential power of the inmate society. Assertions made about prisoners' relatively powerful position in earlier prison sociologies are contradicted by the very nature of supermax prisons, as prisoners are atomized and their cooperation, as individuals, becomes almost redundant for the daily running of the units. Rules and regulations further enforce compliance. When these measures are not sufficient and there are individual acts of prisoner disobedience, they are immediately answered with a range of weapons, restraints and brute force.

The official reason for all of these steps of hypercontrol, are security considerations. These encompass architectural, environmental, situational and physical controls on prisoners' bodies, movements, communications and provisions. But rather than controlling violence, as they officially aim to do, such highly controlled environments may breed it and, as the following chapter demonstrates, they also cause severe suffering for prisoners.

Notes

1 Relly 1999.
2 This is not a groundless fear. In California, between 1989 and 1998 alone, 36 prisoners were killed and 207 wounded by firearms used by CDC employees in prisons across the state (CDC Data Analysis Unit 1998).
3 MTAs are prison officers who have received 1-year medical training. In California, guidelines require that a fully qualified doctor visit SHU prisoners at least once a week, but prisoners reported that in practice this is not the case.

4 Regulations in Washington state stipulate that 'individuals who have used food or food service equipment in a manner that is hazardous to self, staff, or other offenders' will be served with 'alternative meal service' consisting of food loaves (Washington Department of Corrections, policy DOC 320.255, rev. 5/22/08). In New Mexico, this can be done for up to 7 days and extended further after a day's break.

5 CDCR Authorized Personal Property Schedule (APPS), Section 54030.20, Effective August 2007.

6 For fuller discussion, see Jewkes (2002).

7 For a discussion of medical ethics as applied in the prison setting with particular emphasis on medical ethics in segregation units, see Shalev (2008: 57–68).

8 Early prison sociologies in the USA include the works of Clemmer (1940), Sykes (1958), McCleery (1961), Irwin (1980), Jacobs (1977), and, in the UK, Morris and Morris (1963) and Cohen and Taylor ([1972] 1981).

9 Simon (2000: 301). Kauffman (1988: 78) similarly noted that 'only the forceful restraints offered by a prison-wide system of solitary confinement or the psychological isolation offered by pharmaceutical means of control make domination by force or coercion truly practical. At most prisons, however, only a small proportion of inmates can be held for long in the solitude of their cells or their minds.'

10 If the inmate society, as Sykes and others have suggested, is a functional adaptation to the 'pains of imprisonment', by fragmenting it prisoners are stripped also of a tool of coping with the harsh conditions of their imprisonment.

11 Prisoners have traditionally found ways of communication even in the strictest of conditions, as by tapping on water pipes and walls (see Sykes 1958).

12 See also Rhodes' (2004b: 43–9) analysis of the use of the body as a form of resistance in supermax prisons.

13 CDC Use of Force Policy, 1997 revisions.

14 CDC, Pelican Bay State Prison Use of Force Policy, revised 1997. Following the *Madrid* ruling and subsequent reports by the court-appointed Special Master (Hagar 2004), the CDCR made further changes to its policy and clarified when and how force may be used. Incidents involving the use of force are now also reviewed by a special analyst (Pelican Bay Use of Force Policy revised 2003). See also Corrections Independent Review Panel report, 30 June 2004.

Chapter 8

The dynamics of control: views from the control room, views from the cells

They say that you're a violent inmate, you're violent to yourself, you're violent to everybody, that … it's unsafe for the institution to have you out there in general population. So every day, you know, they're [saying] you're a trouble maker, you're real violent, you're too violent, you know, and you're handcuffed, you're shackled, you got two officers side by side by you, it's like, you know, you're the biggest threat around. Eventually it goes into your head you know … [it] starts sinking in 'Am I violent? Maybe I'm violent' and after a while, you know, all you're doing is thinking about this over and over. I mean, you got twenty-four hours to think of what they're saying to you, what they believe you are, eventually, you know, you're going to feel that hey, well maybe I am violent, and you see the officers sort of scared of you so you put on your role, yeah, I'm a tough guy, until eventually, you know, you're cell extracted and you realise you ain't all that tough, or you're in a cell by yourself and you're down on your knees praying, you know, 'Please let me out.' And then you realise you're not that tough. [former prisoner]

So far I have described daily life in a typical supermax prison and the rules, regulations and guidelines which prescribe its operation. I have demonstrated how these administrative guidelines and the architectural arrangements in supermaxes join together to enable constant and thorough control and monitoring of prisoners, and how 'security' considerations are paramount in every aspect of daily life in a supermax. I have argued that, to a large extent, those who work in supermax prisons are also tightly controlled through strict timetabling, security arrangements and administrative guidelines. Such structural conditions not only allow, but require, prison staff to be completely separated from prisoners, not to engage in any communication with them, and to treat them in an impersonal, arbitrary and sometimes violent manner. Despite conscious attempts to make the operation of supermax units as automatic as possible, however, prison officers are not robots, and prisoners are, after all, human beings. In what follows, I examine some of the situational and socio-psychological processes which enable one social group to act in a way which involves treating other human beings as objects or non-humans. I then turn to focus on the experiences and consequences of supermax confinement from the perspective of prisoners, and examine how the social isolation, reduced environmental stimulation, and 'totality of control' (Haney 2003) typical of all solitary confinement units, and brought to an extreme in supermax prisons, are experienced by them, and some of the health consequences of their confinement.

Guarding super-predators and evildoers: views from the control room

> [ADX] guards say they are just doing their job, which they will gladly do for an annual entry level salary of $32,000, a nice benefit package and a bully pulpit to boot. Some do it with benign neglect, others do it with perverse cruelty. In a Faustian contract with the government, they work the cages and in return get to send their kids to college and take Caribbean vacations. (ADX prisoner, Levasseur 1998: 201)

Solitary confinement and control units have traditionally been particularly violence prone, since by nature they are closed, almost hidden, places, with little external supervision or scrutiny. Arbitrary treatment and guard brutality have been heightened in solitary confinement units from the days of the hole to present-day segregation units, and the high-tech supermax prisons are no exception. Since their introduction in the late 1980s, a constant stream of horror stories of guard violence including rape, the release of members of rival gangs from their isolated cells to participate in staged 'gladiator fights', and old-fashioned beatings have come to light throughout the USA. While reports by prisoners, voluntary organisations and prison activists are often discredited by officials as grossly exaggerated, testimonies and evidence given under oath in a court of justice are more difficult to deny. One particularly harrowing account of brutality in a supermax unit was that of Vaughn Dortch, a mentally ill prisoner and a 'gasser' held at Pelican Bay SHU, whose fate was recounted in detail by the court

> Dortch ... suffered second and third-degree burns over one third of his body when he was given a bath in scalding water in the prison infirmary. The week before the incident Dortch bit an officer. Dortch had also created a nuisance by smearing himself and his cell with his own faecal matter. Although there was a shower near Dortch's cell, which would have provided a more efficient method of cleaning Dortch than a bath (even assuming Dortch was uncooperative), the officers instead forcibly escorted Dortch to a bathtub in the SHU infirmary, located some distance away in another complex.... Five or six correctional officers then arrived with Dortch. Although a nurse would normally run the water for a therapeutic bath, Dortch's bath was managed solely by correctional staff ... [the nurse on duty] later observed, from her nurse's station, that Dortch was in the bathtub with his hands cuffed behind his back, with an officer pushing down his shoulder and holding his arms in place ... she overheard the officer say about Dortch, who is African-American, that 'it looks like we're going to have a white boy before this is through, that his skin is so dirty and rotten, it's all fallen off'. (*Madrid* 1995: 1166–7)

Vaughn Dortch's horrifying ordeal was perpetrated by a group of five or six guards who were directly involved, and at least one onlooker. As Dortch was forcibly removed from his cell and escorted to the infirmary (which would have involved passing through several corridors, gates and control rooms), other staff members must have also witnessed his forceful removal. Furthermore, the preparation of the scalding bath must have required agreement and coordination between the participating guards. In other words, it could not be said that the event was the result of the guards' temporarily irrational state of mind and a heated response to Dortch's 'gassing'.

If court testimonies are difficult to refute, physical evidence of extreme brutality is impossible to ignore. In Dortch's case, such evidence included second- and third-degree burns on his body. In one case involving nine Florida State Prison guards who beat a prisoner, Frank Valdez, to death, the evidence included broken ribs and boot prints left on his body.[1] Sometimes, the perpetrators of violence may also be so blasé about their actions that they provide the evidence themselves – witness the graphic photographs of the abuse of Iraqi detainees by US military personnel at Abu Ghraib Prison in Iraq.[2]

But how can such brutal acts be explained, and what are some of the conditions that allow them to take place and, often, go unpunished? One possible explanation is that some prison staff are sadistic individuals who thrive in the violent world of the supermax and similar prisons. It could indeed be assumed that prison guards, as a social group, have their own share of 'rotten apples', to use a term more commonly applied to prisoners. In the wider context of a strong code of silence among prison staff, a small number of violent individuals can abuse their position and cause much damage without being held accountable. This was the view of the Special Master appointed by the *Madrid* court to monitor the implementation of its orders regarding Pelican Bay SHU:

> A minority of rogue officers can establish a code of silence, threaten the majority, damage cars, isolate uncooperative co-workers, and create an overall atmosphere of deceit and corruption. And if the minority are supported by a powerful labor organization, and the union as well as management condones the code of silence, the consequences are severe. (Hagar 2004: 75)

Certainly, the California Correctional Peace Officers Association (CCPOA), as illustrated in Chapter 3, falls into the category of a 'powerful labour organisation' and it devotes substantial energy and resources to protecting its members. In the few cases when prison officers are investigated for allegations of misconduct, the CCPOA not only funds their legal costs but also reportedly maintains pressure on investigators. The head of an investigation into charges of guard misconduct, including brutality, unnecessary shootings and staging 'gladiator fights' between members of rival gangs, at Corcoran Prison, for example, commented that

> The union and the governor's office ran the investigation.... We would try to question a witness, and the union was there blocking us. The union even told us how many interviews we could do, and our bosses in Sacramento (central government)

backed them. This was no independent inquiry. It was just a sham. (Arax and Gladstone 1998)

Reporting his findings following an investigation of shooting incidents at Pelican Bay State Prison (PBSP) SHU, the Special Master appointed by the *Madrid* court described similar interference in his investigation:

> During the ... criminal interviews at PBSP, the CCPOA put out a memo notifying staff that Internal Affairs was going to be at PBSP and that staff did not have to talk to them if they did not want to. Thus, the union sent a message to correctional officers not to cooperate with IA no matter what position they were in (in other words, even if a correctional officer was a witness to an abuse of force) ... because of the code of silence one officer did not come forward with any information until he left the CDC's employment for fear of his safety. (Hagar 2004: 75–7)

The code of silence went beyond the prison under investigation,

> There is a code of silence about the code of silence in the CDC's Central Office, an attitude of benign neglect concerning the history of CCPOA's interference with criminal investigations, which in turn allows continued interference by the union that causes many investigations and adverse action cases to end without success. (Hagar 2004: 75)

Rather than 'correcting' prisoners, the institutional culture created by a blanket defence of violent prison staff through a code of silence seeps into recently recruited staff,

> The young men and women who seek CDC employment are not taking peace officer jobs to commit crimes or lie or cover-up the abuses of their co-workers. Somehow, however, the rookie correctional officers who go to work for the CDC are forced to adopt the code of silence. Rather than CDC staff correcting the prisoners, some correctional officers acquire a prisoner's mentality: they form gangs, align with gangs, and spread the code of silence. The code of silence is taught to new recruits because of a longstanding CDC culture; thereafter, good officers turn bad. The Department has failed to address the situation in any effective manner; indeed, the evidence demonstrates

that the Directorate turned its head when confronted with the code of silence, especially if the CCPOA is involved. It cannot be emphasized too strongly that the code of silence is always accompanied by corruption. It serves no legitimate penological purpose. (Hagar 2004: 76).[3]

Criminal prosecutions of prison staff are extremely rare, and convictions even rarer, as the investigating authorities face the 'daunting task of breaking through officer solidarity and a code of silence and of prosecuting prison guards before juries drawn from the rural communities in which the guards lived, and in which the prisons were a major source of employment' (Human Rights Watch 2001: 433–4).

The existence of sadistic individuals protected by a strong code of silence, however, can only partially explain the extremity of some acts of guard brutality. It is just as plausible that the prison environment itself actively brutalises its inhabitants and facilitates the occurrence of arbitrary treatment and violent behaviour. Indeed, this was the main conclusion of the Stanford prison experiment researchers, who noted that:

> The most dramatic and distressing to us was the ease with which sadistic behaviour could be elicited in individuals who were not sadistic types ... the abnormality here resided in the pathological nature of the situation and not in those who pass through it. (Haney *et al.* 1973: 84–5)

In supermax environments, violence is not a by-product, but an inherent part of their *modus operandi*, reinforced through the rules and regulations that govern these prisons, their architectural design, and the daily routines and interactions in them. To a large extent, such environmental and situational factors affect guards' perception of the prisoners under their charge and predetermine their attitudes and reactions to them. This creates an 'ecology of cruelty' where

> At almost every turn, guards are implicitly encouraged to respond and react to prisoners in essentially negative ways – through punishment, opposition, force, and repression.... When punishment and repression continue – largely because of the absence of any available and sanctioned alternative approaches – they become functionally autonomous and often disproportionate in nature. (Haney 2008: 958)

The 'culture of control' (Riveland 1999) in supermax prisons and the potential problems arising from the limited interactions between prisoners and staff, and their mechanical nature, are known to prison officials. One unit manager likened these interactions to dealing with a product rather than an individual human being:

> Staff, because they're dealing with these guys daily on such a sterile level – lock them up, keep them locked up, don't touch them, keep yourself safe, search, search, it's a very, very mechanical, non-human process – staff get used to dealing with the inmates that way ... we deal with him as a product. We are a people business, and we're moving him and we're searching him and we're keeping him fed and safe and warm and healthy. He's not an item. He's a person.

She then went on to say that in her role, she attempts to resolve the problem by reminding staff that prisoners are human beings, albeit dangerous ones:

> I try to teach them to remember this person has a mom and a dad and they're probably very unhappy that he's in prison. He probably deserves to be here and don't forget it ... he's dangerous. But he has a mom and a dad, so when he's talking to you about wanting to visit with his mother or his father, you need to remember how you would feel if you hadn't seen you mom and dad in fifteen, twenty years. How would you feel? Don't just tell him, hey, he's got nothing coming. Talk to him about it.... Ask him if he writes. Ask him if he ever gets a phone call. Ask him about his parents' health. I try to keep balanced with this very, very sterile security the element of the people issue.

According to this officer, staff maintain the balance between the sterile environment and prisoners' humanity so well that 'if the average person in the public spent a couple of days [here] they would be shocked at how warm and caring the staff here are.' My impressions of staff attitudes during my visits to supermax units were rather different. Prisoners and former prisoners also described a very different reality:

> I've seen officers on their first day, you know, 'How are you doing today?', and then you see that officer three months later,

you know, it ain't nothing. Now, it's, you know, just give you your tray and you try to ask … you go 'Hey, can I …?' 'No, no, no. I don't wanna hear it.' The same officer that was new eventually grows the attitude. Maybe it's from other inmates, you know, talking back to the new officer or the unit has effect on him too… I mean they gotta have some kind of feeling. Maybe they learned after the months or after the years working [here] how to ignore the inmate.… Or maybe they're taught by other officers or by administration that remember, these guys are not human. They're the animals. They're [the ones] who we want off the streets. They belong here. They belong in this warehouse. Maybe they figure, hey, why should I talk to him? Why should I give him a conversation? Who cares he's over there banging his head against a wall? He's not human. He's nobody. [former prisoner]

Indeed, the reality of supermax prisons, contrary to claims about the warm and caring treatment of prisoners, is that the division between the two groups, prisoners and guards, is physically, procedurally and symbolically clear, and they do not engage with each other. The strict timetables and brief contact points between them make such interactions near impossible, and in any event they are not part of the atmosphere and ethos in a typical supermax.

Despite all the structural arrangements minimising contact and interactions between prisoners and prison staff, however, prison staff must also make some psychological adjustment in order to carry out daily tasks that are based on a system of near total control of a group of other human beings. Ideologies and official justifications for the need for supermax confinement and the nature of those confined within, play, of course, a crucial role in the way prison staff view themselves and the prisoners in their custody. Additionally, there are a number of techniques for easing the cognitive dissonance that prison staff may experience, and for achieving a sense of psychological and perceptual balance that, in turn, enables them to continue carrying out their duties.

The literature on crimes of obedience is useful in explaining some of these processes and helping to understand the role of staff in the dynamics of control in the extreme environment of isolation units. Applied to supermax prisons, it helps explain some of the social and psychological processes which allow those who work in them to carry out both daily tasks and the related routine use of force discussed above, and occasional acts of extreme 'spontaneous' violence. Kelman and Hamilton (1989: 6) identify three main social processes that create conditions which weaken moral inhibitions against violence:

[T]hrough authorisation, the situation becomes so defined that the individual is absolved of the responsibility to make personal moral choices. Through routinization, the action becomes so organized that there is no opportunity for raising moral questions. Through dehumanisation, the actors' attitudes toward the target and toward themselves become so structured that it is neither necessary nor possible for them to view the relationship in moral terms.

In addition to these processes, one also observes various forms of denial or neutralisation (Sykes and Matza 1957), which further ease any psychological tension which staff may experience in performing their jobs. I briefly examine these processes below, starting with authorisation, routinization and dehumanisation, as outlined by Kelman and Hamilton, followed by denial and neutralisation, as outlined by Sykes and Matza and developed by Cohen (2001).

Authorisation

The powerful influence of authority on the individual actor and the very high levels of obedience produced in such situations have long been observed,[4] not least in studies of Nazi Germany and, more recently, in respect of the treatment of 'terror suspects' in Abu Ghraib Prison in Iraq and in other places of detention across the world. In Kelman and Hamilton's account, the term 'authorisation' includes acts of violence that are explicitly ordered, implicitly encouraged and tacitly approved or at least permitted by the legitimate authorities. In situations of authority, individuals are more likely to obey orders without raising issues of morality and necessity.

This process is illustrated in the response of Lynndie England, who featured in some of the notorious photographs depicting prisoner abuse at Abu Ghraib, when asked about her reaction to the abuse:

Of course it was wrong. I know that now. But when you show the people from the CIA, the FBI and the MI [military intelligence] the pictures and they say, 'Hey, this is a great job. Keep it up', you think it must be right. They were all there and they didn't say a word. (*Rumsfeld Knew* 2008)

When asked whether she felt sorry for the detainees, she replied,

> Well, it was kind of weird at first. But once I started to see the big picture, I thought, okay, here come these guys, the OGAs [Other Government Agencies], the MIs or even officers, and they don't even look twice at it. If they approve, then I'm not going to say anything. Who was I to argue? (*Rumsfeld Knew* 2008)

I previously discussed some of the official rules and procedures that guide daily routines in supermax units, as well as the use of varying degrees of force, from cell extractions to 'hog-tying', which are performed on a regular basis. At Pelican Bay SHU, as the *Madrid* court observed, prison officers were implicitly authorised by the highest levels of California's Department of Corrections to use force excessively with the intention of causing harm to prisoners:

> [CDC] knew that unnecessary and grossly excessive force was being employed against inmates on a frequent basis, and that this practice posed a substantial risk of harm to the plaintiff class. Nonetheless, defendants consciously disregarded the risk of harm, choosing instead to tolerate and even encourage abuses of force by deliberately ignoring them when they occurred, tacitly accepting a code of silence, and, most importantly, failing to implement adequate systems to control and regulate the use of force, despite their knowledge that such systems are important to ensuring that the use of force is effectively controlled. (*Madrid* 1995: 1251).

Since supermax guards are directly authorised to perform acts involving the use of force and, as discussed above, 'over-diligence' in carrying their tasks is often tolerated by their superiors, they do not need to engage in soul-searching moral assessments of the treatment of prisoners who are *a priori* labelled as the 'worst of the worst'.

Routinisation

The impoverished regime and rigid timetables in supermax prisons and the detailed guidelines stipulating procedures and tools for the control of prisoners as described throughout this book, regulate interactions and dictate relationships between prisoners and prison staff, and to a large extent also predetermine their perceptions of each other. Through such arrangements, after some time, even the most violent and inhuman treatment seems almost 'normal'. Officers who work for long periods in supermax prisons 'can easily become oblivious to the indignities of the situations that prisoners routinely endure. This comes about not because of the callousness or insensitivity of the officers, but rather because they have 'gotten used to it"' (Haney 2008: 965). Concluding one of the few published studies of prison guards in the USA and 'their world', Kauffman (1988) quotes a former Walpole state prison guard recollecting how he felt when placing prisoners in filthy segregation cells:

> I know it was a real dump now, when I look at it. But at the time it was just where you go. It wasn't like I stood there every time I had to put somebody in there and I was totally emotional or something like that ... the first time I saw it, it bothered me, and now it bothers me, but at the time it was just ... an everyday thing.[5]

Lynndie England similarly explained in an interview that

> When we first got there, we were like, what's going on? Then you see staff sergeants walking around not saying anything [about the abuse]. You think, OK, obviously it's normal. (*Rumsfeld Knew* 2008)

With time, supermax officers become 'increasingly desensitized to these uses of force [and] they are also rendered more susceptible to "behavioral drift" – the tendency in this context for the stress and exigencies of the situation to blur the line between ethical and unethical treatment' (Haney 2008: 971). Once an act is performed, even if it was somewhat troubling at first, the social and psychological pressures to continue performing it are powerful (Kelman and Hamilton 1989: 17).

Dehumanisation

A common technique for neutralising guilt or moral qualms about the treatment of others is to 'postulate that inmates constitute a class of individuals beyond the claims of morality' (Kauffman 1988: 232). Indeed, depersonalisation and dehumanisation have been identified by scholars as common techniques utilised by the powerful in extreme situations including concentration camps, military operations and massacres, as well as prisons. One prison guard recalled how, when he was placing a prisoner in an isolation cell:

> [He] started yelling and screaming like a wild animal. We had to put a towel around his neck and arms and take him down to seclusion ... there was a full moon out, too, big big moon right above seclusion ... he was a wild man. He wasn't human. There was no way. He wasn't a human being. We weren't dealing with a person. He didn't even feel like a person. (Kauffman 1988: 232)

Another prison guard linked the dehumanisation of prisoners to the fear experienced by staff:

> If you put yourself in a frame of mind that they're animals – I'm a human being; I'm a good human being and they're bad human beings ... it's easy to perpetrate the feeling of animosity, hatred, fear. Because there's a lot of fear in guards, believe me – that fear turns into hate. And how do you deal with that fear? by making him feel less than you. (Kauffman 1988: 231)

The dehumanisation of supermax prisoners begins at a very early stage of official justifications for the creation of supermax prisons, which focus on the need to contain a new breed of 'super predators'. It continues with the creation of classificatory categories of 'dangerousness' which objectify prisoners and make more of the 'category' and less of the 'human' in them, and it is reinforced by the tightly controlled and highly regulated routines in supermaxes, treating prisoners as highly dangerous creatures, capable of superhuman acts of violence – not quite human like the rest of us.

The issue of 'gassing' provides a good illustration of this. Viewed by prison officials as demonstrative of the savage nature of supermax prisoners rather than a manifestation of their emotional distress, such incidents are used to justify the extreme measures of control used against them.

> These guys are a-holes plain and simple. They think nothing of, say, defecating on their hands, waiting for a guard to pass by and slinging it through the bars. That's the kind of person we are dealing with. (Texas prison warden referring to supermax prisoners, in Johnson 1997)

The same process is evident in the 'war on terror', where the label of 'terrorists' or, to use one of the terms favoured by former US President George W. Bush, 'evildoers', enemies whose sole purpose is to kill and destroy 'us', is sufficient to justify any treatment meted out to them. Referring to the abuse of detainees in Abu Ghraib Prison, military personnel explained that,

> Like I said, what he was saying to us ['I hate you. I want to kill you'], and when he was thrashing out at us, I didn't even feel sorry for him at the time. And he's probably out there killing Americans now. (*Rumsfeld Knew 2008*)

> [He was a taxi driver] who has a very anti-coalition presence, a very anti-American presence. 'I want to kill you folks. I'm on a Jihad'.... He was very forthcoming ... and he couldn't wait to ... to ... to kill us all, sir. (A-R investigation interview, *Taguba Report* 2004)

The social distancing between 'us' and 'them' allows prison staff to treat prisoners in a way that would have been inconceivable had they viewed them as people like themselves. As Haney (2008: 963) aptly put it,

> The 'worst of the worst' designation defines the inhabitants of supermax as fundamentally 'other' and dehumanizes, degrades, and demonizes them as essentially different, even from other prisoners. It provides an immediate, intuitive, and unassailable rationale for the added punishment, extraordinary control, and severe deprivation that prevail in supermax.

Denial and neutralisation

Another way for prison staff to manage their daily tasks without difficult psychological imbalances is by denying or minimising the extent of the harmful effects of supermax environments on prisoners. Denial and neutralisation work both outward to justify certain acts and inward, to ease any qualms that the actor may have about the act (Cohen 2001). Interviews with supermax staff illustrate this process at work:

> I've heard people describe the environment here is similar to sensory deprivation, and I don't honestly think that I believe

that because they do have human interaction daily. They talk to their counsellor, they talk to their officers, they talk to the people feeding them and escorting them, they have people walking on the tier interacting with them constantly. [prison officer]

One administrator similarly stated that he did not observe any negative effects of supermax confinement on prisoners, and quickly returned to the narrative of 'they've brought it on themselves':

As far as there being a mental or a physical negative as far as health and welfare, I have not noticed anything in that area. I do notice that once they're here for a while, they realise what a huge mistake they made to get here, all of them wish that they could change, and the ones that have an avenue to leave here, do what they need to do to leave here as fast as they can. The ones that are not going to leave here, realise that there's only, you know, it was a conscious choice to get here and they have to live with that choice.

Asked whether sometimes prisoners were unable to cope with the conditions of their confinement, one supermax officer replied that:

It happens on a small scale – outbursts of anger, temper tantrums are a good indication of when I see somebody who's not coping well. Those are small flare ups. Occasionally we'll have an inmate who won't cope well and we'll get him access to the mental health clinicians and such, and occasionally we will move an inmate out of a unit. But to actually have someone who can't cope to the point where we have to move him is pretty rare. I'd say maybe one every two to three months.

It is at least debatable whether one prisoner completely 'losing it' once every 2 months can be considered as a 'rare' occasion, but some staff members go further than that, and claim that not only is the supermax environment not harmful, but also, for certain prisoners, the 'isolation from opportunity to act out', as one officer put it, has a positive effect on them. In fact, 'with us putting up the walls and barriers for them, they [prisoners] almost seem relieved because they don't have to act out.' Another officer expressed similar sentiments and stated that, mostly, life in the unit is better than life in 'general-population' prisons because prisoners do not feel obliged to participate in criminal or other unauthorised activities of the prison society:

> I think for the most part, most inmates find [this] to be a good place to live and I say that because one hell of a lot of inmates tell me that ... there's actually more room inside those cells than there is a in a general population cell, so if they want to do some exercises in their cell they're perfectly able to do so, and there are a significant number of inmates in our system that feel obliged on a general population yard to do things they might not otherwise do. There's a lot of pressure to carry out assaults on other staff, to pay up part of your canteen, or a package you might receive from home, in order to be left alone, and when you're housed alone, you're removed from those pressures and for that reason, for a number of inmates, it's a much less stressful place to be. [administrator]

One is reminded of comments made by Dick Cheney, the former US vice president, in respect of detainees in Guantánamo Bay, who, according to him, had nothing to complain about:

> They're living in the tropics.... They're well fed. They've got everything they could possibly want. There isn't any other nation in the world that would treat people who were determined to kill Americans the way we're treating these people. (CNN 2005)

Beyond such upbeat declarations, which nullify and neutralise the adverse effects of the regime and conditions in supermax prisons, prison staff also made other unintentional but telling comments. Take, for example, one teacher who runs a programme of videotaped courses transmitted to prisoners in their cells. In an interview, she stated that she did not observe any adverse effects of the environment, but went on to describe prisoners who struggle to interact with other human beings or to maintain a sense of time, two 'symptoms' identified by mental health professionals as indicative of mental deterioration:

> Inmates who have been in [supermax] setting for a period of time are not used to interacting with others. So it takes a period of time to feel comfortable with working with a teacher.... The programme lasts approximately a month; however, it's an open interim programme, meaning that they come in at any time during the programme, so they may see parts of it over again and frankly I've found that because some of these folks are not on the same timeframe, they have their days and nights mixed

up, even though the programme starts normally around 8.30 in the morning, they may not be on that, on that time. [supermax teacher]

'Just deserts'

The claim that prisoners have 'earned their way in' and have done something truly appalling to be placed in a supermax accompanies each and every aspect of these prisons, from their underlying justifications through to the prisoner classification system, their architectural design, and their daily routines. Summing up what supermax confinement entails for prisoners, one officer said:

> Less access to staff, less personal comfort in their cell, less exposure to opportunity to programme. However, they're all things that the inmates have earned. Nobody is here for not having done something. They've done something to earn their way here.

All the discomforts of life in a supermax unit, then, have been brought upon prisoners by their own behaviour. The alliance between prison officers and victim groups (see Chapter 3) and prison officials' frequent recourse to horror stories about prisoners' dangerousness (see Chapter 7) also help to 'shift' the blame over anything that happens to them in supermaxes onto the prisoners themselves. This technique of 'condemning the condemners' (Sykes and Matza 1957) allows prison workers to further neutralise any criticisms of their chosen policies and practices and helps them to justify, to themselves and others, the harsh treatment of supermax prisoners.

The processes identified above – authorisation, routinization, dehumanisation, neutralisation – and the sense that prisoners are getting their just deserts, enable staff not to question the treatment they mete out to prisoners, its moral implications and its effects. Free of moral dilemmas, they go about their jobs with occasional outbursts of extreme violence. Where such outbursts occur, the strong code of silence and backing of their powerful unions often mean that violent and arbitrary treatment of prisoners goes unpunished. In an environment where the relationship between the ruled and their rulers is predetermined and hugely unbalanced, the violent treatment of prisoners may not be a by-product but an inherent feature of supermax environments. In what follows, I examine how prisoners experience isolated confinement, and how they are affected by it.

Degraded and alone: views from the cells

And never a human voice comes near
  To speak a gentle word:
And the eye that watches through the door
  Is pitiless and hard:
And by all forgot, we rot and rot,
  With soul and body marred.

And thus we rust Life's iron chain
  Degraded and alone:
And some men curse, and some men weep
  And some men make no moan:
But God's eternal Laws are kind
  And break the heart of stone.

(Oscar Wilde, *The Ballad of Reading Gaol*, 1896)

All forms of imprisonment involve some restriction of prisoners' movement, social interactions and sensory stimulation, which is likely to cause them a certain degree of stress and discomfort. Sykes' (1958) classic study of a New Jersey maximum security prison drew attention to the impact of prison environments on the psychological well-being of prisoners and identified five deprivations experienced by prisoners as the main causes of what he termed the 'pains of imprisonment': deprivation of liberty, deprivation of autonomy, deprivation of goods and services, deprivation of heterosexual relationships, and loss of security. Isolated prisoners suffer an aggravated form of the deprivations listed by Sykes: the deprivation of liberty is extended to include liberty within the prison as they rarely leave their cell; the deprivation of personal autonomy is extended, as previously discussed, to every detail of the prisoner's life; the deprivation of goods and services is similarly substantially worse than that experienced by prisoners in general population prisons; the deprivation of heterosexual relationships in regular prisons extends to include, in solitary confinement, also homosexual relationships, and any other form of human touch, as prisoners do not have any physical contact with others; finally, the loss of security which in Sykes' typology refers to threats by other prisoners, takes an interesting turn in isolated environments in that the potential threat to prisoners' safety and security is posed by guards, not other prisoners.

In addition to suffering an aggravated form of the deprivations suffered by all prisoners, isolated prisoners suffer a unique deprivation which is potentially one of the most painful deprivations that we can experience as social beings: the deprivation of human contact and social interactions, even ones of a hostile nature. Sykes noted that 'the deprivations and frustrations of prison life cannot be eliminated, it is true, but their consequences can be partially neutralized' by the presence of a cohesive inmate society (1958: 107). This option is not available to prisoners isolated in supermax prisons, who can suffer the deprivations listed above for very prolonged periods of time. The psychological assault on them thus works in two parallel dimensions: isolation increases levels of frustration and anxiety, and it also decreases the available avenues for releasing such tensions.

Throughout the long history of its use in prisons – from the 'silent' and 'separate' penitentiaries of the nineteenth century through to modern segregation units and supermax prisons – health practitioners and researchers have observed the adverse effects of solitary confinement on prisoners' health.[6] These are so severe that, in the context of coercive interrogation, international experts have identified solitary confinement as psychological torture.[7] Prisoners, too, have reported profound effects and the unusual techniques they have employed to combat them. The cumulative findings of these reports present unequivocal evidence of the damaging effects of solitary confinement, particularly for those with pre-existing mental health disorders, and indicate that it may also actively cause mental illness.

The extent of psychological damage varies and will depend on individual factors (e.g. personal background and pre-existing health problems), environmental factors (e.g. physical conditions and provisions), regime (e.g. time out of cell, degree of human contact), and the context of isolation (e.g. punishment, own protection, voluntary/ non-voluntary, political/criminal) and its duration. Notwithstanding variations in individual tolerance and environmental and contextual factors, there is nonetheless remarkable consistency in the accounts of prisoners and in research findings on the health effects of solitary confinement throughout the decades, up to and including studies of supermax prisons. In what follows, I examine some of these findings and prisoners' accounts of how they were affected by life in perpetual isolation and under strict control.

The pains of isolation

How do I explain desperation to one who is not desperate? ... Try to imagine living in a room the size of your bathroom ... try to imagine the stress of keeping oneself both mentally and physically healthy in a place where physical movement is completely limited, where there is little stimulation except one's own thoughts ... try to imagine coping with this day after endless day for almost 11 years ... [Texas Management Control Unit (MCU) prisoner] (Lutalo 1995)

I hold this slow and daily tampering with the mysteries of the brain, to be immeasurably worse than any torture of the body. (Dickens 1842: 147)

For most prisoners, being held in solitary confinement is a stressful experience. The prisoner is socially isolated from others, and his human contacts reduced to superficial transactions with staff and infrequent contact with family and friends. He is almost completely dependent on prison staff – even more than is usual in the prison setting – for the provision of all his basic needs and his few movements are tightly controlled and closely observed. Confined to a small sparsely furnished cell with little or no view of the outside world and with limited access to fresh air and natural light, he lives in an environment with little stimulation and few opportunities to occupy himself.

Each of the three main factors inherent in solitary confinement and brought to an extreme in supermax prisons – social isolation, reduced environmental stimulation, and loss of control over almost all aspects of daily life – is potentially distressing. Together they create a potent mix whose effects are most acutely felt by those with less resilient personalities. Prisoners are a particularly vulnerable population, with more than half of the total prison and jail populations in the USA reported to suffer from a mental health problem and large numbers of prisoners with learning difficulties.[8]

The prevalence of mental illness in supermax prisoners has been found to be particularly high. Haney's study of 100 randomly selected prisoners at Pelican Bay SHU reported a very high prevalence of symptoms of psychological trauma, with 91 per cent of the prisoners sampled suffering from anxiety and nervousness, more than 80 per cent suffering from headaches, lethargy and trouble in sleeping, and 70 per cent fearing impending breakdown. More than half of the prisoners suffered from nightmares, dizziness and heart palpitations. Other reported mental health problems included ruminations, irrational anger and confused thought processes (more than 80 per cent of prisoners sampled), chronic depression (77 per cent), hallucinations (41 per cent) and overall deterioration (Haney 1994, 2003). A survey of 131 randomly selected prisoners in Washington state's supermax units, found that 45 per cent of them suffered from serious mental illness (Lovell 2008). Forensic psychiatrist Terry Kupers notes that

> Every prisoner placed in an environment as stressful as a Supermax unit, whether especially prone to mental breakdown or seemingly very sane, eventually begins to lose touch with reality and exhibit some signs and symptoms of psychiatric decomposition. (Kupers 1993: 56)

Below, I briefly examine how prisoners experience the three main aspects inherent in solitary confinement units and brought to an extreme in supermax prisons, namely social isolation, reduced sensory input, and the totality of control.

Social isolation

Isolated prisoners are removed from the company of others and deprived of most forms of meaningful and sympathetic social interaction, as well as physical contact with other human beings.[9] Social learning theories highlight the importance of social contact with others not just for pleasure and play but also for the individual's very sense of 'self', which is shaped and maintained through social interactions. Social contact is crucial for forming perceptions, concepts, interpreting reality and providing support.

> The self ... is essentially a social structure and it arises in social experience. After a self has arisen, it in a certain sense provides for itself its social experiences, and so we can conceive of an absolutely solitary self. But it is impossible to conceive of a self arising outside social experience. When it has arisen we can think of a person in solitary confinement for the rest of his life, but who still has himself as a companion, and is able to think and to converse with himself as he had communicated with others.... *This process of abstraction cannot be carried on indefinitely* [my emphasis] (Mead 1934: 140)

Paradoxically, social isolation can lead to further withdrawal from contact with others. Many isolated prisoners protect themselves by 'going mute', or what we may term 'protective apathy': If prisoners cannot physically escape their reality, they can at least escape it psychologically (Sykes 1958: 80). One study found support for the hypothesis that the 'shut-in' or 'seclusive' personality, 'generally considered to be the basis of schizophrenia, may be the result of an extended period of 'cultural isolation', that is, separation from intimate and sympathetic social contact' (Faris 1934: 155). Faris adds that 'seclusiveness is frequently the last stage of a process that began with exclusion or isolation which was not the choice of the patient' (1934: 159). Hans Toch coined the term 'isolation panic' to describe the experiences of isolated prisoners. Symptoms of this syndrome include

A feeling of abandonment ... dead-end desperation ... helplessness, tension. It is a physical reaction, a demand for release or a need to escape at all costs.... [Isolated prisoners] feel caged rather than confined, abandoned rather than alone, suffocated rather than isolated. They react to solitary confinement with surges of panic or rage. They lose control, break down, regress. (Toch 1992: 49)

Prisoners who have been isolated commonly report that they found it hard to distinguish between reality and their own thoughts, or found reality so painful that they created their own fantasy world. Researchers link such incidents to the absence of external stimuli, which results in the brain starting to create its own stimulation, manifesting in fantasy and hallucinations. One study of prisoners who were isolated for periods ranging from 11 days to 10 months reported both auditory and visual hallucinations. One interviewee described how 'the cell walls start wavering ... everything in the cell starts moving; you feel that you are losing your vision.' Others reported auditory hallucinations: 'I overhear guards talking. Did they say that? Yes? No? It gets confusing. Am I losing my mind?' Prisoners also reported high sensitivity to noise and smells: 'You get sensitive to noise. The plumbing system ... the water rushes through the pipes – it's too loud, gets on your nerves. I can't stand it. Meals – I can't stand the smells.... The only thing I can stand is the bread' (Grassian 1983). Others, including my interviewees, have reported similar experiences, including hypersensitivity to sound and smell, having imaginary conversations, hallucinations and fear of impending death.

Your vision was highly restricted, so you live by sound ... you could hear every creaking of the place, you know, the building. It was almost amplified ... not that our hearing was better, it was just that we paid more attention because sound had to do with ... with life. [former prisoner]

Sometimes I felt like I was losing my mind, or that I have lost it already, you know.... Holding conversations with myself ... I had conversations with people. I mean dialogues, long dialogues with people. Some of them I knew, and some of them I didn't know. There were times when the darkness wasn't dark. I could see faces ... I think that I found out that I may be hallucinating when I touched my eyes and my eyes were open so I kind of knew I wasn't dreaming. After a while I thought that maybe I will die there. I really thought I would. [former prisoner]

[You] start talking to yourself. Who do you ... who else are you going to talk to, you know? And start answering yourself back, like a crazy person, you know. I thought that I would be probably going off the deep end. [former prisoner]

I found solitary confinement the most forbidding aspect of prison life. There is no end and no beginning; there is only one's mind, which can begin to play tricks. Was that a dream or did it really happen? One begins to question everything. (Mandela 1994)

Similar experiences were reported in Siegel's (1984) study of 31 people who were subjected to isolation, visual deprivation and restraint on physical movement as hostages, prisoners of war or convicted prisoners over varying periods. All interviewees reported visual and auditory hallucinations that appeared within hours of being isolated and became more and more elaborate as time went by. Prisoners participating in Toch's (1992) large-scale study of the psychological effects of incarceration reported similar experiences in solitary confinement. One interviewee, for example, described his first days in isolation:

And then I lay on the mattress, and then after I sit there I feel the walls coming in around me. And then when the guards come in and I am screaming, they say: 'What the fuck is going on here?' and I say 'The walls are closing in on me' and they say 'That's tough, you're going to die anyway. We'll strangle you' ... I was thinking that if I don't get the hell out of there, they're going to kill me. And I don't feel like fighting them. (Toch 1992: 150)

A former prisoner who spent two years in a supermax prison chose to refer to 'seeing others lose it' and described similar scenes:[10]

I have seen inmates lose their mind completely because of the sound of a light where they are yelling at the light, cursing at the light, believing that for some reason the [authorities] planted some kind of noise inside the light purposely ... and so the inmates that ain't strong-minded, don't have something to hang on to, the light, the sound of the door, can make them lose their mind.... I found it strange, you know, how can a grown man, a very big, grown man, break down to a light. But that's what [that place] can do. And once you lose your mind, you don't know right from wrong. You don't know that you're breaking a rule. You don't know what to do exactly.

Seeing and hearing other prisoners break down is a stressful experience in itself, as Henri Charrière (*Papillon*) found during his time in isolation on 'Devil's Island', a penal colony in French Guiana: 'A great many suicides and men going raving mad around me ... it's depressing to hear men shouting, weeping or moaning for hours or even days on end.' He himself survived 8 years in solitary confinement through fantasy: 'Thanks to my wandering amongst the stars it was very rare that I ever had a lasting despair. I got over them pretty fast and quickly invented a real or imaginary voyage that would dispel the black ideas' (Charrière 1970: 354–6).

One of the problems with such techniques is that the boundaries between fantasy and reality can become dangerously blurred, as was the case for one former female prisoner, who regularly 'left her body' to 'travel' in the outside world. These were not daydreams, but out-of-body experiences from which at times, according to her, it was 'really hard to come back':

The first four years of prison was such a fantasy world ... I was in segregation. I could be in my cell and shut everyone out and I would go travelling. I would go up and out of prison and fly over the beaches and mountains of Okinawa, where I used to live. Sometimes it was really, really hard to come back.

As her time in isolation grew longer, so did the intensity and frequency of her 'travels', until one day the prison chaplain saw her lying on her cell floor in a near catatonic state and took her under his wing. British prisoner Doug Wakefield had somewhat less pleasant hallucinations after a period in isolation, 'usually in the form of spiders and insects crawling over the floor, the bed and walls, and at such times it is common to hear voices and strange noises' (Wakefield 1980: 28). Describing himself as a 'graduate of 1000 days in segregation', he wrote: 'Fantasising and day-dreaming become prevalent pastimes and the obvious danger here is that this activity could become a permanent feature of the mind with the consequent disadvantage of not knowing at times whether you are in reality or fantasy' (*ibid.* at p. 30).

In supermax settings, where the prisoner has no contact with his fellow prisoners and very limited contact with prison staff, prisoners are reluctant to seek help and may deteriorate without anyone noticing.

> I never had that problem before where ... where [at] the front of [the] cell I saw the mesh, and I was just standing there and looking out, and all of a sudden it just starts moving like going like waving. And I was like, Woaw, you know, what is all that, you know. And then I, I opened my eyes some more and tried to check it out again, and it would, it would move. It, it just, it was strange. I never experienced anything like that before except if I was on drugs or something. But I wasn't under any drug. And I ... I didn't think to ask anybody else if they were experiencing that because I thought well they'll think I'm crazy if I say something like that, then they just take it as a weakness, you know, and laugh at you. So I didn't say anything about that. [former prisoner]

Reduced activity and sensory input

Monotony, reduced sensory input and boredom are part and parcel of the experience of isolation. Even in the isolation prisons of the nineteenth century, where prisoners had access to work, great care was taken to ensure that they were given intentionally dull jobs, performed in complete silence. Supermax prisoners are held in their sparsely furnished cells for at least 22.5 hours a day, with little sensory or mental stimulation. They have no access to work and limited, if any, access to educational programmes and other diversions such as hobby and craft materials. Prisoners' accounts illustrate the effects of monotony and boredom on their mental state after a period of isolation:

> Boredom is a major enemy. Sensory deprivation is a way of life. There is simply nothing to do. Sit in your bathroom alone with none of your intimate possessions and try to imagine years of it, week after week. Slowly it tears you down, mentally and physically. (a prisoner in Florida's supermax, cited in the Campaign to Stop Control Units Report 1997)

> The utter and monstrous boredom that becomes so obvious after a short period of isolation is an all-powering one ... in order to fight off the tendency to complete idleness and to retain a hold on the senses, it is necessary to make great exertions.... Yet no matter how successful a prisoner may be in staving off the effects of ... isolation, it is only a matter of time before it catches up with him. (Wakefield 1980: 28)

> You sit in solitary confinement stewing in nothingness, not merely your own nothingness but the nothingness of society, others, the world. The lethargy of months that add up to years in a cell, alone, entwines itself about every 'physical' activity of the living body and strangles it slowly to death, the horrible decay of the truly living dead. You no longer do push-ups or other physical exercise in your small cell; you no longer pace the four steps back and forth across you cell. You no longer masturbate; you can call forth no vision of eroticism in any form ... time descends in your cell like the lid of a coffin in which you lie and watch it as it slowly closes over you ... solitary confinement in prison can alter the ontological makeup of a stone. (Abbott 1982: 44–5).

These personal accounts are supported by studies which indicate that reduced sensory input may lead to reduced brain activity. Building on the input-output theory, one study suggested that sensory input and motor-mental output work in parallel:

> A drop in sensory input through sensory restriction produces a drop in mental alertness, an inability to concentrate, a drop in planning and motivation, together with a drop in physical activity in the speech and motor systems.... In prison life

boredom generates boredom. A drop in stimulus input results in mental sluggishness, a disinclination to learn and a correlated drop in planning, motivation and physical activity. (Scott and Gendreau 1969: 338)

To evaluate this hypothesis, the brain activity of isolated prisoners was measured daily. Researchers found that after 7 days in isolation there was a decline in brain activity. This decline 'was correlated with apathetic, lethargic behaviour... and with a reduction in stimulation seeking behaviour. Up to seven days the EEG decline is reversible, but if deprived over a long period this may not be the case' (Scott and Gendreau, *ibid.*). To counteract the effects of boredom and restricted sensory input, the researchers suggested that it was crucial that prisoners have access to an adequate programme of activities in captivity, particularly in high-security prisons: 'The greater the security of an institution, the more intense must be its activity program. Maximum prison lock-up without an appropriate activity program is detrimental to the inmate's health and his rehabilitative prognosis.' Ideally, such programmes should be offered in association with other prisoners, but where association is impracticable, in-cell provisions can also be of value (Scott and Gendreau 1969: 341). Most prison systems operate security classification systems which not only ignore such recommendations, but also are designed to operate in a diametrically opposite way, as prisoners' access to programmes and other sources of stimulation declines as their security classification increases and, in supermax prisons, is reduced to an absolute minimum. The monotonous atmosphere, impoverished regime and limited provisions in supermax prisons may thus potentially result in reduced brain activity and the associated symptoms as described above.

The totality of control

They [Department of Corrections] ... take control of the rest of the inmates' body as far as they have 'em, they already have them isolated, they already have his body, they already took his freedom, they already took his clothing, they took most of his pride and now they're working on the mind – and that would be the last thing that they would take. [former prisoner]

I'm not going to allow them to destroy my sense of hope, because there's always a greater picture, you know, they could

destroy your physical body but not your spirit ... that's how I
look at it. [supermax prisoner]

A third aspect of segregated confinement is the rigid regime and
exceptionally high level of control over all aspects of prisoners' lives.
In the case of supermax prisons, as discussed throughout this book,
this control is extreme, as prisoners are completely dependent on staff
for the provision of all their basic needs and have few avenues to
exercise personal autonomy. When this degree of control is exercised
over long periods of time, the psychological impact is proportionally
greater. Studies examining the socio-psychological aspects of long-term
imprisonment in highly controlled environments have identified some
common psychological reactions.[11] These typically range from apathy
to aggression: 'Either reaction to the system of rigid discipline tends
to become something very much like insanity – apathy, listlessness,
vagaries, or else irritability, hatred and nervous instability' (Sutherland
and Cressey 1955: 473). Another study similarly noted that over time,
symptoms experienced by isolated prisoners are 'likely to mature into
either homicidal or suicidal behaviour' (McCleery 1961: 265).

Since prisoners are confined to their isolated cells and have
no contact with others, the main possible outlet of aggression is
towards oneself. Historical reports of nineteenth-century isolation
prisons repeatedly describe acts of autoaggression, self-mutilation,
and suicide. Contemporary studies have also shown that self-harm
and suicides are more common in isolation units than in the general
prison population (Haney and Lynch 1997: 525). In California, for
example, a reported 69 per cent of prison suicides in 2005 occurred
in segregated housing units (*USA Today*, 27 December 2006).

Other forms of self-harm are also prevalent in solitary confinement.
Researchers have noted that self-mutilation or cutting is often 'a result
of sudden frustration from situational stress with no permissible
physical outlet.... Self-addressed aggression forms the only activity
outlet' (Scott and Gendreau 1969: 341). Another study found that
self-mutilation was a means to 'liberate the self from unbearable
tension – the physical pain becomes a compensatory substitute for
psychic pain or shame' (Dabrowski (1937) cited in McCleery 1961:
303). Former prisoners have testified that self-harm played another
role for them when they were isolated – it asserted that they were
still alive.

I was totally frustrated ... I started smashing up the cell. I
refused to eat. I started refusing water. I was totally paranoid.

I started sipping my own urine because I thought they were trying to poison me. I resorted to self-injury, was put in a body belt. You become so angry. It's an outlet, but you have to vent it out. Even your own blood is something real.

I found myself curled up in a foetal position rocking myself back and forth and banging my head against the wall. In the absence of sensation, it's hard sometimes to convince yourself that you're really there.

Rather than controlling violence, then, supermax confinement can lead to irritability, anger and violent outbursts, often unprovoked. In the absence of contact with others, such violent outbursts are mostly turned upon the prisoner himself. Where the prisoner does become more docile and apparently conforms to the rules, it may, in fact, be a pathological reaction in the form of withdrawal, emotional numbing and apathy. Further, the 'totality of control' means that some prisoners become so reliant on the prison to organise their lives and daily routines that they lose the capacity to exercise personal autonomy. This may render them dysfunctional in society upon their release.

Isolation and mental illness

Most observers agree that for mentally ill prisoners, isolation can be a determinate factor.[12] The courts, as previously noted, increasingly order departments of corrections to remove the mentally ill from isolated settings, though, so far, they have been less willing to find that supermax conditions can actively cause mental illness. The *Madrid* court found that for certain categories of prisoners, placement at Pelican Bay SHU violated the Eighth Amendment's prohibition of cruel and unusual punishment: [13]

Such inmates consist of the already mentally ill, as well as persons with borderline personality disorders, brain damage or mental retardation, impulse-ridden personalities, or a history of prior psychiatric problems or chronic depression. For these inmates, placing them in the SHU is the mental equivalent of putting an asthmatic in a place with little air to breathe. The risk is high enough that we have no hesitancy in finding that the risk is plainly 'unreasonable'. (*Madrid* 1995: 1265)

Kupers observes that

> The forced idleness and isolation in these units cause many previously stable men and women to exhibit no signs of serious mental illness. But for people who already suffer from mental disorders, the segregation environment is totally intolerable. Meanwhile, a significant proportion of prisoners with psychiatric problems are selectively funnelled into segregated housing. In other words, they misbehave on account of their mental illness, but since they are not likely to be diagnosed and treated adequately, they are punished with time in 'the hole'. If they attempt suicide or self-mutilation, they are punished for their illegal attempts to harm themselves with more time in the punitive segregation. (Kupers 1999: 33)

Since isolated prisoners have little interaction with others, their deterioration may go unobserved. Even when prisoners 'act out' or completely shut off psychologically, they are more likely to be viewed by guards and, more worryingly, by prison medical professionals, as malingering, or being 'bad' rather than 'mad'.[14] Incidents of 'gassing' (see Chapters 5 and 7), for example, can be viewed as a reaction to the supermax environment, and as a manifestation of mental illness. In psychoanalytical terms, 'gassing' may signify emotional breakdown and perhaps regression to a primal childhood trauma. While in a supportive environment such regression is an important stage in the therapeutic process, in the behaviourist-orientated supermax environments it signifies a disciplinary problem that calls for punishment. As a former supermax prisoner observed,

> Like an inmate who wipes himself with human faeces, I mean, just shows he don't got a mind. I mean if you're gonna wipe yourself with faeces there's something wrong with you. But as [the Department of Corrections] looked at it, he was breaking a rule.

Some of the 'pains of imprisonment' described above are also suffered, albeit to a lesser degree, by prisoners in general-population prisons, particularly high-security facilities. The critical difference, however, is that supermax prisoners do not have contact with each other and little contact with prison staff, and therefore the survival mechanism of social interaction is not available to them. To be sure, one of the purposes of supermax prisons, as noted, is to fragment the prison society.

The acute and chronic pains of imprisonment, including in some cases mental disintegration, experienced by those in supermaxes, may have lasting consequences. In what follows I examine how prisoners react to being released from supermax confinement. These reactions are important not only to understand some of the socio-psychological scars of solitary confinement, but also to assess the possible implications of prolonged solitary confinement on recidivism rates and the rehabilitation and reintegration prospects of large numbers of prisoners.

Release from isolation

So now you're out here, you know, just spending let's say two years in isolation by yourself not even talking to nobody and all of a sudden, boom, they kick you out the door, boom you're right there in a bus, a bus depot, people around you … freedom, you know, people going by you fast, people looking at you, somebody bumps into you, I mean you have to, boom, go into the bathroom, gather your thoughts, gather yourself and realise that wait a minute, wait a minute, there's other people that live out here in this world, I'm not in a cell no more. [former prisoner]

My character and personality have undergone many negative changes and I am now a very paranoid and suspicious person. The paranoia has become so extensive that I find it impossible to trust anyone anymore and I have developed a tendency to hate people for no apparent reason. (Wakefield 1980: 30)

You just become so you can't be around other people. [former prisoner]

Being locked away in like a dark place like that, has made me feel a lot of different about who I am, you know. I mean, I will carry that with me no matter what. I have those memories. I mean, they're gonna be long lasting memories in my mind – a lesson learned. [former prisoner]

I mean, while they are isolating individuals, they're feeding them 'You're violent. You're violent. You don't belong in society' … This all sinks into your mind and you know, you have to pull yourself away from all this negative talk, you know, you're the animal. No. I'm not an animal. I'm a human being. Although they had me inside a real cage like an animal, I'm not. I'm a human being. [former prisoner]

Many prisoners find the transition from life in solitary confinement to coexistence with others, be it in general-population prisons or in free society, sharp and unsettling. Some of the very survival skills that they adopted in reaction to their painful environment while isolated, such as 'going mute', are dysfunctional upon their release. They become so dependent on the structure and routines of the prison for controlling their behaviour that they find it difficult to function without them. One prisoner who was due to be released from a supermax unit directly back to the community a week later expressed some apprehension about life as a free man:

> I'm just conditioned, you know, after so many years of being on [here] it's, it's just basically conditions you ... you know, you got your same routine every, you know, day in and day out. I'm not used to that, all that freedom and stuff like that ... I'm more used to be confined, just because I've been doing it for so long, because I've been structured since I was like thirteen years old, you know ... it's just part of the programme for me now. It's hard to explain, you know.

The problem of having become institutionalised is, of course, experienced by many prisoners upon their release, but it takes on a much more acute form when the transition is from years of social isolation. In this sense, the effects of social isolation *and* near total control are much more profound than what Clemmer (1940) termed 'prisonization', in that in addition to 'taking on, in greater or lesser degree the folkways, mores, customs and general culture of the prison', supermax prisoners take on the mores of social recluses who have learned how to 'live inside their own head'. Researchers asserted long ago that the shock of leaving highly restricted environments and re-entering free society may be so overwhelming that some formerly isolated prisoners will seek to return to prison:

> The deprived inmate cannot adjust to a sudden release into free society because his mental and emotional mechanisms are adjusted to the deprivation circumstances. He cannot tolerate the myriad sensory input in normal environments with its pace, noise, confusion and instant decision making. Anxiety, restlessness, sleeplessness and irritability become so great in the released ex-inmate that he may seek means to return to prison with its retarded input and routine existence. (Scott and Gendreau 1969: 340)

Other studies similarly reported long-lasting symptoms in formerly isolated individuals, including sleep disturbances, nightmares, depression, anxiety, phobias, emotional dependence, confusion, and impaired memory and concentration (Hocking 1970: 4–26). But the lasting effects of solitary confinement are perhaps most evident in social settings and with interpersonal relationships:

> Although many of the acute symptoms suffered by inmates are likely to subside upon termination of solitary confinement many [prisoners], including some who did not become overtly psychiatrically ill during their confinement in solitary, will likely suffer permanent harm ... this harm is most commonly manifested by a continued intolerance to social interaction, a handicap which often prevents the inmate from successfully readjusting to ... general population prison and often severely impairs the inmate's capacity to reintegrate into the broader society upon release from imprisonment. (Grassian 2006: 332)

Unable to regain the necessary social skills for leading a 'normal' life, many former prisoners continue to live in relative social isolation after their release. Indeed, this was a common thread in the experiences of the former prisoners whom I interviewed. They all reported that they cannot handle big social gatherings, and tend to live in relative seclusion. With one exception, none of them developed a lasting intimate relationship since their release. The one exception was a man who was held in punitive isolation for a relatively short time in the 1960s and now leads a 'normal' work and family life. But even for him, the experience of isolation resurfaced when, more than 30 years later, he had to undergo an MRI scan.

> I laid back and tried to relax. When the machine moved and I was inside it, I started screaming; I was back there, back inside that cell. The nurse got me out as fast as she could but the memories all came back.

A female former prisoner who was isolated for 4 years and was released from prison 2 years earlier said that once in a while she has to lock herself in a small room in her home, where she stays for a few hours in complete silence. She still feels bouts of inexplicable rage, and has joined a local church for support. Another former supermax prisoner lives in a tiny studio flat not much bigger than his cell and spends most of his time working during the day and watching TV in the evening. He said that he still feels uncomfortable in large crowds:

> I mean there are still times where I may go to the walk-in and after the movie's over and they turn on the light, you know, it's like I've been in the dark and all of the sudden the light comes on and boom all these millions of people around me, I'm like, you know, looking around like, okay, okay, who's gonna hit me, what's gonna happen, you know. I mean, you feel real uncomfortable and then all of a sudden you start shaking, you know, you feel your heart beat and then you realise, wait a minute, I'm at a theatre, what am I tripping on? There ain't nobody out here all crazy. I'm not in prison. It gets real uncomfortable when I'm around a big crowd. Like sometimes even going to the grocery store I feel uncomfortable, you know, when people look at me, and I'm wondering, you know, wow, what are they looking at?

These former prisoners are a relative 'success' in official terms, as they have not reoffended, nor have they suffered extreme mental illness. But their social skills were, quite clearly, severely eroded, and they lived a relatively lonely, secluded life.

Many former prisoners are simply unable to adjust and return to prison shortly after their release. Others who were released after years in isolation go on to commit truly horrible crimes. One parolee who was released from Pelican Bay SHU was arrested a day after his release and charged with raping and viciously beating a young woman with a tyre iron. Prior to his incarceration in the SHU, the man was a small-time car thief (Cummins 1994: 274). A young man who was released from a supermax unit in Arizona slaughtered his mother and three local people in a small motel hours after his release. Such incidents are used by prison staff as evidence of how dangerous 'those' prisoners are, but, as one supermax prisoner pointed out, the prison environment may be equally and directly responsible:

> It's like the same thing about Frankenstein creating the monster, and the monster ends up turning on Frankenstein … so in this instance here, Frankenstein ends up turning on the citizens.

The logic behind this familiar claim seems obvious; as a former prisoner said, 'If you treat someone like a dog they will act as one.'

When asked what he thought of the practice of releasing prisoners from isolation directly back to the community, a senior supermax administrator suggested that the practice would endanger the public:

> If it were a matter of inmate Jones going to [supermax] and spending ten years there, and then you walk up, then you put him in handcuffs, put him in leg-irons, walk him up to the front gate, take the leg-irons off, take the handcuffs off and say, 'Okay, try not to hurt anybody today,' that's a scary thing. I think that most citizens would be [worried], and I think that ... the fear could be well founded.

Although this suggestion ignores the inadequacy of pre-release programmes, where any are offered at all,[15] clearly some form of preparation for prisoners who have been isolated for years is more beneficial than none at all. Research has shown that recidivism rates of supermax prisoners who were released directly back to the community were significantly higher than those of prisoners who left a supermax 3 months or more before their release, as well as those of non-supermax prisoners (Lovell *et al.* 2007). Yet some prison administrators maintain a narrower view. When asked whether he was concerned about the release of isolated prisoners directly back to the community, the response of another supermax official reflected the short-term view of a prison bureaucrat:

> Once an inmate leaves this facility, he is a citizen, he's earned his right to go back into society and he's not a concern of mine any longer. I am totally focused on the individuals that are here.

The consequences of bureaucratic attitudes such as those expressed above may be felt not only by prisoners, but also by society at large. In the case of supermax confinement, administrative and managerial decisions and practices may have some serious implications well beyond the institutional level in which they operate. The public may or may not be concerned about the mental well-being of its prisoners, or have moral qualms about how they are treated in the name of its protection. Surely, though, 'high crime societies' (Garland 2001) should be concerned about recidivism rates and the prospect of tens of thousands of former prisoners, who have lived in a world devoid of social interaction and human contact being released, without any preparation for the transition, from being 'entombed in steel and concrete' (Lutalo 1995) to the overwhelming stimulation of modern life.

Notes

1 Frank Valdez died on 17 July 1999. Three guards were later charged with second-degree murder, but acquitted of all charges on 16 February 2002, because the jurors (drawn from rural towns whose economies are dependent on prisons) could not determine which one of them was responsible for the fatal blow.

2 At least two of the key people involved, Charles Garner and 'Chip' Frederick, previously worked as prison guards in the USA. Some of the reported acts of abuse included 'Punching, slapping, and kicking detainees; jumping on their naked feet; Videotaping and photographing naked male and female detainees; Forcibly arranging detainees in various sexually explicit positions for photographing; Forcing detainees to remove their clothing and keeping them naked for several days at a time; Forcing naked male detainees to wear women's underwear; Forcing groups of male detainees to masturbate themselves while being photographed and videotaped; Arranging naked male detainees in a pile and then jumping on them; Positioning a naked detainee on a MRE Box, with a sandbag on his head, and attaching wires to his fingers, toes, and penis to simulate electric torture; Placing a dog chain or strap around a naked detainee's neck and having a female Soldier pose for a picture; A male MP [military police] guard having sex with a female detainee; Using military working dogs (without muzzles) to intimidate and frighten detainees, and in at least one case biting and severely injuring a detainee; Taking photographs of dead Iraqi detainees' (*Taguba Report*, 2004).

3 In February 2004, the California Department of Corrections issued a 'code of silence memo' to all its employees, introducing a 'zero tolerance policy' concerning it. Enacting recommendations made by the Corrections Independent Review Panel (2004), new recruits now also receive special training in ethics and how to deal with the 'code of silence', and all employees are required to sign a code of conduct detailing penalties for not reporting violations of the code.

4 Milgram's (1974) experiment powerfully demonstrated the high levels of obedience achieved in authority situations. The experimental subjects were told that they were participating in a learning experiment, and were instructed to administer electric shocks to a person carrying out a learning task whenever he made an error. To measure obedience, Milgram used the extent to which the subject complied with the experimenter's request to increase the level of 'shock' given to the person doing the learning task for each successive error they made. Sixty-five per cent of the subjects complied even when they believed that they were delivering

dangerous levels of electric shocks, although doing so clearly distressed them.

5 Kauffman 1988: 226. The study focused on the Massachusetts prison system during a period which was 'violent and tumultuous' in US prisons, 1976–80, and is based on interviews with 60 prison officers working in the four major state prisons for men, including Walpole prison.

6 Some of the reported symptoms of solitary confinement include physical manifestations (such as poor appetite, back and other joint pains, insomnia, migraine headaches, lethargy and profound fatigue) and psychological symptoms, including anxiety (ranging from feelings of tension to full-blown panic attacks), depression (varying from low mood to social withdrawal to major depression), anger (ranging from irritability to outbursts of physical and verbal violence against others, self and objects and full-blown rage), cognitive disturbances (ranging from lack of concentration to confusional states), perceptual distortions (ranging from hypersensitivity to noises and smells to hallucinations affecting all five senses), and paranoia and psychosis (see Shalev (2008) for fuller discussion).

7 Reyes (2007), Human Rights Watch (2008), Physicians for Human Rights (2005), United Nations Committee Against Torture (2000).

8 Bureau of Justice Statistics (2006a). By way of comparison, 11 per cent of the general US population were reported to suffer a mental health problem during the same time.

9 Some argue that because supermax prisons are modern and well equipped, and prisoners are provided with adequate food and shelter, allowed to have a TV and so on, it cannot be said that prisoners are subjected to sensory or social isolation in the traditional sense. I would argue that technological advances allow stricter isolation and tighter control of prisoners, and that the careful planning of supermax facilities by professional architects, who intentionally design them in a way which maximises isolation and reduces sensory input, and the nuanced attention to every detail of prisoners' daily lives and provisions, make confinement in supermax prisons less humane and more damaging than ever before.

10 As Toch notes 'personal breakdown in isolation does not square with manly self-images and reputations' (1992: 152), so prisoners may find it easier to refer to others 'losing it'. Indeed, independent mental health professionals who had interviewed isolated prisoners noted that they initially expected prisoners to exaggerate their experiences, but instead found that prisoners tended to play them down.

11 See Sutherland and Cressey (1955), Sykes (1958), Goffman (1961) and McCleery (1961). See also Cohen and Taylor's ([1972] 1981) study of prisoners in Durham Prison's maximum-security wing in the late 1960s and Toch's (1992) study of prisoners' reactions to the 'psychological strain of imprisonment'.

12 Despite the clear evidence that solitary confinement is particularly destructive for mentally ill prisoners, Human Rights Watch (2003) found that many jurisdictions held mentally ill prisoners in supermax prisons and other segregated settings.

13 A psychologist who worked at Pelican Bay SHU between 1989 and 1991 estimated that 10–20 per cent of prisoners were mentally disordered and in need of treatment during that period (cited in Kupers (1993: 64)). Kupers notes that the actual number is 'double that figure or more' (*ibid*.). See also Grassian (1993, 1995, 2006), and Haney (1994, 2003).

14 The problem of misdiagnosis of prisoners is an age-old one. In 1943, the Prison Medical Reform Council in the UK published a report identifying 'grave defects' in the Prison Medical Service, including 'an assumption that every prisoner was a malingerer' (cited in Sim 1995: 108). A report on mentally ill prisoners in the USA similarly found that mental health staff working in prisons are 'unduly quick in concluding that prisoners who request psychiatric assistance are malingering … and may be also unduly quick to assign diagnoses of personality disorders rather than Axis I diagnoses' (Human Rights Watch 2003). It should be noted that prisoners with 'personality disorders' are considered to be untreatable and therefore not eligible for specialised medical treatment.

15 In some states, prisoners about to be released from supermax units to general-population prisons or back into the community are offered special programmes, or housed in special units aimed at facilitating the transition. In others, isolated prisoners are released directly back into the community or general-population prisons. Where programmes are offered, they are often very limited in scope and, since security considerations take precedence over therapeutic and rehabilitative considerations, are usually offered to prisoners in their cells via a CCTV system, thus failing to address the main problem facing isolated prisoners: how to live alongside others.

Chapter 9

Evaluating supermax confinement

This chapter pulls together the different threads discussed throughout this book and evaluates supermax confinement and its costs and benefits. This, it seems to me, is an appropriate way to look at contemporary penal systems that claim to operate on a broad cost-benefit rationale, and evaluate themselves accordingly.[1] I also measure the 'proportionality', in its legal sense, of supermax prisons.[2] That is, I examine whether the measures of control (means) used in supermax prisons are proportionate to their official goals (ends).

I start by assessing the success of supermax prisons in achieving their goals as articulated in official objectives as discussed in Chapter 4. I then examine some of the costs of supermax confinement, financially and in terms of their psychological and societal effects, as discussed in Chapters 7 and 8. I then question the utilitarian necessity of some of the additional measures of control used in supermax prisons, and their proportionality to the end they seek to achieve.

Operational success?

How do you measure the success of supermax prisons, and what criteria should be used for evaluating their operation? One obvious measurement is their success in achieving their declared objectives, which emphasise controlling violent and disruptive prisoners and managing risk. As we will recall, it is claimed that by removing 'predators' from the general prison population and holding them in solitary confinement in separate, specially designed facilities (the 'concentration' model), the entire prison system will be safer. Security arrangements in general-population prisons can then be relaxed and programme delivery improved, enabling prisons to operate without disruptions while maintaining prisoner and staff safety. Consistent with this line of reasoning and with 'new penology' discourses, one supermax administrator suggested that

> You measure the success of supermax based on the ability of the rest of the prison system to programme in a functional manner ... that the majority of time the inmates are allowed to go out to their programme – to go to work, to get education, to be out on their yards without having to suffer violent activities out there.

Many prison staff members claim that in these respects supermax prisons are very successful:

> The unit has been an incredible success.... In the ... [since] we've been open, the violence rate in the other prisons has dropped dramatically even while our population in those other prisons has gone up. So what we've done is fulfil the purpose by pulling the predators out. [prison officer]

> I definitely think [that] isolating the violent inmates from a general population setting is a very effective tool for us. Approximately ten years ago when we isolated many of the leaders of the various gangs and moved them [here] ... the violence in all other mainline institutions went down markedly. [administrator]

> One of the most obvious avenues for me to say that this unit not only is a necessity but is a very positive avenue and a very positive management tool ... is because violence among other units within this state has decreased drastically; homicides, serious assaults, any type of crime that can be committed on the streets cannot be committed virtually except, you know, one or two. The crime intimidation, extortion – all those have declined, it's real obvious. The gangs do not have the opportunity to prey on the individuals that choose to come here and try to programme, do what they need to do, pay their debt to society, finish their time and go home and become a responsible individual in society. They have the opportunity now because

they do not have the predators that were once upon a time on those yards making it impossible to do it. [administrator]

How does the rhetoric, though, measure up in practice? Has prison violence decreased since the introduction of supermax prisons? Is there less gang activity? Are prisoners in general-population prisons offered more educational and vocational programmes? Are prison staff and the public safer? Below, I evaluate and refute some of these claims, using, among other sources, official data on prison violence.

Reducing overall prison violence

Focusing on California and using CDCR's own benchmarks of success and its own statistical data, we see that the introduction of supermax prisons has not, in fact, succeeded in reducing violence throughout the prison estate, and may have even contributed to its increase. The *Madrid* court reached similar conclusions, noting that '[CDC] presented the Pelican Bay SHU as a centrepiece of their program to decrease violence in the California prison system. However, evidence regarding the SHU's significance is inconclusive' (*Madrid* 1995: 1263, n. 204).

As Table 9.1 demonstrates, in the first 2 years of Pelican Bay's SHU operation (1990–91) there was a small decrease in overall prison violence, measured by prisoner-on-prisoner and prisoner-on-staff assaults, but since this period of stabilisation, prison violence on these two measures has been steadily increasing. The one indicator that has decreased is the rate of escapes, which can be prevented through fortified perimeter security rather than the strict internal security of supermaxes.

Official data on prison violence do not, then, support claims that the introduction of SHU facilities in California's prison system has reduced prisoner violence. A study of the effects of supermax prisons on levels of institutional violence, carried out by Briggs *et al.* (2003) in three other jurisdictions in the USA (Arizona, Illinois and Minnesota) similarly found no support for the hypothesis that supermax reduces levels of inmate-on-inmate violence system-wide.

Furthermore, past experience with isolation units should have made such findings predictable, as studies assessing their success have revealed mixed results at best. One study which examined the occurrence of prison violence (more specifically, incidents of stabbing and assaults on staff) before and after the introduction of an earlier incarnation of supermax units, the 'special security' or 'lockdown'

Table 9.1 Incidents in CDCR prisons and jails (rate per average 100 prison population) 1980–2006[3]

Year	Total inmate incidents	Inmate-on-staff assaults			Inmate-on-inmate assaults			Escapes	Fatal prisoner injuries (Total numbers)	
		Total	With weapon	Without weapon	Total	With weapon	Without weapon		Shot	Total
1980	12.2	1.4	0.2	1.2	2.0	1.2	0.8	0.45	0	13
1981	11.8	1.4	0.2	1.2	2.1	1.2	0.9	0.50	1*	17
1982	11.7	1.5	0.2	1.3	2.0	1.2	0.9	0.44	0	14
1983	10.9	1.5	0.3	1.2	2.2	1.2	1.0	0.32	0	10
1984	12.7	1.7	0.3	1.4	3.0	2.0	1.0	0.20	1	16
1985	11.6	1.6	0.4	1.3	2.4	1.7	0.7	0.18	1	15
1986	9.6	1.4	0.2	1.2	2.2	1.5	0.7	0.16	1	21
1987	8.5	1.5	0.2	1.2	2.0	1.3	0.6	0.14	7	20
1988	7.1	1.2	0.2	1.0	1.8	1.2	0.6	0.10	2	8
1989	6.5	1.1	0.2	0.9	2.3	1.0	1.3	0.10	5	9
1990	4.7	1.0	0.2	0.7	1.6	0.8	0.8	0.09	3	11
1991	4.3	1.0	0.3	0.7	1.6	0.8	0.8	0.08	1	4
1992	5.0	1.2	0.5	0.7	1.6	0.9	0.8	0.08	3	9
1993	5.7	1.3	0.6	0.7	2.0	1.1	0.9	0.07	8*	11
1994	5.9	1.4	0.6	0.8	2.0	1.0	1.1	0.05	8	13
1995	5.3	1.0	0.5	0.6	2.1	0.8	1.4	0.06	1	5
1996	5.1	1.1	0.5	0.6	2.2	0.7	1.5	0.04	3	11
1997	6.8	1.5	0.7	0.8	2.8	0.8	2.0	0.04	1	16
1998	6.7	1.6	0.7	0.8	2.7	0.7	2.0	0.02	3	15
1999	7.1	1.7	0.8	0.9	2.7	0.7	2.0	0.01	0	12
2000	7.8	1.9	0.8	1.0	2.9	0.8	2.1	0.02	1	9
2001	7.7	1.8	0.7	1.1	2.7	0.6	2.1	0.01	0	13
2002	7.8	1.9	0.7	1.2	2.7	0.6	2.1	0.01	0	9
2003	8.0	1.9	0.6	1.3	2.8	0.6	2.2	0.01	2	12
2004	7.9	1.8	0.5	1.3	2.8	0.6	2.2	0.01	1	8
2005	8.7	2.2	0.6	1.7	3.0	0.6	2.4	0.01	1	17
2006	9.2	2.4	0.6	1.8	3.2	0.6	2.6	0.01	2	14

*One prisoner shot during an attempted escape.

regimes, in California's prisons in the early 1970s, found that in half of the general-population prisons the overall rate of stabbings declined, but it almost doubled in 'special-security' prisons. The author speculated that this could be explained by the concentration of violent prisoners in special-security prisons, but also noted that 'with limited exercise available in security units, the energies and tensions which inmates formerly released in general population exercise periods and other available diversions may have found an outlet in violent activity' (in Bottoms 1999: 239). An earlier study of isolation in the 'incorrigible units' at Hawaii's Oahu Prison and North Carolina's Central Prison concluded that 'the overall impact of the incorrigible unit in penal practice probably is one that intensifies tendencies to criminal attitudes and behavior' (McCleery 1961: 306). Other studies identified segregation and 'lockdown' regimes as central factors in events leading to prison riots.[4]

In addition to an increase in prisoner violence since the introduction of SHUs in California, there has also been a substantial increase in the number of prisoners assaulted or killed by guards, an important factor in measuring prison violence which is missing from most standard reports and statistical data sets. In California, between 1975 and 2006, 57 prisoners were shot dead by prison staff. Only two of them were attempting to escape at the time.[5] Thirty-eight of the deaths occurred between 1990 and 2006, after the introduction of SHUs. In addition to fatal injuries, allegations of guard brutality, as previously discussed, are rife in many supermax prisons in the USA, not least in California's SHUs.

Reducing prison gang activity

Gang activity is one of the main sources of prison violence and its reduction is one of the official goals of supermax prisons. I demonstrated above that the introduction of supermax prisons has not reduced the overall occurrence of violent incidents in California's prisons. Did the placement of alleged and confirmed gang members in strict solitary confinement in SHUs, however, assist in addressing the problem of prison gangs in California? Here, again, there is some indication that the answer may be 'no'. One study of California's prison gangs found that gang activity increased as gang members were removed and housed in SHUs, as 'efforts to contain the spread of gangs led, unintentionally, to a vacuum within the prison population within which new prison groupings developed' (Hunt et al. 1993: 403). Leadership struggles among these new groupings

then resulted in gang-related murders in general-population prisons
(Parenti 1999a: 209). Although such a causal relationship is difficult
to prove, studies from other jurisdictions and other periods have
made similar observations. Colvin's (1992) study of events leading to
the 1980 riot in the New Mexico Penitentiary, for example, attributed
the riot to the strategy of isolating prisoner leaders, leading to the
fragmentation of prisoner solidarity, which in turn led to growing
violence.

One supermax administrator acknowledged the existence of new
factions of prison gangs since the introduction of supermax units,
though he did not attribute their emergence to the policy of isolating
gang leaders, but rather to the importation of street violence to
prison:

> The approach to identifying gangs is not as clear cut as it
> always was. I mean, it used to be real simple when you had
> six prison gangs – you had the Mexican Mafia, the New Astra
> Familiar, the Arian Brotherhood, Black Guerrilla Family, the
> Vanguard and the Texas Syndicate and somebody fell into that.
> Well, now you don't have that anymore. With Hispanics you
> have Suraneos (southerners), Nortaneos (northerners) and they
> don't easily fit into that, yet they're out there committing a lot
> of violence. Even with a lot of the black inner city gangs, the
> Kripps, the Bloods, people like that – well, they're not real Black
> Family, they're not the old Vanguard that was out there, and
> it's arguable that they're even being controlled by the Black
> Guerrilla Family. A lot of these splinter groups, these factional
> groups aren't being controlled by anybody but themselves.

Following the same line of reasoning, the official conceded that gang
activity continued despite the isolation of gang leaders, but again,
attributed this to the increasingly predatory nature of prisoners rather
than the failure of the policy:

> Inmates in the [unit] still wield some influence over general
> populations and it is real safe for those guys to do it. They're
> sitting in the safety of the [supermax] telling inmates on a
> general population, 'We want you guys to go out and, and
> do this violence out there' and the guys in [supermax] don't
> have to suffer the consequences of it, and so we're seeing larger
> numbers of inmates getting involved in riotous situations, and
> if you look you can't say, 'Well these guys are members of this

prison gang or that prison gang'. The fictionalisation is getting bigger out there.

When the consequences do not measure up to the declared intentions in official discourses, in a way that it by now familiar, a new breed of the dangerous individual appears on the stage, a 'super-predator' who requires super-maximum-security confinement. Supermaxes do not fail to reduce gang activity because their founding concepts are faulty, but because prisoners are increasingly dangerous. It follows from this line of official reasoning that the answer is tightening controls over prisoners even further.

Increasing prison programmes

Another official goal of supermax prisons is to enable better pro-gramme delivery in general-population prisons. It is claimed that without the disruptive few, the majority of prisoners will be able to participate in prison programmes without fear of being attacked, thus making more of their time in prison. Research certainly suggests that educational programmes have a positive effect on prisoner behaviour, whereas reduced privileges may result in an increase of violent behaviour. A literature review of over 90 studies of prison programmes concluded that:

> Without adequate [statistical] control techniques it is difficult to speak definitively about the impact of correctional education programmes ... [but] research shows a fair amount of support for the hypotheses that adult academic and vocational correctional education programs lead to fewer disciplinary violations during incarceration, reductions in recidivism, increases in employment opportunities, and to an increase in participation in education upon release.[6]

In other words, participation in prison programmes (vocational, educational, recreational) is cited as an important factor in promoting some of the behaviours which prison systems officially seek to achieve, whereas the lack of such programmes may slow down if not shut off altogether prisoners' chance of breaking out from the vicious cycle of crime and imprisonment. Despite this knowledge, and despite the claim that isolating high-risk prisoners in supermax settings will enable improved programme provision in the general-population prison, the budgetary allocation to prison programmes speaks volumes on the (lack of) importance attached to them. In California, the provision of prison programmes counts for less than 4.7 per cent of CDCR's budget (2008/9 budget year), a reduction from an already low starting point in previous years. There is little evidence, then, at least in California, that the introduction of supermax confinement has had a positive impact on the availability of programmes in general-population prisons.

Furthermore, although research indicates that they may benefit most from prison programmes, high-security and supermax prisoners typically have little, if any, access to prison programmes. The lack of programmes and related activities in supermax environments may lead quite directly to violent acts committed by frustrated prisoners, turning them into the dangerous individuals they are said to be.

Increasing staff safety

Another stated objective of isolating prisoners labelled as dangerous or disruptive is increasing staff safety across prison estates. This objective, at least in California, as the data on prison violence above clearly illustrates, has not been met since rates of prisoner-on-staff assaults have risen constantly since the 1990s.

Do prison staff who work inside supermax units, at least, *feel* safe? Does the design of supermax prisons succeed in this sense? An architect who designs supermax prisons expressed great satisfaction with his designs in terms of staff safety, and reiterated where his loyalties lay:

> We know from our interviews with staff in the design of the multiple facilities that they feel pretty comfortable working inside these facilities, and as far as I'm concerned, the staff and the safety of staff is a number one priority.

Prison staff who work in supermax prisons largely agree that these prisons provide a safe working environment:

> The staff who've come to work here that worked in other [supermax units] are absolutely wide-eyed at how safe this system is ... the vast majority of staff here find this to be so non-stressful that they want to continue work [here] rather than work in the main areas of the prison. [administrator]

As far as physical issues, as far as an individual being physically harmed by an inmate or inmates, it's relatively impossible. If an officer follows established policy and procedure in this unit, they cannot physically be harmed by an inmate one on one, or several on one – it is that secure. So, you know, on a scale from one to ten as far as staff safety, I give it an eleven. [unit manager]

These positive reactions are not surprising. Supermax prisoners are subjected to such extreme control measures that, with the exception of 'gassing' incidents, the possibility of an assault on another prisoner or a member of staff is almost non-existent. Because supermax prisons are safe working environments, there is no shortage of staff wanting to work in them, and many departments of corrections do not enforce the policy of rotating their staff between institutions every few years:[7]

We have been pleasantly surprised by the number of staff who wanted to come here, for a number of reasons. One is it is in a beautiful setting.... There's fishing, hunting, etc.... Because [the unit] is unique in the system, staff have an interest in it and a number of people wanted to come work here because it is a one of a kind unit and it gives an experience you won't get anywhere else. [administrator]

In addition to the beautiful rural setting, prison staff enjoy good salaries, job security and the backing of a strong union, particularly in California. Staff working in supermax prisons may also experience less 'role conflict' and therefore less stress than that experienced by prison staff in lower-security prisons, where 'the relative freedom and lower classification of the prisoners lead to an ambiguous definition of the situation' (Owen 1988: 127).[8]

We may conclude, then, that staff working inside supermax prisons do feel safe. Measured system-wide, however, the introduction of supermax prisons, at least in California, does not improve staff safety, as the overall rate of violent incidents is constantly increasing. Findings from other jurisdictions are mixed. A study carried out by Briggs and colleagues in Arizona, Illinois and Minnesota found 'mixed support for the hypothesis that supermax increases staff safety: the implementation of a supermax had no effect on levels of inmate-on-staff assaults in Minnesota, temporarily increased staff injuries in

Arizona, and reduced assaults against staff in Illinois' (Briggs *et al.* 2003: 1341).

Protecting the public

The final stated goal of supermaxes is 'protecting the public', an amorphous objective which is difficult to measure or refute. If 'protecting the public' means preventing prison escapes, then the internal security arrangements and devices in supermax prisons are broadly irrelevant, as escapes can be prevented through external (perimeter) security. If the aim is to cut off communications relating to crimes committed outside the prison, it should be noted that street gangs and prison gangs are two different entities and thus isolating prison gang members does not necessarily have a bearing on crimes committed outside the prison. Further, as one supermax administrator conceded, communications can never be completely cut off:

> Just because you remove them from this population and isolate them to this population, doesn't necessarily cut off their communication back to that population, it makes it more difficult; they still have access to the mail, they still have access to visitors who communicate with other people, and so there is a communication from the unit to General Populations – [supermax] just makes it more difficult.

The connection between supermax confinement and 'protecting the public', then, is tenuous if not entirely fictitious. I would also argue that even if this were not the case, this aim does not require, nor justify, the extreme conditions of internal control in supermax prisons. I would go even further and suggest that, as most prisoners eventually return to society, holding them in prolonged, highly controlled, solitary confinement may in fact endanger the public.

Putting objective measurements aside, does the public *feel* safer and are they reassured by the existence of supermax prisons? While it is difficult to gauge with any accuracy what 'the public' thinks about these prisons, there is at least some indication that the public is not oblivious to the potential damage of supermax confinement and would like to see prisoners in them receive some form of programmes to facilitate their reintegration into the community, or at least minimise the risk of violence stemming from years of isolation. Following the broadcast of the documentary film on supermax prisons in the USA which I was involved in making, the television network which commissioned it opened a forum on its website, where members of the public were asked to address the question, 'Are supermax prisons too cruel?' There were hundreds of responses, some of which were posted within minutes of the film's broadcast.[9] Some of the respondents had direct contact with the prison world, either as prison employees, former prisoners or as relatives of prisoners. Respondents who identified themselves as prison employees were mostly in favour of supermax confinement, with some notable exceptions, including prison officers who chose the forum to expose the inner workings of, and abuse within, supermax prisons. Many postings, both in favour and against supermaxes, used the analogy of caged animals, the former to emphasise the animalistic behaviour of prisoners and the latter to condemn the treatment of supermax prisoners as worse than that of animals. The punitive attitudes discussed in Chapter 3 were manifested in 'lock them up and throw away the key' responses, ranging in tone from muted to obscene, many invoking the violent prisoner versus victim equation. Those opposing supermaxes based their argument on moral considerations (no one should be treated this way), pragmatic considerations (they do not 'work'), and human rights considerations (solitary confinement is torture). As with those supporting supermaxes, responses from those opposing supermax prisons ranged from the mild to the outraged. Others accepted that supermax confinement may be necessary, but only with a very small, select group of extremely dangerous prisoners, and many expressed concern about the prospects of former supermax prisoners when they are released back to the community.

These responses indicate that the public would like to be better informed on what is happening inside prisons. They also provide some indication that members of the public would like to see some rehabilitation efforts made rather than the purely punitive regime of supermax prisons. It is interesting to note that the official discourse on the nature of prisoners that end up in supermax prisons, in the absence of an informed discussion, was mostly accepted at face value by both supporters and opponents of these prisons. Many respondents assumed that supermax prisoners are extremely dangerous individuals who have committed the most atrocious crimes. I encounter similar assumptions when I speak about supermax prisons and a genuine surprise when I explain that this assumption is often unfounded. In short, the public may not be as eager to 'lock prisoners up in supermaxes and throw away the key' as it is assumed to be, and there is little indication that supermax prisons contribute to perceptions of public safety.

Costs?

So far, I have discussed the alleged benefits of supermax prisons and refuted some claims regarding their success in achieving their official goals. I now address some of the costs of supermax confinement.

Human costs

The main cost of supermax confinement is its devastating and potentially irreversible impact on prisoners' health and well-being. Such adverse effects alone present a powerful and compelling argument against supermax prisons.[10]

Financial costs

The cost of constructing and equipping supermax prisons is very high, as are the costs of running them, since they are very staff intensive (one prison officer for every 3.5 to 7 prisoners). To illustrate, the construction of the Pelican Bay prison in California cost some $224 million, with the construction cost per SHU bed being $74,000.[11] The cost of housing a prisoner in segregated housing costs, on average, $14,600 more annually than housing a prisoner in general-population settings (Office of the Inspector General 2009). Bearing in mind that most state prison systems across the USA are severely overcrowded, there is an absurdity in the expensive single-cell accommodation in supermax prisons. The short-term financial savings made by the lack of any vocational, educational or therapeutic programmes in supermaxes only partially cover the costs of maintaining the tight security and close surveillance in these prisons. If the money spent on isolating, monitoring and controlling supermax prisoners were spent on prisoner treatment and education, reduced recidivism rates would almost certainly result, and the financial costs of prisons would be greatly reduced. However, as long as the political benefits of punitive rhetoric and policies continue to outweigh those of rehabilitation and reintegration efforts, this is unlikely to change, and departments of corrections opt for enlarging the prison estate rather than tackling problems of recidivism and improving delivery of programmes in prisons. Further, although the wish to protect prison staff from assaults by prisoners is legitimate, the legitimacy and necessity of spending so much money on the excessive prisoner controls in supermaxes are at least debatable.

In addition to the direct financial costs of supermax and other prisons, and of criminal justice expenditures in general, we must also consider the loss of spending on other public-sector areas, including education, health, welfare and so on. Prisons are costing taxpayers enormous amounts of money annually. In 2003 (most recent data available), state corrections expenditures in the USA nationwide totalled $39.2 billion, or $209 a year per US resident (Bureau of Justice Statistics 2006b). For the average annual cost of imprisoning one prisoner in California's prison system, for example, approximately five students could have attended the California State University (Centre on Juvenile and Criminal Justice 1998).

Societal costs

The 'failure of correctional systems to correct' and the notion that 'prisons call upon the individual to succeed virtually in spite of such settings rather than because of them' (Moyer 1975: 54) have been persistent themes in discourses on the roles of prisons. That prisoners can become institutionalised and experience difficulties in adapting to free life, was similarly observed long ago. This outcome is magnified in the case of supermax prisons, where the totality of the environment and regime holds little hope for prisoners. They become accustomed to solitude, are completely dependent on the structure and routines of the institution, and are ill equipped to function outside that environment.

One can only speculate how communities may be affected by the release of prisoners whose social skills have been eroded during years of isolation. Some prisoners carry with them the psychological harm of solitary confinement long after their release. This harm may manifest itself in ways that affect not only these former prisoners, but also their communities. I previously discussed the symptoms of the 'isolation syndrome' and prisoners' reactions (or adaptations) to conditions in supermax confinement. One of these reactions is overwhelming rage, which can manifest itself in violence. It is plausible, indeed almost predictable, that some of the prisoners who are released from the harsh supermax environment directly back to the community will react violently. As Toch (2001: 381) aptly put it,

Perception of capricious deprivation and custodial overkill predictably engenders bitterness and alienation. For this reason, supermax prisons may turn out to be crucibles and breeding grounds of violent recidivism. The graduates of such settings (often released directly into the community) may be time bombs waiting to explode. They may become 'the worst of the worst' because they have been dealt with as such.

Others may simply be unable to adapt to free life and reoffend soon after their release. Supermax prisons may thus also affect society as a whole through contributing to a general increase of recidivism rates, one of the traditional measures of the success (or failure) of prisons.

Human rights violations

Supermax confinement gives rise to serious human rights concerns and, in addition to breaching numerous international standards relating to the administration of prisons and the treatment of prisoners, may constitute a violation of the international prohibition of torture or inhuman treatment. The UN Human Rights Committee (1992) stated that 'prolonged solitary confinement of the detained or imprisoned person may amount to acts prohibited by Article 7 of the International Covenant on Civil and Political Rights (ICCPR)' (the prohibition of torture or cruel, inhuman or degrading treatment or punishment), and expressed concern over 'conditions of detention in certain maximum security prisons [in the USA] which are incompatible with article 10 of the Covenant and run counter to international human rights law standards' (UN Human Rights Committee 1995).[12] The UN Committee Against Torture (2000) and the UN Special Rapporteur on Torture expressed similar concerns regarding the compatibility of supermax prisons with international human rights law. I have discussed the human rights view of solitary confinement in some detail elsewhere (Shalev 2008). The point to make here is that most aspects of isolated confinement are brought to an extreme in the design and operation of supermax prisons, and they violate, by their very nature, the obligation to treat prisoners 'with humanity and with respect for the inherent dignity of the human person' (Article 10 of the ICCPR), a fundamental human right enshrined in numerous international law instruments.

Proportionate and rational?

Supermax prisons fail to meet most of their declared goals. They impose a heavy human, financial and societal cost, and by operating on what even a non-interventionist judicial system considers to be the verge of psychological torture, raise profound moral questions about whether they befit a civilised society. One may wonder, then, at their proliferation in a contemporary penal system which claims to make rational decisions in the management and operation of prisons, and where ideological justifications have largely been removed from official discourses, which are now constructed of 'target points', 'cost-effectiveness', and other terms borrowed from the global business culture to indicate objectivity, uniformity and rationality.

This conflict between the discourses of rationality and actual practices is apparent in the design of, and regime in, supermax prisons. In terms of their institutional behaviour, prisoners are assumed to be rational actors. Official discourses emphasise that those who are placed in solitary confinement have made a rational decision: they 'earned their way in', and need to 'earn their way out'. The fear of isolation is also claimed to act as a deterrent to institutional misbehaviour by prisoners in the general prison population, a philosophy that is rooted in the assumption that prisoners are rational actors motivated by the wish to maximise gain and minimise pain. Yet, regimes in supermax prisons, furthered by architectural measures, treat prisoners, in practice, as irrational, dangerous and unpredictable actors, organising their every move across time/space to minimise the risk of violence.

Supermax prisons are extreme places. Their design accommodates a strict regime that responds harshly and swiftly to the smallest instances or threats of disobedience, which in supermax prisons rarely mean more than a prisoner refusing to return his food tray at the end of a meal. Recalling the questionable success of the classification process in 'identifying' prisoners correctly, even if we were to accept that solitary confinement is the only way to manage difficult or dangerous prisoners, 'It beggars belief that there are sufficient numbers of them in the USA to fill the vast number of spaces now to be found in supermax facilities' (King 2007: 349). We must also enquire whether 'dangerous' or 'disruptive' prisoners – real or alleged – should be penalised so heavily and subjected, on top of their isolation, to all the additional deprivations and measures of control, surveillance and inspection typical of supermax regimes. I would argue that these measures are not only disproportionate to the stated purposes of supermax prisons, which evidence indicates are in the most part not met, but are also highly excessive and irrational. Consider the following.

Do supermax prisoners really need to be secured behind 10 layers of tightly controlled and closely monitored physical barriers that separate them from the outside world (see Figure 6.1)? What legitimate purpose is served by prohibiting them from using hobby and craft materials, listening to music, and participating in educational programs, or by limiting the number of books they may keep and foodstuffs they may eat? Is it really necessary to move prisoners around the prison in full body restraints at all times? Is it necessary to strip search a prisoner who has left his cell for a medical appointment, had no contact with any other prisoner, and was watched by two guards at all times? Is it necessary to conduct medical examinations while the prisoner is handcuffed and in the presence of two armed guards, in violation of basic principles of medical confidentiality and ethics? Is it necessary to remove all recreational equipment from the solitary, closed and constantly monitored exercise yards? Is it necessary to regulate so carefully the types of food and canteen goods that prisoners may receive, or the items of personal hygiene they may use? Do spicy crackers, lip balm and hair conditioner really present a danger to prison 'safety and security'? Similar questions arise regarding the design of supermax units, such as the lack of windows and views of the outside. Is any legitimate penological purpose served by these measures, or are they punitive measures aimed at something different than the control of 'high-risk' prisoners? Recalling the official insistence that supermax prisons are merely a 'management tool', these questions become all the more pressing.

What next?

Isolation is as old as punishment itself, and predates the prison as a penal practice. Pressures for segregation, isolation and separation of prisoners have always been, and are likely to remain, part of the inner logic of prison systems, the ultimate form of physical and mental control. Indeed, despite decades of failure to achieve their declared aims, high financial costs, and devastating health effects, the chosen strategies for managing prisoners identified as 'core troublemakers' in all their different incarnations, have involved solitary confinement.

The explosion in the use of isolation through the proliferation of supermax prisons at this specific historical time is the result of a confluence of administrative convenience, political and economic interests, societal attitudes and cultural sensibilities, all pushing penal attitudes and practices in the same direction, as described in Chapter 3. A judicial tradition of 'hands-off' and reluctance to intervene in prison practices has meant that there has been no effective legal brake. As the authors of a report by Human Rights Watch, a non-governmental organisation which has been monitoring prisons and reporting on conditions in supermaxes since the early 1990s, note,

> There has been scant public debate about the penological justifications for Supermax confinement, its high price in terms of the misery and suffering it inflicts, and the likelihood that it reduces an inmate's ability to make a successful transformation to society upon release. The public has either been indifferent or has uncritically accepted the punitive penal views of those who endorse the Supermax approach. Judicial scrutiny has been limited by both the courts' tradition of deference to the judgement of prison officials and by jurisprudence that sets an extraordinarily high threshold for finding prison conditions to be unconstitutional.... Prolonged segregation that previously would have been deemed extraordinary and inconsistent with concepts of dignity, humanity, and decency has become a corrections staple. (Human Rights Watch 2000: 3)

Certainly, even when courts are very critical of prison conditions in general, and conditions in supermax prisons in particular, they have fallen short, so far, of declaring them to be unconstitutional. The *Madrid* (1995) court, for example, was clearly outraged by conditions at Pelican Bay SHU, but felt unable to rule that the SHU, in its entirety, was unconstitutional:

> Defendants [CDC] have unmistakably crossed the constitutional line with respect to some of the claims raised by this action. In particular, defendants have failed to provide inmates at Pelican Bay with constitutionally adequate medical and mental health care, and have permitted and condoned a pattern of using excessive force, all in conscious disregard of the serious harm that these practices inflict. With respect to the SHU, defendants cross the constitutional line when they force certain subgroups of the prison population, including the mentally ill, to endure conditions at the SHU, despite knowing that the likely consequence for such inmates is serious injury to their mental health, and despite the fact that certain conditions in the SHU have a relationship to legitimate security interests that is tangential at best ... defendants have subjected plaintiffs to 'unnecessary and wanton infliction of pain' in violation of the Eighth Amendment.... We observe that while this simple phrase articulates the legal standard, dry words on paper can

> not adequately capture the senseless suffering and sometimes wretched misery that defendants' unconstitutional practices leave in their wake.... Conditions in the SHU may well hover on the edge of what is humanly tolerable for those with normal resilience, particularly when endured for extended periods of time. They do not, however, violate exacting Eighth Amendment standards, except for the specific population subgroups identified in this opinion. (*Madrid* 1995: 1279–80)

Where courts do intervene, departments of corrections do not always comply, and institutions have their own survival mechanisms in response to changes enforced by external bodies: a condemned 'adjustment centre' is reincarnated as a 'decompression unit'; court-sanctioned 'group therapy' is provided in individual holding cages arranged in a semicircle; a special committee for investigating incidents involving the use of force is established, but it only has two members and always finds that the use of force was justified in any given case. These and other such institutional adaptations engage prisoners, departments of corrections and the courts in ongoing and costly circular lawsuits which, while sometimes leading to real changes in prison conditions and the treatment of prisoners, mostly fail to affect change in the principal operation of prisons.

Bar a radical change in penal *thinking* and concepts, we are unlikely to witness, in the near future, a substantial decrease of imprisonment rates and by implication prisoner numbers. Against this background, existing prison space, including that available in supermaxes, will be used, regardless of the 'fit' between its security arrangements and those incarcerated in it. Supermax prisons immortalise solitary confinement by their very existence. Their legacy is ensured in brick and mortar, regardless of the costs of isolating large segments of the prison society. The design of supermax prisons predetermines the activities and interactions that can take place within them, and therefore little can be done to improve the conditions of confinement in them. As supermax prisons are a convenient penal tool that also serves some powerful interests, we can only conclude that the suffering inflicted on prisoners through the use of solitary confinement is still generally accepted as a 'just measure of pain' (Ignatieff 1978).

So long as supermax prisons continue to be legitimised despite their failures, they will continue to be used and may become the tools of first resort for more groups of prisoners. The security and control standards set by supermax prisons are not the 'end of the line'. There can always be even more isolation, regulation and deprivation. As previously noted, there already are special measures for prisoners who misbehave inside supermax prisons, segregation units within segregation prisons. One of the dangers is that the entire prison system will gradually move towards more control and deprivation, slowly turning former tools of last resort into tools of first resort, or into the standard in prison conditions, moving the entire prison system to a new extreme which will then become its own *de facto* justification. Another possible development is that, as a result of growing pressures for prison beds, departments of corrections will begin to hold two prisoners to a cell, in the conditions described in this book. Whether such a move would be cynically justified as an effort to ease the pains of isolation remains to be seen, but studies of 'small-group confinement' indicate that the health effects and possible consequences of incarcerating two people in a small space may be even worse than those of solitary confinement.[13] We can but hope that this will not be the case, but lessons from the past indicate that prison systems do not always pay heed to expert advice and adopt measures previously condemned as dangerous and counterproductive. To be sure, the failures, costs and consequences of highly controlled and isolated prison environments discussed here have been continuous themes and the subject of numerous studies, dating back to the nineteenth century.

Not only are strategies which failed in the past still being used despite their failure, but they are also 'exported' from the US criminal justice system to other countries and to settings outside the prison. Though on a much smaller scale than their US counterparts, other countries, including Australia, Brazil, Peru and South Africa now operate at least one supermax-like prison. The design of two of the detention facilities used by the US military at Guantánamo Bay, Cuba, is modelled directly on supermax prisons in the USA (Joint Task Force Guantánamo 2009) and, as more information filters out on the regime and some of the practices at Guantánamo Bay, it becomes clear that these, too, are modelled in part on supermax regimes in the USA. The strategy of identifying and excluding the 'uncontrollable', 'incurable', 'dangerous' and 'disruptive' has also been proposed in settings outside the prison.[14] Calls to introduce special schools in the UK for children with 'behavioural difficulties', rather than keeping them in mainstream schools where they are 'increasing disruption and putting pupils in danger' (Ward 2004: 4), are one example. As with prisons, it is claimed that by excluding 'increasingly aggressive children' who are a 'danger to themselves and others' from regular schools, teachers will be able to focus on teaching rather than 'dealing with these kids' (Ward, *ibid.*). The managerial argument is supported by professional discourses and new syndromes and disorders, such as attention deficit and hyperactivity disorder, which help to justify the need for such special measures.

Perhaps, nonetheless, there are glimmers of hope. At the time of writing (early 2009), the newly elected US president, Barack Obama, has ordered the closing of Guantánamo Bay, and there are some early signs of a shift in the penal ideologies which have dominated the administration of justice in the USA for almost three decades. Most states have adopted in recent years some reforms in the areas of sentencing, drug policy, parole revocation and racial justice to tackle expanding prison populations and budget deficits (King 2009).[15] The language of rehabilitation and reintegration of prisoners seems to be creeping back into official discourses, exemplified by the California Department of Corrections' addition of 'and Rehabilitation', to its name and listed purposes in July 2005. Whether or not these early signs will mature into meaningful changes on the ground remains to be seen. What is clear, though, is that a serious rethink of the very principle of prolonged solitary confinement as a prison strategy – in supermax prisons and other units, by whatever name they are called – particularly when applied to a large number of prisoners, is urgently needed. It is time to acknowledge the failures of solitary confinement and the immense pain it causes, and reject its use as a legitimate prison practice in all but the most exceptional circumstances and subject to stringent safeguards and external scrutiny.

Notes

1 The discussion here does not constitute a structured cost-benefit analysis in the traditional sense, but for one such analysis, see Lawrence and Mears (2004).
2 Proportionality is defined as an examination of 'whether the effect of a law exceeds what is necessary to be achieved and whether it is proportionate to the specific objective', *Curzon Dictionary of Law*.
3 The data are drawn from CDCR Data Analysis Unit Reports through to September 2007.
4 See Adams 1994; Colvin 1992; Haney and Lynch 1997.
5 CDCR Data Analysis Unit Population reports through to September 2007. Additionally, between 1975 and 1999, a reported 200 prisoners were seriously injured in California (Human Right Watch 1999).
6 Gaes *et al.* 1999: 411. See also California Legislative Analyst Office (LAO) 2001.

7   This policy, officially aimed at reducing the levels of stress suffered by staff and increasing their professionalism, undoubtedly also aims to minimise the risk of special 'accommodations' between prison staff and prisoners and the development of personal relationships.

8   I should add, nonetheless, that some of the supermax officers to whom I chatted informally said that they found their job a bit boring, as 'there was very little to do' and their tasks were mostly routine.

9   Appendix 1 contains excerpts from some of these responses.

10 Another possible human cost of supermax environments is the brutalisation of those who work in them. Staff may carry with them the 'style' and behaviour they are encouraged to exercise in their work onto their homes and communities.

11 Pelican Bay Public Information Office, December 1993.

12 See also International Psychological Trauma Symposium (2007). For fuller discussion of the application of human rights standards in prisons, see Coyle 2002; Office of the United Nations High Commissioner on Human Rights 2005; Penal Reform International 2001.

13 Amnesty International 1980. Grassian (1993: 37) noted that 'confined groups comprising of just two individuals may be the most pathogenic of all, associated with especially high rates of mutual paranoia and violent hostility.' Similar observations were made in Arctic environments (Zubek 1969).

14 See Mason (1999: 155) on the creation of a 'psychiatric supermax' for a core group of 'mentally disordered offenders who are considered too dangerous to move elsewhere or transfer to lesser levels of security'.

15 In California, as previously discussed, voters rejected proposals for policy reforms, but in February 2009 the Department of Corrections was ordered by a panel of three federal judges to enact such reforms and reduce its prisoner population by more than a third within 3 years (Moore 2009).

Appendix

Responses to documentary film on supermaxes

The excerpts below are taken from online responses to the documentary film on supermax prisons which I was involved in making, to give a flavour of the language, tone and arguments for and against these prisons. Some of the respondents had direct contact with the prison world, either as prison employees, former prisoners or relatives of prisoners. Where the respondent identified their profession or their connection to the prison world, I indicate that in brackets following the quotation.

Many of the respondents who identified themselves as correctional officers were in favour of supermax confinement, with some notable exceptions.

> People do not know the real deal about what goes on in there. I worked in a correctional facility and half these officers are just as bad as the inmates they watch. They just get away with it because of people like the ones that say these inmates deserve what they get. Many of these [supermax] cells are being used for minor offences where there was no way a threat to anyone. The Department of Corrections just wants justification for all the money that is spent from the taxpayers.... I saw abuse of inmates from officers on a daily basis.... Corrections Officers (and I use that title loosely) are not held accountable for anything and they cover up everything that really goes on in there. Then the taxpayers are the ones to pay because they think we need more supermax prisons. If you held the Department of Corrections to any kind of professionalism and made them

justify their actions, the problems in our prisons would definitely drop considerably.... There is just as much brutality inside our prisons and that makes these officers no better than the inmates. [correctional officer]*

Additional responses are reproduced below, broadly divided into those in favour of supermax prisons, those who oppose them, and those who think that supermax prisons should be used more selectively.

In favour of supermax prisons

People are sick of all of the crap, they are sick of their kids not being able to safely walk the streets, it seems we must send some sort of message to these criminals. If that means we taxpayers have to pay more, so be it. I'd rather that than have more of them out on the street. We give them too many chances to 'do the right thing' ... these people are there for a reason.

Do you know what these people did to be in prison? What if it were you who was raped or your child who was killed? Would you think of the constitution then????????? God forbid that the prisoners be violated the rights of FREE people, people who do not victimize, rob, steal, murder and kill. The question is what if you were the Victim?

When you deal with animals that don't value human life or the rights of others, how can you treat them otherwise? I believe they shouldn't have any rights whatsoever, they did not think of the rights of the people they murdered or their families. I say put them in a cage like the animals they are.

---

*This posting led to heated debate, which degenerated into the exchange of insults. Many responses were from prison officers expressing doubts as to whether the writer was indeed a former prison employee. There were also a few responses from other guards who said the description was accurate and congratulated the man for breaking the 'code of silence'. One such reply was from a retired guard, who stated that he could not remain silent any more, and reaffirmed what was said in the message. This posting, too, received scalding responses.

It seems that people with overwhelming violent tendencies should be dealt with in a more severe manner; if he was violent before this incident, his eyes should have been removed; it would have then made it more difficult for him to commence an attack. In total isolation now, he should be immobilized to a bed or a chair at all times, so that he is unable to move. These are fair and humane punishments.

I work in a maximum security institution ... I totally agree with the 'Super Max' systems ... we run into some offenders who are just dangerous. Some are difficult to deal with, even at a maximum-security institution. There has to be another step, and I believe 'Super Max' is it. ... Yes, the system is flawed, but it is that system that is keeping ... children from being raped and killed.... I know that is harsh, but that is reality, and the real reality is that some of these guys in prison are DANGEROUS.

The people locked up in maximum security prisons are VIOLENT FELONS! By the time they get to this point, they've probably been through countless 'rehabilitation programs' ... especially if they began their criminal careers as youngsters. The rate of recidivism for violent felons is somewhere around 80%. Some people need to be away from society where they cannot harm others. How many times do we hear about felons being paroled or sent to halfway houses and they commit the exact same violent crime and destroy another life because of our bleeding heart, soft prison system? Why don't you try having compassion for the victims?

This country blows so much money on the scums. They need to take any good organs from these scums and give them to people who are waiting for organ transplants ... look at all the money that can be used for good instead of wasting it on these useless maggots ... oops sorry... maggots are higher life forms than these people.

I have had urine, and feces thrown on me. I have been hit, kicked, and spit on several times. If for nothing else but officer safety I lean towards the harder lock down style prison. Sadly though, the good offenders must live in these conditions. I think it is important for us all to try to see both sides of the coin. People aren't put in prison for missing Sunday school too many times. They have committed a serious crime. In other words they have made an innocent person a victim, and they have to learn not to repeat this type of behavior. [correctional officer]

We ... attempt to put into place what works and is best for everyone.... We really try hard and our intentions are honourable. We don't torture anyone. Unfortunately they do it themselves and we try to correct that behaviour. Some people are so bad that they need to be separated. [correctional officer]

It's all about choices.... Inmates that are sent to a supermax facility are sent because of choices, wrong choices, that they have made while in general population. Rules and consequences of said rules are very clear in a correctional environment. If a rule is broken repeatedly or severely then the system provides a more structured environment with which to manage the non-conforming offender ... ie the supermax facility. The goal is not to dehumanize or demoralize the offender but to manage the offender in a safe and effective manner that poses as little threat as possible to the staff and other offenders within that facility. [former correctional officer/manager]

I do not think supermax prisons are too cruel, I believe we need more of them. [correctional officer]

Inmates placed in a lock down situation are there because after given the choice to program they did not. Inmates housed in 'SUPERMAX' facilities are typically the worst of the worst. I have been assaulted by inmates physically and verbally. I have seen fellow officers assaulted by inmates. As correctional professionals we only use the amount of force necessary to control the situation. We are not the 'guards' as we are too often portrayed on TV and the movies. I pride myself as a corrections professional and am very disappointed with the fact that the general public does not realize what we go through day after day. [correctional officer]

These inmates that are locked up in a special housing unit are there for a reason because they cause so much trouble they cannot be out in general population. They also are a threat to public safety which is our main goal in corrections. [correctional officer]

232

These people were not chosen randomly for solitary confinement. They have committed additional crimes which have led them to this point. I am tired of people in this country feeling sorry for people who have never cared about anyone else a day in their life. Our prison systems should be harsher; we need to get rid of all these 'bleeding-heart' psychologists who are so concerned about the mental health of violent criminals. These people forfeited their right to pity when they chose the path that they did.

Against supermax prisons

They are inhuman and not intended to create a better society or to deter crime. It is just cruel and inhuman punishment. Shame on us!!!

This is torture not punishment. Were I in that situation I would say that I'd rather be shot than to endure that for a lifetime or even a year for that matter.

I do not believe that we are doing anything right or just by treating anyone, prisoners or otherwise, in an inhumane manner, no matter who they are or what they have done. I don't believe doing so serves any purpose. We should use whatever means necessary to control them (and in this day of sophisticated gadgets, that's not too difficult), and we should segregate them as necessary to control their violence. That does not mean that it is acceptable to stick them in a hole in the ground and deprive them of sunlight or any form of human interaction, especially if it is likely that they will someday be set loose back into open society, for I think that will only make them worse. I think that is the height of stupidity.

And we want to believe that we are the greatest country in the world, that we care, that we would never do what dictators the world over do with their concentration camps ... [in] Supermax inmates [are] being beaten, dehumanized, and treated worse than we would treat an animal. ... Wake up people. No one deserves to be treated the way these people were being treated, and unbelievably, there was no shame in what they were doing, even afterward, when the blood stopped boiling. Something should be done to stop these Supermax prisons, use them for a nunnery or monastery. I can't think of anything else they would be good for.

I feel that supermax prisons are a waste of money and time. They are a political toy for state officials.... We have inmates that want to go to the supermax, like its [*sic*] a badge they can wear. (I'm bad, I've been to the supermax.) [correctional officer]

Supermax Prisons are excessive. The way we treat our criminals reflects who we are as a society.... Total isolation is too distractive to the human psyche. During wars, these methods are used to destroy the will and sense of individual identity of prisoners-of-war. These methods should not be used in our prisons, especially for minors.... Of course, dangerous people should be removed from society, but isolation in the Supermax prisons is being used primarily for convenience and ... for political play with the public, who primarily wants easy, quick answers.

Most people would shrivel up in one of these supermax prisons. This would be especially true for young people. If these prisons represent the BEST we can do as a society, then we are a sorry lot!

How do you teach compassion by forgetting that it exists? How do you rehabilitate a man by treating him like an animal?

Isolation in this form brings out the worst of the worst. This is mental cruelty ... these guys are left to rot or go insane.

These Super Max Pens are designed specifically to torture and dehumanize the inmates through sensory deprivation and isolation. I mean why would you put somebody in a cell with no windows and no opportunity to see the outside world for literally years? What purpose does it fulfil? ... Who thought up this sadistic system?

Isolation of prisoners can be an effective tool if used correctly. But I have seen with my own eyes how easy it is to, and IS abused every single day. ['corrections veteran']

How can punishment be defined by being isolated from reality? ... how can we expect him to behave when he is released?... Provide something 'new' and something 'educational' to these S.H.U. inmates, give them reason to not want to be angry instead of giving them the reason to be. [SHU relative]

I was horrified seeing not only how they 'lock down' prisoners but the type of prisoners they do it to. This should be reserved for the vilest of serial killers.... We know that even animals will die without contact with either humans or other animals of their kind. Their rationale was to 'let them decide' and 'let them learn' what kind of person they want to be. With thousands of prisoners locked in cages with no human contact, all we are guaranteeing is that we will be setting free on our society people who have lost all ability to cope with other people and the basic daily skills of living. We are making people insane and turning them into people who most likely will become more violent than ever simply by being among other people again. ['Inquisitive who cares']

Fine, if prisons are for punishment then so be it. But don't talk about rehabilitation. They don't rehabilitate anyone. And if they are for punishment then once a sentence is served drop the matter. Don't throw it back in my face every time I ask for a job, or get pulled over at a Stop Check, come up for jury duty, or any of the other things I am now excluded from or denied access to. I served my time. Must I also serve for the rest of my life? Yes I do. So how am I being rehabilitated? How can I prove myself? How can I ever be a productive member of society if I'm never given a chance. Give me a break. I don't even dare admit what I did or I will have to bear greater punishment. Do you think I like the man who looks back at me from the mirror every morning? Well I don't and I don't need anyone telling me that I deserve what I got. I already know that. So please put me to death or let me kill myself instead of constantly reminding me that I am less than human.

It is with great sadness that I read some of the reactionary, uninformed, and simply ignorant posts in this forum. If tonight's documentary revealed anything, it was the systemic barbarism of a penal culture that has abandoned any ethic of either 'rehabilitation' or 'correction.' These so-called 'Supermax' prisons, with their solitary-confinement infrastructures, are simply regressive adaptations of past failed penal experiments. The 'Pennsylvania' system didn't work, it simply aggravated the brutalization of already disturbed people, and so will the 'Supermax' system. It always amazes me that the narrow-minded conservative majority seeks to justify the treatment of prisoners by referring to the suffering of their victims. Exacting 'punishment' in the form of revenge accomplishes nothing ... even victims understand that. One act of barbarism and cruelty certainly does not justify another.... Thanks for a stimulating documentary.

In favour of a more selective use of supermax prisons

As long as it is 'just' those inmates who 'cannot' or 'will not' be controlled in general population, I believe that SuperMax has a place ... I think that SuperMax is like anything else where bureaucracy is concerned... there will be many instances where it will be abused because it is too 'convenient' as a 'political' tool.

I agree that it is beneficial to all involved if [problem prisoners] are removed as quickly as possible. But the design of the Super Max facilities ensures that many of its inmates will never be successfully integrated into society after their release, effectively dooming them to mental instability and possible violence. Is it justified to use such drastic measures on inmates that prison guards simply can't deal with? I think that other alternatives must be examined before a prisoner is condemned to an indefinite portion of his or her sentence in isolation.

Solitary confinement can create criminals and cause extreme psychological damage. This form of punishment should be used for extreme cases of violence, if it used at all because these prisoners should not be released back into society after keeping them from human interaction for so long.

There has to be a place to put these problem offenders so that the rest of the population doesn't suffer.... I think if we use 'Super Max' as a tool and not a punishment it can be effective. [correctional officer]

Bibliography

Abbott, J.H. (1982) *In the Belly of the Beast: Letters from Prison*. New York: Vintage Books.

Abramsky, S. (2002) 'Return of the madhouse'. *The American Prospect* [online], 13 (3), 11 February 2002. Available at: http://www.prospect.org/cs/articles?article=return_of_the_madhouse [accessed on 1 April 2009].

Ackroyd, C., Margolis, K., Rosenhead, J. and Shallice, T. (1977) *The Technology of Political Control*. Harmondsworth: Penguin Books.

Adams, R. (1994) *Prison Riots in Britain and the USA* (2nd edn). London: Macmillan.

Adams, R. (1998) *The Abuses of Punishment*. London: Macmillan.

Adler, M. and Longhurst, B. (1994) *Discourse, Power and Justice: Towards a New Sociology of Imprisonment*. London: Routledge.

Adshead, J. (1845) *Prisons and Prisoners*. London: Longman, Brown, Green and Longman.

Alexander, J. and Austin, J. (1992) *Handbook for Evaluating Objective Prison Classification Systems*. Washington, DC: US Department of Justice, National Institute of Corrections.

Allchin, A.M. (ed.) (1977) *Solitude and Communion: Papers on the Hermit Life*. London: Fairacres Publication No. 66.

Allen, F. (1981) *The Decline of the Rehabilitative Ideal: Penal Policy and Social Purpose*. New Haven, CT: Yale University Press.

American Institute of Architects, Committee on Architecture for Justice (1999a) Proceedings of conference on *Doing Justice to Design/Build*, 18–20 March, Washington, DC.

American Institute of Architects, Committee on Architecture for Justice (1999b) Proceedings of conference on *Justice in the Next Millennium*, 14–17 October, Los Angeles.

Amnesty International (1980) *Prison Conditions of Persons Suspected or Convicted of Politically Motivated Crimes in the FRG: Isolation and Solitary Confinement.* AI Index: EUR 32/01/80.

Amnesty International (1997) *United Kingdom: Special Security Units: Cruel, Inhuman or Degrading Treatment.* AI Index: EUR45/006/1997.

Amnesty International (1998) *United States of America: Rights for All.* AI Index: AMR/51/35/98.

Amnesty International (2000) *United States of America: A Call to Action by the UN Committee Against Torture.* AI Index: AMR51/107/2000.

Amnesty International (2003) *Combating Torture: A Manual for Action.* AI Index: ACT 40/001/2003.

Arax, M. and Gladstone, M. (1998) 'The poison in the lifeblood of the nation: the consequences of the police state', *Los Angeles Times, Orange County Edition,* 5 July, p. 1.

Arendt, H. (1965) *Eichmann in Jerusalem: A Report on the Banality of Evil.* New York: Penguin books.

Austin, J. (1996) 'The effect of "three strikes and you're out" on corrections', in D. Shichor and D. Sechrest (eds), *Three Strikes and You're Out: Vengeance as Public* Policy. Thousand Oaks, CA: Sage, pp. 155–76.

Austin, J. and Chan, L. (1994) *Survey Report on Internal Offender Classification Systems.* Washington, DC: US Department of Justice, National Institute of Corrections.

Austin, J. and Irwin, J. ([1994] 2000) *It's About Time: America's Imprisonment Binge* (3rd edn). Belmont, CA: Wadsworth.

Barker, A. (1998) 'Political responsibility for UK prison security: ministers escape again', *Public Administration,* 76: 1–23.

Bauman, Z. (2000) 'Social issues of law and order', *British Journal of Criminology,* 40 (1): 205–21.

Beck, U. (1992) *Risk Society.* London: Sage.

Becker, H. (1963) *The Outsiders: Studies in the Sociology of Deviance.* New York: Free Press.

Benjamin, T.B. and Lux, K. (1977) 'Solitary confinement as psychological punishment', *California Western Law Review,* 13: 265–96.

Bentham, J. (1791) 'Panopticon or the inspection house', in J. Bowring (ed.) (1843) *The Works of Jeremy Bentham,* vol. 4. Edinburgh: William Tart.

Berk, R.A., Ladd, H., Graziano, H. and Baek, J.H. (2003) 'A randomized experiment testing inmate classification systems', *Criminology and Public Policy,* 2 (2): 215–43.

Berk, R.A., Kriegler, B. and Baek, J.H. (2006) *Forecasting Dangerous Inmate Misconduct.* Berkeley, CA: California Policy Research Center, University of California.

Berkman, A. (1995) *Address to a meeting of the Campaign to End the Marion Lockdown,* 21 October 1995. Available at: http://www-unix.oit.umass.edu/kastor/fallprogram/fall-main.html [accessed on 1 April 2009].

Biderman, A.D. (1962) 'The image of brainwashing', *Public Opinion Quarterly*, 26 (4): 547–63.

Binda, H. (1975) 'Effects of increased security on prison violence', *Journal of Criminal Justice*, 3: 33–46.

Blumstein, A. and Beck, A.J. (1999) 'Population growth in U.S. prisons 1980–1996', in M. Tonry and J. Petersilia (eds), *Crime and Justice: A Review of Research*, vol. 26, *Prisons*. Chicago and London: University of Chicago Press, pp. 17–61.

Bone, E. (1957) *Seven Years Solitary*. London: Hamish Hamilton.

Bottomley, K. (1973) *Decisions in the Penal Process*. Oxford: Martin Robertson.

Bottomley, K. and Hay, W. (eds) (1991) *Special Units for Difficult Prisoners*. Hull: University of Hull Centre for Criminology and Criminal Justice.

Bottoms, A. (1995) 'The philosophy and politics of punishment and sentencing', in C. Clarkson and R. Morgan (eds), *The Politics of Sentencing Reform*. Oxford: Oxford University Press, pp. 17–49.

Bottoms, A. (1999) 'Interpersonal violence and social order in prisons', in M. Tonry and J. Petersilia (eds), *Crime and Justice: A Review of Research*, vol. 26, *Prisons*. Chicago and London: University of Chicago Press, pp. 205–81.

Bottoms, A.E. and Light, R. (eds) (1987) *Problems of Long Term Imprisonment*. Cropwood Round-Table Conferences, Cambridge Studies in Criminology. Aldershot: Gower.

Bottoms, A.E. and Willes, P. (1997) 'Environmental criminology', in R. Maguire, R. Morgan and R. Reiner (eds), *The Oxford Handbook of Criminology* (2nd edn). Oxford: Clarendon Press, pp. 305–59.

Boxall, B. (2000) 'Video visiting is latest jail trend', *Los Angeles Times, Orange County Edition*, 18 January, p. 3.

Braswell, M., Dillingham, S. and Montgomery, R. (eds) (1985) *Prison Violence in America*. Cincinnati, OH: Anderson Publishing Company.

Briggs, C.S., Sundt, J.L. and Castellano, T.C. (2003) 'The effects of supermaximum security prisons on aggregate levels of institutional violence', *Criminology*, 41 (4): 1341–76.

Brockes, E. (2009) 'What happens in war happens', *Guardian Weekend Magazine*, 3 January 2009, 14–21.

Brodie, A., Croom, J. and Davies, J. (1999) *Behind Bars: The Hidden Architecture of England's Prisons*. Swindon: English Heritage.

Brown, M. and Pratt, J. (eds) (2000) *Dangerous Offenders: Punishment and Social Order*. London: Routledge.

Buchanan, R.A., Unger, C.A. and Whitlow, K.L. (1988) *Disruptive Maximum Security Inmate Management Guide*. Washington, DC: US Department of Justice, National Institute of Corrections.

Bureau of Justice Statistics (1999) *Mental Health and Treatment of Inmates and Probationers*. Washington, DC: US Department of Justice (NCJ 174463).

Bureau of Justice Statistics (2001) *Sourcebook of Criminal Justice Statistics* [online]. Available at: http://www.albany.edu/sourcebook [accessed on 10 January 2005].

Bureau of Justice Statistics (2004) *State Prison Expenditures, 2001*. Washington, DC: US Department of Justice (NCJ 202949).

Bureau of Justice Statistics (2006a) *Mental Health Problems of Prison and Jail Inmates*, September 2006. Washington, DC: US Department of Justice.

Bureau of Justice Statistics (2006b) *Justice Expenditure and Employment in the United States in 2003*. Washington, DC: US Department of Justice (NCJ 212260) (rev. 5 October 2006).

Bureau of Justice Statistics (2008) *Prisoners in 2007*, Washington, DC: US Department of Justice (NCJ 224280).

Bureau of Justice Statistics (2009) *Crime Rates by State*. Available at: http://bjsdata.ojp.usdoj.gov/dataonline/Search/Crime/State/RunCrimeStatebyState.cfm [accessed on 5 March 2009].

Burrell, I. (1999) 'Fate of Alcatraz Prison in doubt', *The Independent*, 21 January, p. 11.

Burton-Rose, D., Pens, D. and Wright, P. (1998) *The Celling of America: An Inside Look at the U.S. Prison Industry*. Monroe, ME: Common Courage Press.

Bustamente, G. (1995) *Letter Sent to a Meeting of the Campaign to End the Marion Lockdown*, 21 October 1995 [online]. Available at: http://www-unix.oit.umass.edu/kastor/fallprogram/fall-main.html [accessed on 1 April 2009].

Byrd, R.E. (1938) *Alone*. Garden City, NY: International Collectors Library.

California Blue Ribbon Commission on Inmate Population Management (1990) Sacramento, CA.

California Board of Corrections (2000) *Gassing Incidents Report*. Available at: http://www.bdcorr.ca.gov/fsod/gassing_report/gassing_report.htm [accessed on 27 November 2000].

California Board of Corrections (2001) *Minimum Standards for Local Detention Facilities*. Sacramento, CA.

California Correctional Peace Officers Association (2003) *History of CCPOA* [online]. Available at: http://www.ccpoa.org/ccpoa_hist/History_of_CCPOA.htm [accessed 19 February 2003].

California Department of Corrections and Rehabilitation, Regulations and Policies Manuals. Available at: http://www.cdcr.ca.gov/Regulations/index.html [accessed on 1 April 2009].

California Department of Corrections and Rehabilitation, Regulations and Policies Manuals. Notice of Change to the Director's Rules, 27 March 2000.

California Department of Corrections and Rehabilitation, Regulations and Policies Manuals (2009) *Career Opportunities*. Available at: http://www.cdcr.ca.gov/Career_Opportunities/POR/COIndex.html [accessed on 14 January 2009].

California Department of Corrections and Rehabilitation, Data Analysis Unit, Offender Information Services Branch Reports [online]. Available at: http://www.cdcr.ca.gov/Reports_Research/Offender_Information_Services_Branch/index [accessed on 1 April 2009].

California Department of Corrections and Rehabilitation, Data Analysis Unit, Offender Information Services Branch Reports [online] (2008) CDCR Facts and Figures, Third Quarter 2008. Available at: http://www,cdcr.ca.gov/Division_Boards/Adult_Operations/Facts_and_Figures.html [accessed on 16 February 2009].

California Department of Corrections and Rehabilitation, Data Analysis Unit, Offender Information Services Branch Reports [online] (2009) Second and Third Striker Felons as of 31 December 2008. Available at: http://www.cdcr.ca.gov/Reports_Research/Offender_Information_Services_Branch/index [accessed on 30 January 2009].

California Department of Finance, Performance Review Unit (1996) *California Department of Corrections, A Performance Review*. Sacramento, CA.

California Legislative Analyst's Office (LAO), Sacramento, CA. Analysis of Budget Bills 1994–5; 1995–6; 1996–7; 1997–8; 1998–9; 1999–2000; 2000–01; 2001–02; 2002–03; 2003–04; 2005–06; 2007–08. Available at: http://www.lao.ca.gov [accessed on 1 January 2009].

California Legislative Analyst's Office (LAO), Sacramento, CA (1997) *Addressing the State's Long-Term Inmate Population Growth*. Available at: http://www.lao.ca.gov/pb052097_addressing_inmate_pop.html [accessed on 1 April 2009].

California Legislative Analyst's Office (LAO), Sacramento, CA (1999 update) *The Three Strikes and You're Out Law*. Available at: http://www.lao.ca.gov/1999/cal_update/oct_99/oct_99_calupdate.html [accessed on 1 April 2009].

California Legislative Analyst's Office (LAO), Sacramento, CA (October 2005) *A Primer: Three Strikes: The Impact After More Than a Decade*. Available at: http://www.lao.ca.gov [accessed on 1 April 2009].

California Legislative Analyst's Office (LAO), Sacramento, CA (2007) *California's Criminal Justice System: A Primer*. 31 January 2007. Available at: http://www.lao.ca.gov [accessed on 1 April 2009].

California Prison Focus (1998a) 'Control units in the U.S.: part 1', *Prison Focus*, 2(2).

California Prison Focus (1998b) 'Control units in the U.S.: part 2', *Prison Focus*, 2(3).

California Prison Focus (2001) Press Release and Fact Sheet on Hunger Protest for Human Rights at Pelican Bay State Prison, 16 July. Available at: http://www.prisons.org/fact_sheet.htm [accessed on 4 October 2001].

Cambra, S. (1997) Address to participants of conference on supermax custody held on 13 August 1997 at Pelican Bay State Prison. Pelican Bay State Prison Public Information Office.

Caplow, T. and Simon, J. (1999) 'Understanding prison policy and population trends', in M. Tonry and J. Petersilia (eds), *Crime and Justice: A Review of Research*, vol. 26, *Prisons*. Chicago and London: University of Chicago Press, pp. 63–120.

Carlson, P. (1996) 'Corrections trends for the 21st century: our future behind the walls and wire', *The Keeper's Voice*, 17 (1): 5–8.

Carrabine, E. (2000) 'Discourse, governmentality and translation: towards a social theory of imprisonment', *Theoretical Criminology*, 4 (3): 309–31.

Carroll, L. (1974) *Hacks, Blacks and Cons: Race Relations in a Maximum Security Prison*. Lexington, MA: Lexington Books.

Carroll, L. (1998) *Lawful Order: A Case Study of Correctional Crisis and Reform*. New York and London: Garland.

Centre on Juvenile and Criminal Justice (1998) *Class Dismissed: Higher Education vs. Corrections During the Wilson Years*. September 1998. Available at: http://www.cjcj.org/files/classdis.pdf [accessed 1 April 2009].

Centre on Juvenile and Criminal Justice (2002) *California Correctional Facility Growth*. CJCJ Report, 27 March 2002.

Chadbourne, R. (1998) 'Prison architecture: the building is a tool', *Correctional Technology Magazine* (CTM), 14 December 1998.

Champion, D.J. (1994) *Measuring Offender Risk: A Criminal Justice Sourcebook*. Westport, CT: Greenwood Press.

Charrière, H. (1970) *Papillon*. London: Panther Books.

Christianson, S. (1998) *With Liberty for Some: 500 Years of Imprisonment in America*. Boston: Northeastern University Press.

Christie, N. (1993) *Crime Control as Industry: Towards Gulags, Western Style?* London: Routledge.

Clarke, R. (1980) '"Situational" crime prevention: theory and practice', *British Journal of Criminology*, 20 (2): 136–47.

Clay, W. (1861) *The Prison Chaplain – A Memoir of the Rev. John Clay*. London: Macmillan.

Clements, C. (1985) 'Towards an objective approach to offender classification', *Law and Psychology Review*, 9: 45.

Clemmer, D. (1940) *The Prison Community*. New York: Holt, Rinehart and Winston.

CNN (2005) 'Cheney: Iraq will be "enormous success story"'. Available at: http://www.cnn.com/2005/POLITICS/06/23/cheney.interview/index. html [accessed on 30 January 2009].

Cohen, S. (1985) *Visions of Social Control*. Cambridge: Polity Press.

Cohen, S. (1993) 'Human rights and crimes of the state: the culture of denial', *Australian and New Zealand Journal of Criminology*, 26 (2): 97–115.

Cohen, S. (2001) *States of Denial: Knowing About Atrocities and Suffering*. Cambridge: Polity Press.

Cohen, S. and Taylor, L. ([1972]1981) *Psychological Survival: The Experience of Long-Term Imprisonment* (2nd edn). Harmondsworth: Penguin Books.

Collins, W.C. (1998) *Jail Design and Operation and the Constitution: An Overview*. Washington, DC: US Department of Justice, National Institute of Corrections.

Colvin, M. (1992) *The Penitentiary in Crisis – From Accommodation to Riot in New Mexico*. Albany, NY: State University of New York Press.

Commission on Safety and Abuse in America's Prisons (2006) *Confronting Confinement*. Vera Institute of Justice, New York, June 2006.

Committee on the Judiciary, United States Congress (1974) *Individual Rights and the Federal Role in Behavior Modification*. A study prepared by the Subcommittee on Constitutional Rights. Second Session, November 1974. Washington, DC: US Government Printing Office.

Corrections Independent Review Panel (2004) *Reforming Corrections*. State of California, Sacramento, 30 June 2004. Available at: http://cpr/ca/gov/Review_Panel.html [accessed on 8 January 2009].

Coyle, A. (2002) *A Human Rights Approach to Prison Management*. London: International Centre for Prison Studies.

Cummins, E. (1994) *The Rise and Fall of California's Radical Prison Movement*. Stanford, CA: Stanford University Press.

Currie, E. (1998) *Crime and Punishment in America*. New York: Metropolitan Books.

Dewitt, C. (1997) *Building on Experience: A Case Study of Advanced Construction Financing Methods for Corrections*. Washington, DC: US Department of Justice, National Institute of Corrections.

Dickens, C. (1842) *American Notes for General Circulation*. London: Penguin Books (Reprint 1985).

Dilulio, J. (1987) *Governing Prisons: A Comparative Study of the Correctional Management*. New York: Free Press.

Dixon, W. (1850) *The London Prisons*. London: John Murray.

Downes, D. (1997) 'The buckling of the shields: Dutch penal policy 1985–1995', in R.P. Weiss and N. South (eds), *Comparing Prison Systems: Toward a Comparative and International Penology*. International Studies in Global Change, vol. 8. Amsterdam: Gordon and Breach, pp. 143–74.

Downes, D. (2001) 'The macho penal economy: Mass incarceration in the United States – a European perspective', *Punishment and Society*, 3 (1): 61–80.

Du Cane, E. (1885) *The Punishment and Prevention of Crime*. London: Macmillan.

Evans, R. (1982) *The Fabrication of Virtue: English Prison Architecture 1750–1840*. Cambridge: Cambridge University Press.

Fairweather, L. (2000) 'Psychological effects of the prison environment', in L. Fairweather and S. McConville (eds), *Prison Architecture: Policy, Design and Experience*. London: Architectural Press, pp. 31–48.

Fairweather, L. and McConville, S. (eds) (2000) *Prison Architecture: Policy, Design and Experience.* London: Architectural Press.

Fardon, R. (ed.) (1985) *Power and Knowledge: Anthropological and Sociological Approaches.* Edinburgh: Scottish Academic Press.

Faris, R.E. (1934) 'Cultural isolation and the schizophrenic personality', *American Journal of Sociology,* 40 (2): 155–64.

Fay, M. (2000) 'Meeting current challenges with inmate classification', *The Corrections Connections* [online]. Available at: http://www.corrections.com/news/security/012400.htm [accessed on 17 April 2000].

Federal Bureau of Prisons, US Department of Justice (1995) *Guidelines for Control Unit Programs.* 29 August 1995, Document No. PS5212.06.

Federal Bureau of Prisons, US Department of Justice (2001) *Program Statement on Control Unit Programs.* 20 February 2001, Document No. PS 5212.07.

Feeley, M. and Simon, J. (1992) 'The new penology: notes on the emerging strategy of corrections and its implications', *Criminology,* 30 (4): 452–74.

Fleisher, M.S. (1989) *Warehousing Violence.* London: Sage.

Foster, D. (1987) *Detention and Torture in South Africa.* Cape Town and Johannesburg: David Philip.

Foucault, M. (1977) *Discipline and Punish: The Birth of the Prison.* Harmonsworth: Penguin Books.

Foucault, M. (1980) *Power/Knowledge – Selected Interviews and Other Writings 1972–1977* (ed. C. Gordon). Brighton: Harvester Press.

France, P. (1996) *Hermits: The Insights of Solitude.* London: Pimlico.

Franke, H. (1992) 'The rise and decline of solitary confinement: socio-historical explanations of long-term penal changes', *British Journal of Criminology,* 32 (2): 125–43.

Franke, H. (1995) *The Emancipation of Prisoners: A Socio-Historical Analysis of the Dutch Prison Experience.* Edinburgh: Edinburgh University Press.

Freiberg, A. (2000) 'Guerrillas in our midst? Judicial responses to governing the dangerous', in M. Brown and J. Pratt (eds), *Dangerous Offenders: Punishment and Social Order.* London: Routledge, pp. 51–71.

Fry, E. (1847) *Memoir of the Life of Elizabeth Fry with Extracts from Her Journal and Letters.* London: Hatchard.

Gaes, G., Flanagan, T., Motiuk, L. and Stewart, L. (1999) 'Adult correctional treatment', in M. Tonry and J. Petersilia (eds), *Crime and Justice: A Review of Research,* vol. 26, *Prisons.* Chicago and London: University of Chicago Press, pp. 361–426.

Gaes, G., Wallace, S., Gilman E., Klein-Saffran, J. and Suppa, S. (2002) 'The influence of prison gang affiliation on violence and other prison misconduct', *Prison Journal,* 82 (3): 359–86.

Garland, D. (1985) *Punishment and Welfare.* Aldershot: Gower.

Garland, D. (1990) *Punishment and Modern Society: A Study in Social Theory.* Oxford: Clarendon Press.

Garland, D. (2000) 'The culture of high crime societies: some preconditions of recent "law and order" policies', *British Journal of Criminology*, 40: 347–75.

Garland, D. (2001) *The Culture of Control: Crime and Social Order in Contemporary Society*. Oxford: Oxford University Press.

Gaseau, M. (1999a) 'Balancing needs and the budget in corrections construction', 12 April. *The Corrections Connection Magazine* [online]. Available at: http://www.corrections.com [accessed on 18 January 2000].

Gaseau, M. (1999b) 'Construction aesthetics: building a facility that fits staff needs', 19 April. *The Corrections Connection Magazine* [online]. Available at: http://www.corrections.com [accessed on 18 January 2000].

Gaseau, M. (1999c) 'Overcoming the challenges of corrections construction', 26 April. *The Corrections Connection Magazine* [online]. Available at: http://www.corrections.com [accessed on 18 January 2000].

Gendreau, P. and Bonta, J. (1984) 'Solitary confinement is not cruel and unusual punishment: people sometimes are!', *Canadian Journal of Criminology*, 26: 467–78.

Geniella, M. (2001) 'Inside Pelican Bay', *The Press Democrat* [online] 22 April 2001. Available at: http://www.sfbappa.org/Awards/picturestory/picstory28.ex2.html [accessed on 23 November 2008].

Goffman, E. (1961) *Asylums: Essays on the Social Situation of Mental Patients and Other Inmates*. Garden City, New York: Anchor Books.

Goffman, E. (1963) *Stigma*. Englewood Cliffs, NJ: Prentice-Hall.

Gottfredson, S. and Gottfredson, D. (1985) 'Screening for risk among parolees: policy, practice and method', in D. Farrington and R. Tarling (eds), *Predictions in Criminology*. Albany, NY: State University of New York Press, pp. 151–82.

Gottfredson, D. and Tonry, M. (eds) (1987) *Prediction and Classification*. Chicago: University of Chicago Press.

Grassian, S. (1983) 'Psychopathological effects of solitary confinement', *American Journal of Psychiatry*, 140 (11): 1450–54.

Grassian, S. (2006) 'Psychiatric effects of solitary confinement', *Journal of Law and Policy*, 22: 325–83.

Grassian, S. and Friedman N. (1986) 'Effects of sensory deprivation in psychiatric seclusion and solitary confinement', *International Journal of Law and Psychiatry*, 8: 49–65.

Gunderson, E.K. and Palinkas, L.A. (1991) 'Psychological studies in the US Antarctic program: a review', *SPRI Polar Symposia*, 1: 5–8.

Gunn, J., Maden, T. and Swinton, A. (1990) *Mentally Disordered Prisoners*. London: Institute of Psychiatry.

Hagar, J. (2004) *Special Master's Draft Report re Department of Corrections 'Post Powers' investigations and Employee Discipline*. Sacramento, CA, 15 January.

Hall, D.A., Townsend, R.E. and Knippa, J. (1980) *Changes in Mood, Fatigue, and Work-Rest Cycles Associated with Deep Submersible Operations*. San Diego, CA: Naval Health Research Center, Report No. 80–5.

Haney, C. (1994) 'Infamous punishment: the psychological consequences of isolation', *National Prison Project Journal*, 9: 3–21.

Haney, C. (2003) 'Mental health issues in long-term solitary and "supermax" confinement', *Crime and Delinquency*, 49 (1): 124–56.

Haney, C. (2008) 'A culture of harm: taming the dynamics of cruelty in supermax prisons', *Criminal Justice and Behaviour*, 35 (8): 956–84.

Haney, C., Banks, W. and Zimbardo, P. (1973) 'Interpersonal dynamics in a simulated prison', *International Journal of Criminology and Penology*, 1: 69–97.

Haney, C. and Lynch, M. (1997) 'Regulating prisons of the future: psychological analysis of supermax and solitary confinement', *New York University Review of Law and Social Change*, 23 (4): 477–570.

Hannah, M. (1997) 'Space and the structuring of disciplinary power: an interpretative review', *Geografiska Annaler*, 70B (3): 171–80.

Hanson, R. and Daley, H. (1995) *Challenging the Conditions of Prisons and Jails: A Report on Section 1983 Litigation.* US Department of Justice Discussion Paper, January 1995 (NCJ-151652).

Hardyman, P. and Adams-Fuller, T. (2001) *Prison Classification Peer Training and Strategy Session: What's Happening with the Prison Classification System?* Conference Proceedings, 7 September 2000. Washington DC: US Department of Justice, National Institute of Corrections.

Hayes, L. (1995) 'Prison suicide: an overview and a guide to prevention', *Prison Journal*, 75 (4): 431–56.

Hazelrigg, L.E. (ed.) (1968) *Prison Within Society: A Reader in Penology.* New York: Doubleday.

Hinkle, L. and Wolff, H. (1956) 'Communist interrogation and indoctrination of "enemies of the states"', *A.M.A. Archives of Neurology and Psychiatry*, 76: 115–74.

Hirst, P. (1985) 'Constructed space and the subject', in R. Fardon (ed.), *Power and Knowledge: Anthropological and Sociological Approaches.* Edinburgh: Scottish Academic Press, pp. 171–91.

Hocking, F. (1970) 'Extreme environmental stress and its significance for psychopathology', *American Journal of Psychiatry*, 24: 4–26.

Hodgins, S. and Cote, G. (1991) 'The mental health of penitentiary inmates in isolation', *Canadian Journal of Criminology*, April: 175–82.

Hoffmann, J. (1999) 'Don't let your food loaf', *Corrections Technology Magazine*, 2 (August): 5.

Hunt, G., Reigel, S., Morales, T. and Waldorf, D (1993) 'Changes in prison culture: prison gangs and the case of the Pepsi generation', *Social Problems*, 40 (3): 398–409.

Human Rights Watch (1991) *Prison Conditions in the United States.* New York: Human Rights Watch.

Human Rights Watch (1993) *The Human Rights Watch Global Report on Prisons.* New York: Human Rights Watch.

Human Rights Watch (1995) *Prison Conditions in Japan.* New York: Human Rights Watch.

Human Rights Watch (1997) *Cold Storage: Super-Maximum Security Confinement in Indiana*. New York: Human Rights Watch.

Human Rights Watch (1999) *Red Onion State Prison: Super-Maximum Confinement in Virginia*. New York: Human Rights Watch.

Human Rights Watch (2000) *Out of Sight: Super-Maximum Security Confinement in the United States*. New York: Human Rights Watch.

Human Rights Watch (2001) *World Report 2000*. New York: Human Rights Watch.

Human Rights Watch (2003) *Ill-Equipped: U.S. Prisons and Offenders with Mental Illness*. New York: Human Rights Watch.

Human Rights Watch (2008) *Locked Up Alone: Detention Conditions and Mental Health at Guantanamo*. New York: Human Rights Watch.

Ignatieff, M. (1978) *A Just Measure of Pain: the Penitentiary in the Industrial Revolution 1750–1850*. New York: Pantheon Books.

Ingram, G.L. (1987) 'The American federal system: control and classification', in A.E. Bottoms and R. Light (eds), *Problems of Long Term Imprisonment*. Cropwood Round-Table Conferences, Cambridge Studies in Criminology. Aldershot: Gower, pp. 202–13.

Ingram, G.L. and Wellford, C.F. (1987) 'The totality of conditions test in eighth-amendment litigation', in S.D. Gotterfredson and S. McConville (eds), *America's Correctional Crisis: Prison Populations and Public Policy*. Contributions in Criminology and Penology, Number 17. Westport, CT: Greenwood Press, pp. 13–37.

International Psychological Trauma Symposium (2007) *Istanbul statement on the use and effects of solitary confinement*. Available at: http://solitaryconfinement. org/istanbul [accessed on 1 April 2009].

Irwin, J.K. (1980) *Prisons in Turmoil*. Boston: Little Brown.

Irwin, J.K. (1981) 'Sociological studies of the impact of long-term confinement', in D.A. Ward and K.F. Schoen (eds), *Confinement in Maximum Custody: New Last-Resort Prisons in the United States and Western Europe*. Lexington, MA: Lexington Books and D.C. Heath, pp. 49–60.

Irwin, J.K. and Cressey, D.R. (1962) 'Thieves, convicts and the inmate culture', *Social Problems*, 10: 142–55.

Jackson, M. (1983) *Prisoners of Isolation*. Toronto: Toronto University Press.

Jacobs, J.B. (1977) *Stateville: The Penitentiary in Mass Society*. Chicago: University of Chicago Press.

Jacobs, J.B. (1983) *New Perspectives on Prisons and Imprisonment*. Ithaca and London: Cornell University Press.

James, A., Bottomley, K., Liebling, A. and Clare, E. (1997) *Privatising Prisons: Rhetoric and Reality*. London: Sage.

Jebb, J. (1844) *Modern Prisons: Their Construction and Ventilation*. London: John Weal.

Jewkes, Y. (2002) *Captive Audience: Media, Masculinity and Power in Prisons*. Cullompton: Willan Publishing.

Johnson, K. (1997) 'Serving superhard time: new prison isolates worst inmates', *USA Today*, 4 August 1997, p. 01A.

Johnston, N. (2000) *Forms of Constraint: A History of Prison Architecture*. Chicago: University of Illinois Press.

Joint Task Force Guantánamo (2009) http://www.jtfgtmo.southcom.mil/about.html [accessed on 6 March 2009].

Kauffman, K. (1988) *Prison Officers and Their World*. Cambridge, MA: Harvard University Press.

Keenan, B. (1992) *An Evil Cradling*. London: Vintage Books.

Kelman, H.C. and Hamilton, V.L. (1989) *Crimes of Obedience: Toward A Social Psychology of Authority and Responsibility*. New Haven, CT: Yale University Press.

King, R. (1987) 'New generation prisons: the prison building programme and the future of the dispersal policy', in A.E. Bottoms and R. Light (eds), *Problems of Long Term Imprisonment*. Cropwood Round-Table Conferences, Cambridge Studies in Criminology. Aldershot: Gower, pp. 115–38.

King, R. (1999) 'The rise and rise of supermax: An American solution in search of a problem?', *Punishment and Society*, 1 (2): 163–86.

King, R. (2007) 'Security, control and the problems of containment', in Y. Jewkes (ed.), *Handbook on Prisons*. Cullompton: Willan Publishing, pp. 329–55.

King, R. and Maguire, M. (1994) *Prisons in Context*. Oxford: Clarendon Press.

King, R. and McDermott, K. (1995) *The State of Our Prisons*. Oxford: Clarendon Press.

King, R.S. (2009) *The State of Sentencing 2008*. Washington, DC: The Sentencing Project. Available at: http://www.sentencingproject.org [accessed on 1 April 2009].

Kingsmill, J. (1854) *Chapters on Prisons and Prisoners and the Prevention of Crime* (3rd edn). London: Longman, Brown, Green, and Longmans.

Krantz, S. (1988) *The Law of Corrections and Prisoners Rights in a Nutshell* (3rd edn). St. Paul, MN: West Publishing.

Kupers, T. (1993) Declaration in the case of *Coleman v. Wilson*, District Court of Eastern California, No. CIV S 90-0520 LKK-JFM, 16 February 1993.

Kupers, T. (1996) 'Trauma and its sequelae in male prisoners: effects of confinement, overcrowding and diminished services', *American Journal of Orthopsychiatry*, 66 (2): 189–96.

Kupers, T. (1999) *Prison Madness: The Mental Health Crisis Behind Bars and What W Must Do About It*. San Francisco: Jossey-Bass.

Kurki, L. and Morris, N. (2001) 'The purposes, practices and problems of supermax prisons', in M. Tonry (ed.) *Crime and Justice: A Review of Research*, vol. 28. Chicago: University of Chicago Press, pp. 385–424.

Larsen, D., Hudnall-Stamm, B., Davis, K. and Magaletta, P. (2004) 'Prison telemedicine and telehealth utilization in the United States', *Telemedicine and e-health Journal*, 10 (2): S81–S90.

Lawrence, S. and Mears, D.P. (2004) *Benefit–Cost Analysis of Supermax Confinement: Critical Steps and Considerations.* Urban Institute, Justice Policy Center, Washington, DC.

Lenz, N. (2002) '"Luxuries" in prison: the relationship between amenity funding and public support', *Crime and Delinquency*, 48 (4): 499–525.

Levasseur, R.L. (1998) 'From USP Marion to ADX Florence (and back again): the fire inside', in D. Burton-Rose, D. Pens and P. Wright (eds), *The Celling of America: An Inside Look at the U.S. Prison Industry.* Monroe, ME: Common Courage Press, pp. 200–5.

Levasseur, R.L. (1995) *Letter sent to a meeting of the Campaign to End the Marion Lockdown,* 21 October 1995. Available at: http://www.unix.oit.umass.edu/~kastor/fallprogram/florence-letters.html [accessed on 10 January 2005].

Liebling, A. (2000) 'Prison officers, policing and the use of discretion', *Theoretical Criminology*, 4 (3): 333–57.

Liebling, A., Price, D. and Elliot, C. (1999) 'Appreciative inquiry and relationships in prison', *Punishment and Society*, 1 (1): 71–98.

Little Hoover Commission (1998) *Beyond Bars: Correctional Reforms to Lower Prison Costs and Reduce Crime.* Report No. 144. Available at: www.lhc.ca.gov/lhcdir/144/TC144.html [accessed on 1 April 2009].

Locke, J. (1710) *Essay Concerning Human Understanding.* London.

Lovell, D. (2008) 'Patterns of disturbed behaviour in a supermax population', *Criminal Justice and Behaviour*, 35 (8): 985–1004.

Lovell, D., Johnson, C. and Cain, C. (2007) 'Recidivism of supermax prisoners in Washington State', *Crime and Delinquency*, 52 (4): 633–56.

Lynch, M. (2000) 'Rehabilitation as rhetoric: the ideal of reformation in contemporary parole discourse and practices', *Punishment and Society*, 2 (1): 40–65.

Lynch, M. (2002) 'Selling "securityware": transformations in prison commodities advertising 1949–99', *Punishment and Society*, 4 (3): 305–19.

Lutalo, O. (1995) 'Letter sent from MCU, Texas, to a meeting of the Campaign to Stop Control Units meeting held in Chicago, Illinois on 21 October 1995'. Available at: http://www-unix.oit.umass.edu/-kastor/fallprogram/florence-letters.html [accessed on 31 January 2009].

Lyon, D. (1994) *The Electronic Eye: The Rise of Surveillance Society.* Minneapolis, MN: University of Minnesota Press.

MacKenzie, D. (1989) 'Prison classification: the management and psychological perspectives', in L. Goodstein and D. MacKenzie (eds), *The American Prison: Issues in Research and Policy.* Law, Society, and Policy Series, vol. 4. New York: Plenum Press, pp. 163–89.

Maguire, R., Morgan, R. and Reiner R. (eds) (1997) *The Oxford Handbook of Criminology* (2nd edn). Oxford: Clarendon Press.

Mandela, N. (1994) *Long Walk to Freedom*. Boston: Little Brown.

Mason, T. (1999) 'A psychiatric "Supermax"? Long-term high-security psychiatric services', *International Journal of Law and Psychiatry*, 22 (2): 155–66.

Mathiesen, T. (1965) *The Defences of the Weak*. London: Tavistock.

Mathiesen, T. (1990) *Prison on Trial*. London: Sage.

Mathiesen, T. (2001) 'Television, public space and prison population', *Punishment and Society*, 3 (1): 35–42.

Matthews, R. and Francis, P. (eds) (1996) *Prisons 2000*. Basingstoke: Macmillan.

Mauer, M. (1998) *'Three Strikes' Laws: Five Years Later*. Washington, DC: The Sentencing Project.

Mauer, M. (1999) *The Race to Incarcerate*. New York: The New Press.

Mauer, M. (2001) 'The causes and consequences of prison growth in the United States', *Punishment and Society*, 3 (1): 9–20.

McCleery, R. (1961) 'Authoritarianism and the belief system of the incorrigibles', in D. Cressey (ed.), *The Prison*. New York: Holt, Rinehart and Winston, pp. 260–306.

McConville, S. (1981) *A History of English Prison Administration*. London: Routledge and Kegan Paul.

Mead, G.H. (1934) *Mind, Self and Society*. Chicago: University of Chicago Press.

Mears, D.P. (2005) *Evaluating the Effectiveness of Supermax Prisons*. Washington, DC: The Urban Institute Justice Policy Center.

Megargee, E.L. and Bohn, M.J. (1979) *Classifying Criminal Offenders: A New System Based on the MMPI*. Beverly Hills, CA: Sage.

Melossi, D. and Pavarini, M. (1981) *The Prison and the Factory: Origins of the Penitentiary System*. London: Macmillan.

Melvin, M.A. (1992) 'Individual coping strategies countering the effects of solitary confinement', *Torture*, 2 (2): 59–61.

Meranze, M. (1996) *Laboratories of Virtue: Punishment, Revolution, and Authority in Philadelphia, 1760–1835*. Chapel Hill, NC: University of North Carolina Press.

Milgram, S. (1974) *Obedience to Authority: An Experimental View*. New York: Harper & Row.

Millender, M.J. (1998) 'The road to Eastern State: liberalism, the public sphere and the origins of the American penitentiary', *Yale Journal of Law and the Humanities*, 10 (1): 163–89.

Miller, J. (1996) *Search and Destroy: African-American Males in the Criminal Justice System*. Cambridge: Cambridge University Press.

Miller, J. (2000) 'American gulag'. *Yes Magazine* [online], Fall 2000. Available at: http://www.yesmagazine.org/15prisons/miller.htm [accessed 30 January 2001].

Millett, K. (1994) *The Politics of Cruelty*. London: Viking Press.

Mitford, J. (1974) *Kind and Usual Punishment: The Prison Business*. New York: Alfred Knopf.

Molden, J. (n.d.) 'FLO: the big one', *Correctional Technology Magazine* (CTM). Available at: http://infobase.thirdcoast.net [accessed 30 January 2001].

Monahan, J. (1981) *Predicting Violent Behaviour: An Assessment of Clinical Techniques.* Beverly Hills, CA: Sage.

Monitoring Project of the National Campaign to Stop Control Units (1997) *The Use of Control Unit Prisons in the United States.* Coulder, CO: The Rocky Mountain Peace Project.

Moore, S. (2009) 'Court orders California to cut prison population', *The New York Times,* 10 February 2009, p. A12.

Morris, N. (2000) 'Prisons in the USA: Supermax – the bad and the mad', in L. Fairweather and S. McConville (eds), *Prison Architecture: Policy, Design and Experience.* London: Architectural Press, pp. 98–108.

Morris, N. and Rothman, D. (eds) (1995) *The Oxford History of the Prison: The Practice of Punishment in Western Society.* Oxford: Oxford University Press.

Morris, T. and Morris, P. (1963) *Pentonville: A Sociological Study of An English Prison.* London: Routledge & Kegan Paul.

Moyer, F. (1975) 'The Architecture of closed institutions', in United Nations Social Defence Research Institute (UNSDRI), *Prison Architecture: An International Survey of Representative and Closed Institutions and Analysis of Current Trends in Prison Design* (prepared by G.D. Gennarro). London: Architectural Press, pp. 53–66.

National Institute of Corrections, US Department of Justice (1991) *Management Strategies in Disturbances and with Gangs/Disruptive Groups.* Longmont, CO: NIC Information Center.

National Institute of Corrections, US Department of Justice (1997) *Supermax Housing: A Survey of Current Practice.* Special Issues in Corrections. Longmont, CO: NIC Information Center.

National Institute of Corrections, US Department of Justice (1999) *MIS Systems in State Prisons.* Special Issues in Corrections. Longmont, CO: NIC Information Center.

National Institute of Corrections, US Department of Justice (2001) *Classification and Training Report.* Longmont, CO: NIC Information Center.

National Institute of Justice Statistics (1997) *Intermediate Sanctions.* Research in Action Report. Washington, DC: Department of Justice.

Neumann, L. (1998) *California Behind Bars* [online]. Available at: http://www.corrections.com/news/misc/california.html [accessed on 20 June 2000].

Newburn, T. (2002) 'Atlantic Crossings: "Policy Transfer" and Crime Control in the USA and Britain', *Punishment and Society,* 4 (2): 165–94.

Nitsche, P. and Williams, K. (1913) 'The history of the prison psychosis', *Nervous and Mental Disease Monograph Series,* No. 13. New York: Nervous and Mental Disease Publishing Company.

Office of the Inspector General (2009) *Special Review: Management of the California Department of Corrections and Rehabilitation's Administrative*

Segregation Unit Population. David R. Shaw, Inspector General. January 2009.

Owen, B. (1988) *The Reproduction of Social Control*. New York: Praeger.

Palinkas, L.A. (1989) *Sociocultural Influences on Psychosocial Adjustment in Antarctica*. Naval Health Research Center Report No. 85–49.

Palinkas, L.A., Gunderson, E.K.E. and Burr, R.G. (1989) *Psychophysiological Correlates of Human Adaptation in Antarctica*. Naval Health Research Center Report No. 89–5.

Parenti, C. (1997) 'Rural prison as colonial master', *Z Magazine* [online]. Available at: http://www.zmag.org/Zmag/articles/june97parenti.htm [accessed on 18 May 2000].

Parenti, C. (1999a) *Lockdown America: Police and Prisons in the Age of Crisis*. London: Verso.

Parenti, C. (1999b) 'The prison industrial complex: crisis and control', *CorpWatch Online*, 1 September. Available at: http://www.corpwatch.org/issues/PID [accessed on 13 February 2003].

Park, R.E. (1925) 'The city: suggestions for the investigation of human behavior in the urban environment', in R. Park, E.W. Burgess and R.D. McKenzie (eds), *The City*. Chicago: University of Chicago Press, pp. 1–46.

PeaceKeeper Magazine (2000) (California Correctional Peace Officers Association, Sacramento, CA), vol. 17 (3, Summer), p. 7.

Pell, E. (ed.) (1972) *Maximum Security: Letters from Prison*. New York: Dutton.

Penal Reform International (2001) *Making Standards Work: An International Handbook on Good Prison Practice*. London: Penal Reform International.

Perkinson, R. (1996) 'Shackled justice: Florence Federal Penitentiary and the new politics of punishment', *Social Justice*, 24 (3): 117–32.

Petersilia, J. (2006) *Understanding California Corrections*. Berkeley, CA: California Policy Research Center, University of California.

Philo, C. (1989) 'Enough to drive one mad: the organisation of space in nineteenth century lunatic asylums', in J. Wolch and M. Dear (eds), *The Power of Geography: How Territory Shapes Social Life*. Boston: Unwin Hyman, pp. 258–90.

Physicians for Human Rights (2005) *Break Them Down: Systematic Use of Psychological Torture by US Forces*. Boston: Physicians for Human Rights.

Pizarro, J. and Stenius, V.M.K. (2004) 'Supermax prisons: their rise, current practices, and the effect on inmates', *Prison Journal*, 84: 248–64.

Pizarro, J., Stenius, V.M.K. and Pratt, T.C. (2006) 'Supermax prisons: myths, realities, and the politics of punishment in American society', *Criminal Justice Policy Review*, 17: 6–21.

Player, E. and Jenkins, M. (eds) (1994) *Prisons After Woolf: Reform Through Riot*. London: Routledge.

Podger, P. (1999) 'Prison control heading high tech: Corrections Dept. considers arming officers with nonlethal devices', *San Francisco Chronicle*, 7 June, p. A–1.

Poole, E.D. and Regoli, R.M. (1980) 'Work relations and cynicism among prison guards', *Criminal Justice and Behavior*, 7 (3): 303–14.

Porter, R. (1982) *English Society in the Eighteenth Century*. Harmondsworth: Penguin Books.

Pratt, J., Brown, D., Hallsworth, S. and Morrison, W. (eds) (2005) *The New Punitiveness: Trends, Theories, Perspectives*. Cullompton: Willan Publishing.

Prendergast, A. (1995) 'The women of supermax: Colorado's highest security prison isn't just for tough guys', *Denver Westword Online*, 8 November. Available at: http://www.westword.com/issues/1995-11-08/news/city limits4.htm [accessed on 13 January 2005].

Prendergast, A. (2000) 'A broken code: the supermax snitch unit was supposed to bust prison gangs, but who is really rolling over?', *Denver Westword Online*, 27 July. Available at: http://www.westword.com/issues/2000-07-27/news/news.htm [accessed on 13 January 2005].

Quay, H. (1983) *Technical Manual for the Behavioral Classification System for Adult Offenders*. Washington, DC: Department of Justice.

Quinsey, V., Harris, G., Rice, M. and Cormier, C. (1998) *Violent Offenders: Appraising and Managing Risk*. Washington, DC: American Psychological Association.

Rakatansky, M. (1991) *Spatial Narratives*. Available at: http://www.haussite.net/haus.0/SCRIPT/txt1999/05/TEXT1.html [accessed on 10 January 2005].

Rasmussen, J. (ed.) (1973) *Man in Isolation and Confinement: Modern Applications of Psychology*. Chicago: Aldine.

Raynor, P. (1997) 'Some observations on rehabilitation and justice', *The Howard Journal*, 36 (3): 248–62.

Reiman, J. (1996) *And the Poor Get Prison: Economic Bias in American Criminal Justice*. Boston, MA: Allyn and Bacon.

Relly, J.E. (1999) 'Supermax – inside, no one can hear you scream', *Tucson Weekly*, 29 April–5 May. Available at http://www.tucsonweekly.com/tw/04-29-99/feat.htm [accessed on 30 January 2009].

Rendon, J. (1998) 'Inside the new high-tech lock-downs', *Salon Online*, 8 September. Available at: http://www.salon.com/21st/feature/1998/09/cov_08feature2.html [accessed on 18 January 2000].

Reyes, H. (2007) 'The worst scars are in the mind: psychological torture' *International Review of the Red Cross*, 89 (867): 591–617.

Rhodes, L.A. (2004a) 'Psychopathy and the face of control in supermax', *Ethnography*, 3 (4): 442–66.

Rhodes, L.A. (2004b) *Total Confinement: Madness and Reason in the Maximum Security Prison*. Berkeley and Los Angeles, CA: University of California Press.

Rice, T. (2003) 'Soundselves: an acoustemology of sound and self in the Edinburgh Royal Infirmary', *Anthropology Today*, 19 (4): 4–10.

Riveland, C. (1999) *Supermax Prisons: Overview and General Considerations*. Washington, DC: US Department of Justice, National Institute of Corrections.

Rock, P. (1996) *Reconstructing a Women's Prison: The Holloway Redevelopment Project 1968–88*. Oxford: Clarendon Press.

Rodley, N. (1987) *Treatment of Prisoners Under International Law*. Oxford: Clarendon Press.

Roscoe, W. (1823) *Additional Observations on Penal Jurisprudence and the Reform of Criminals*. London.

Rosen, E. (2000) 'A captivating success story', *Teleconference Magazine* [online]. Available at: http://www.teleconferencemagazine.com/march april/captivatingsuccessstory.htm [accessed on 18 May 2000].

Rothblum, E. (1990) 'Psychological factors in the Antarctic', *Journal of Psychology*, 124 (3): 253–73.

Rothman, D.J. (1971) *The Discovery of the Asylum: Social Order and Disorder in the New Republic*. Boston: Little, Brown.

Rothman, D.J. (1980) *Conscience and Convenience: The Asylum and Its Alternatives in Progressive America*. Boston: Little, Brown.

Rothman, E. (1995) 'The failure of reform: United States 1865–1965', in N. Morris and D. Rothman (eds), *The Oxford History of the Prison: The Practice of Punishment in Western Society*. Oxford: Oxford University Press, pp. 151–77.

'Rumsfeld Knew' (2008) 'Interview with Lynndie England', *Stern Magazine*, 17 March. Available at: http://www.stern.de/politik/ausland/: Lynndie-England--Rumsfeld-/614356.html [accessed on 28 February 2009].

Rutherford, A. (1986) *Prisons and the Process of Justice*. Oxford: Oxford University Press.

Rutherford, A. (1996) *Criminal Policy and the Eliminative Ideal*. Inaugural Lecture given at the University of Southampton, 8 October 1996.

Scharff-Smith, P. (2004) 'A religious technology of the self: rationality and religion in the rise of the modern penitentiary', *Punishment and Society*, 6 (2): 195–220.

Schein, E. (1960) 'Interpersonal communication, group solidarity, and social influence', *Sociometry*, 23 (2): 148–61.

Schlosser, E. (1998) 'The prison industrial complex', *The Atlantic*, 282 (6): 51–77.

Scott, G.D. and Gendreau, P. (1969) 'Psychiatric implications of sensory deprivation in a maximum security prison', *Canadian Psychiatric Association Journal*, 14 (1): 337–41.

Scott, G.R. (1997) *A History of Torture*. London: Random House.

Scraton, P., Sim, J. and Skidmore, P. (1991) *Prisons Under Protest*. Milton Keynes: Open University Press.

Sestfot, D.M., Andersen, H.S., Lillebaek. T. and Gabrielsen, G. (1998) 'Impact of solitary confinement on hospitalisation among Danish prisoners in custody', *International Journal of Law and Psychiatry*, 21 (1): 99–108.

Shalev, S. (2007) 'The power to classify: avenues into a supermax prison', in D. Downes, P. Rock, C. Chinkin and C. Gearty (eds), *Crime, Social Control and Human Rights: From Moral Panics to States of Denial*. Cullompton: Willan Publishing, pp. 107–19.

Shalev, S. (2008) *A Sourcebook on Solitary Confinement*. London: Mannheim Centre for Criminology, London School of Economics. Available online at: http://www.solitaryconfinement.org.

Shalev, S. and Guinea, D. (2004) 'La détention en isolement dans les prisons européennes', in M. Zingoni-Fernandez and N. Giovannini (eds), *Les régimes spéciaux de détention en Italie et en Espagne et les mesures administratives en France et au Royaume-Uni*. Bruxelles: Bruylant, pp. 63–96.

Shallice, T. (1984) 'The Ulster depth interrogation techniques and their relation to sensory deprivation research', *Cognition*, 1 (4): 385–405.

Sharpe, J.A. (1990) *Judicial Punishment in England*. London: Faber & Faber.

Shearing, C.D. and Stenning, P.C. (1985) 'From the Panopticon to Disney World: the development of discipline', in A. Doob and E. Greenspan (eds), *Criminal Law*. Ontario: Canada Law Books, pp. 335–49.

Sherman, M., Magnani, L. and Kerness, B. (1998) *Torture in the United States: The Status of Compliance by the U.S. Government with the International Convention Against Torture and Other Cruel, Inhuman and Degrading Treatment or Punishment*. Report submitted to the United Nations.

Shichor, D. and Sechrest, D. (eds) (1996) *Three Strikes and You're Out: Vengeance as Public Policy*. Thousand Oaks, CA: Sage.

Siegel, R. (1984) 'Hostage hallucinations: visual imagery induced by isolation and life-threatening stress', *Journal of Nervous and Mental Disease*, 17 (5): 264–72.

Silberman, M. (1995) *A World of Violence: Corrections in America*. Belmont, CA: Wadsworth.

Sim, J. (1995) 'The prison medical service and the deviant 1895–1948', in R. Creese, W.F. Bynum and J. Bearn (eds), *The Health of Prisoners*. Amsterdam/Atlanta, GA: Clio Medica/The Wellcome Series in the History of Medicine, vol. 34, pp. 102–17.

Simon, J. (1993) *Poor Discipline: Parole and the Social Underclass 1890–1990*. Chicago, Illinois: University of Chicago Press.

Simon, J. (2000) 'The "society of captives" in the era of hyper-incarceration', *Theoretical Criminology*, 4 (3): 285–308.

Skinner, B.F. (1953) *Science and Human Behavior*. New York: Macmillan.

Smith, C.E. (2000) 'The governance of corrections: implications of the changing interface of courts and corrections', *Criminal Justice*, 2: 113–66.

Smith, S. and Lewty, W. (1959) 'Perceptual isolation using a silent room', *Lancet*, 2: 342–45.

Solomon, P., Kubzansky, P.E. and Leiderman, P.H. (eds) (1961) *Sensory Deprivation*. Cambridge, MA: Harvard University Press.

Somnier, F.E. and Genefke, I.K. (1986) 'Psychotherapy for victims of torture', *British Journal of Psychiatry*, 149: 323–29

Sparks, R., Bottoms, A.E. and. Hay, W. (1996) *Prisons and the Problem of Order*. Oxford: Clarendon Press.

Stockton, D. (2000) 'Does the tray fit the need? Food service equipment choices'. *Correctional Technology Magazine* (CTM), 21 August. Available at: http://infobase.thirdcoast.net [accessed on 18 January 2003].

Stuab, E. (1989) *The Roots of Evil*. Cambridge: Cambridge University Press.

Suedfeld, P. (1975) 'The benefits of boredom: sensory deprivation reconsidered', *American Scientist*, 63: 60–9.

Suedfeld, P. and Roy, C. (1975) 'Using social isolation to change the behaviour of disruptive inmates', *International Journal of Offender Therapy and Comparative Criminology*, 19: 90–9.

Suedfeld, P., Ramirez, C., Deaton, J. and Baker-Brown, G. (1982) 'Reactions and attributes of prisoners in solitary confinement', *Criminal Justice and Behaviour*, 9 (3): 303–40.

Sutherland, E.H. and Cressey, D.R. (1970) *Principles of Criminology* (8th edn). Philadelphia: J.B. Lippincott.

Sykes, G. (1958) *The Society of Captives: A Study of a Maximum Security Prison*. Princeton, NJ: Princeton University Press.

Sykes, G.M. and Matza, D. (1957) 'Techniques of neutralisation: a theory of delinquency', *American Sociological Review*, 22: 664–70.

Tachiki, S.N. (1995) 'Indeterminate sentences in supermax prisons based upon alleged gang affiliations: a reexamination of procedural protection and a proposal for greater procedural requirements', *California Law Review*, 83: 1115–49.

Taguba Report On Treatment of Abu Ghraib Prisoners in Iraq, released May 2004. Online at: http://www.dod.mil/pubs/foi/detainees/taguba/ [accessed on 28 February 2009].

Tannenbaum, J. (1999) 'Prisons a growth industry: correctional officers union keeping it that way', *San Francisco Chronicle*, 27 September, p. A–24.

Taylor, A.J.W. (1961) 'Social isolation and imprisonment', *Psychiatry*, 24: 373–78.

Toch, H. (1987) 'The disturbed and disruptive inmate: where does the buck stop?', *Journal of Psychiatry and the Law*, 10: 321–49.

Toch, H. (1992) *Mosaic of Despair: Human Breakdown in Prison*. Washington, DC: American Psychological Association.

Toch, H. (2001) 'The future of supermax confinement', *Prison Journal*, 81 (3): 376–88.

Tonry, M. (2001) 'Unthought thoughts: the influence of changing sensibilities on penal policies', *Punishment and Society*, 3 (1): 176–81.

Tonry, M. and Petersilia, J. (eds) (1999) *Crime and Justice: A Review of Research*. Vol. 26, *Prisons*. Chicago: University of Chicago Press.

Travis, A. (1999) 'Prisoners challenge transfer to "brutal' wing", *Guardian*, 21 January, p. 6.

Tyler, T.R. and Boeckmann, R.J. (1997) 'Three strikes and you are out, but why? The psychology of public support for punishing rule breakers', *Law and Society Review*, 31: 237–65.

United Nations Committee Against Torture (2000) Conclusions and Recommendations of the Committee against Torture: United States of America. 15/5/2000, CAT/C/24/6.

United Nations High Commissioner on Human Rights (2005) Human Rights and Prisons, Professional Training Series No. 11. Geneva: United Nations. Available online at: http://www.ohchr.org.

United Nations Human Rights Committee (1990) Selected Decisions of the Human Rights Committee under the Optional Protocol of the ICCPR, vol. 2, 17th to 32nd sessions (October 1982–April 1988), CCPR/C/op/2.

United Nations Human Rights Committee (1992) General Comments no. 20/44 of 3 April and no. 21/44 of 6 April 6.

United Nations Human Rights Committee (1995) Comments on the United States of America. 53rd session, CCPR/C/79/Add 50.

United Nations Social Defence Research Institute (UNSDRI) (1975) *Prison Architecture: An International Survey of Representative and Closed Institutions and Analysis of Current Trends in Prison Design* (prepared by G.D. Gennarro). London: Architectural Press.

United Nations Special Rapporteur on Torture (1996). Report of the Special Rapporteur on Torture, 9 January 1996. UN DOC GENERAL/CN.4/1996/35.

United States Federal Bureau of Justice Statistical Bulletins. Available at: http://www/ojp/usdoj/gov/bjs.

US Bureau of Justice Statistics (2008) *Prisoners in 2007*. Washington, DC: Department of Justice.

Vernon, J. (1963) *Inside the Black Room*. Harmondsworth: Penguin Books.

Vrca, A., Bozikov, V., Fuchs, R. and Malinar, M. (1996) 'Visual evoked potentials in relation to factors of imprisonment in detention camps', *International Journal of Legal Medicine*, 109: 114–17.

Wakefield, D. (1980) *A Thousand Days of Solitary*. London: National Prisoners' Movement (PROP).

Ward, D.A. (1987) 'Control strategies for problem prisoners in American penal systems', in A.E. Bottoms and R. Light (eds), *Problems of Long Term Imprisonment*. Cropwood Round-Table Conferences, Cambridge Studies in Criminology. Aldershot: Gower, pp. 74–96.

Ward, D.A. (1999) 'Supermaximum facilities', in P.M. Carlson and J. Garrett-Simon (eds), *Prison and Jail Administration: Practice and Theory*. Sudbury, MA: Jones and Bartlett, pp. 225–59

Ward, D.A. and Breed, A.F. (1985) Consultants report on the United States Penitentiary Marion, Ilinois, oversight hearing, Committee on the Judiciary, US House of Representatives, Serial No. 26, Washington DC: US Government Printing Office.

Ward, D.A. and Schmidt, A. (1981) 'Last resort prisons for habitual and dangerous offenders: some second thoughts about Alcatraz?', in D.A. Ward and K.F. Schoen (eds), *Confinement in Maximum Custody: New Last-Resort Prisons in the United States and Western Europe.* Lexington, MA: Lexington Books and D.C. Heath, pp. 61–8.

Ward, D.A. and Schoen, K.F. (eds) (1981) *Confinement in Maximum Custody New Last-Resort Prisons in the United States and Western Europe.* Lexington, MA: Lexington Books and D.C. Heath.

Ward, D.A. and Werlich, T.G. (2003) 'Alcatraz and Marion: evaluating super-maximum custody', *Punishment and Society*, 5 (1): 53–75.

Ward, L. (2004) 'Lack of special schools "putting pupils in danger"', *The Guardian*, 17 April, p. 4.

Wener, R. (2000) 'Design and the likelihood of prison assaults', in L. Fairweather and S. McConville (eds), *Prison Architecture: Policy, Design and Experience.* London: Architectural Press, pp. 49–54.

Wolch, J. and Dear, M. (eds) (1989) *The Power of Geography: How Territory Shapes Social Life.* Boston: Unwin Hyman.

Zimring, F.E. and Hawkins, G. (1991) *The Scale of Imprisonment.* Chicago: University of Chicago Press.

Zimring, F.E. (2001) 'Imprisonment rates and the new politics of criminal punishment', *Punishment and Society*, 3 (1): 161–6.

Zubek, J.P. (1969) 'Behavioural and physiological effects of prolonged sensory deprivation', *NATO symposium on Man in Enclosed Space*, Rome.

Zuckerman, M. (1964) 'Perceptual isolation as a stress situation', *Archives of General Psychiatry*, 11 (3): 255–76.

Court cases

Baraldini v. Meese, 691 F. 432 (D.D.C. 1988)

Bruscino v. Carlson 854 F.2d 162 (7th Cir. 1988)

Estelle v. Gamble 429 U.S. 97 (1976)

Holt v. Server, 309 F.Supp. 362 (1970)

Hutto v. Finey, 437 U.S. 678 (1978)

Farmer v. Brennan, 511 U.S. 825 (1994)

Jones'El v. Berge, 164 F.Supp. 1096 (W.D.Wis. 2001)

Madrid v. Gomez, 889 F.Supp. 1146, 1249 (N.D. Cal. 1995)

Re Medley, 134 US 160 (1890)

Rogers v. Peck, 199 U.S. 425 (1905)

Rooney v. State of North Dakota, 196 U.S. 319 (1905)

Ruiz v. Estelle, 503 F.Supp. 1265 (S.D. Tex. 1980)
Sandin v. Connor, 515 U.S. 472 (1995)
Wilson v. Seiter, 501 U.S. 294 (1991)

Index

Added to a page number 'f' denotes
a figure, 't' denotes a table and
'n' denotes notes.